More praise for

THE ART OF CRUELTY

A *New York Times* Editors' Choice and Notable Book of 2011

"The questions that Nelson raises about what it means for artists—and audiences—to delve into cruelty need to be addressed, thought about, discussed, debated. . . . [Nelson] forces us to think for ourselves—which, as Margaret Fuller knew, is often the critic's greatest gift."
—Susie Linfield, *New Republic / The Book*

"This is an important and frequently surprising book. . . . Nelson's opinions can be quirky and hard to square with one another, but they never fail to be interesting. . . . Hopping like a jackrabbit between genres and media, including forays into the swamps of pop culture, Nelson is strongest when at her most rageful, writing with controlled fury at the anti-intellectualism and crassness of the present. . . . This book [is] unpredictable and original." —Laura Kipnis,
New York Times Book Review

"*The Art of Cruelty* is not a book for the squeamish or even the passive reader. It will upset and confuse, and even delight at times."
—Rachel Syme, NPR Books

"[Nelson's] open-mindedness toward questions of catharsis and its demands is what makes her book so fascinating. . . . Nelson is right to urge that we overcome our scruples and preconceptions and listen to what they are trying to tell us. Her struggles to follow her own advice are a useful reminder of just how hard that can be." —Alan Wolfe, *Slate*

"This is criticism at its best: evocative, plainspoken, with an unwavering point of view. As Nelson darts from artwork to artwork, using the lens of cruelty to shine her own particular light, there is a joy in both her conviction and her questions." —Carolyn Kellogg, *Los Angeles Times*

"Nelson is not trying to settle questions of law or policy; in fact, she isn't much concerned with settling anything. What she wants to do is simply think her way carefully and creatively through an area in which sloppy sloganeering and crude moralizing have shut down the more interesting discussions before they could get started." —Troy Jollimore, *Boston Globe*

"In a world increasingly polarized by fundamentalism of various kinds, Nelson makes a compelling case for taking a new look at cruelty." —Patrick Langley, *Times Literary Supplement*

"Nelson . . . breathes life into debates about representations of violence. . . . Recommended." —K. L. Brintnall, *Choice*

"The book's strength lies in [Nelson's] frank, disarming and absolutely personal way of doing theory. Not only does this inevitably draw the reader in but it makes for a good read." —Eva Aldea, *Times Higher Education*

"Maggie Nelson's fascinating and supremely intelligent account asks what the point is of cruelty in art, with reference to these contemporary horrors and cultural representations of them." —Lesley McDowell, *Herald* (Scotland)

"The gory, brutal images that swamp modern culture are stupefying and dehumanizing—or maybe not, argues this richly ambivalent study. . . . Nelson's erudition and wide fluency in artistic and philosophical traditions yield many subtle, insightful readings." —*Publishers Weekly*

"Vivid prose that doesn't hesitate to enthuse and extol one moment, while happily dispensing damning criticism where it's due the next." —J. J. Charlesworth, *ArtReview* magazine

"[Nelson's] generalizations can ring so true that they're like hearing your own half-realized truths in someone else's mouth. . . . Nelson is so strong on this last point—pondering how artists of cruelty hold our attention even as they strive to offend and terrify us." —Parul Sehgal, *Bookforum*

"[Nelson has a] complex, fluidly expressed sensibility. . . . *The Art of Cruelty* is hard to stomach. It is also going to be hard to forget." —*Cleveland Plain Dealer*

"A fine survey recommended for any literary or artistic collection." —*Midwest Book Review*

THE ART OF CRUELTY

THE ART
OF CRUELTY

A RECKONING

Maggie Nelson

W. W. Norton & Company

NEW YORK • LONDON

"Lustmord" by Jenny Holzer. Copyright 2010 Jenny Holzer, member Artists Rights Society (ARS), New York. "Asphodel, That Greeny Flower" by William Carlos Williams, from *The Collected Poems: Volume II, 1939–1962.* Copyright 1944 by William Carlos Williams. Reprinted by permission of New Directions Publishing Corp. "The Ivy Crown" by William Carlos Williams, from *The Collected Poems: Volume II, 1939–1962.* Copyright 1953 by William Carlos Williams. Reprinted by permission of New Directions Publishing Corp. "Her Beckett" from *Decreation* by Anne Carson. Copyright 2005 by Anne Carson. Used by permission of Alfred A. Knopf, a division of Random House, Inc. Brief excerpts from various Sylvia Plath poems from *The Collected Poems of Sylvia Plath,* edited by Ted Hughes. Copyright 1960, 1965, 1971, 1981 by the Estate of Sylvia Plath. Editorial material copyright 1981 by Ted Hughes. Reprinted by permission of HarperCollins Publishers (from "Getting There," "Fever 103," "Elm," "Tulips," "The Surgeon at 2 a.m.," "Lesbos," "Three Women," "Little Fugue," "The Detective," "Lady Lazarus," "Daddy," "The Rabbit Catcher," "The Jailer," "Event," "Poem for a Birthday," "The Moon and the Yew Tree"). Brief excerpts from "Ariel" and "Years" from *Ariel: Poems by Sylvia Plath.* Copyright 1961, 1962, 1963, 1964, 1965, 1966 by Ted Hughes. Foreword by Robert Lowell. Reprinted by permission of HarperCollins Publishers and Faber and Faber, Ltd.

For information about permission to reproduce selections from this book, write to Permissions, W. W. Norton & Company, Inc., 500 Fifth Avenue, New York, NY 10110

For information about special discounts for bulk purchases, please contact W. W. Norton Special Sales at specialsales@wwnorton.com or 800-233-4830

Manufacturing by LSC Harrisonburg
Book design by Dana Sloan
Production manager: Julia Druskin

Library of Congress Cataloging-in-Publication Data

Nelson, Maggie, 1973–
The art of cruelty : a reckoning / Maggie Nelson. — 1st ed.
    p. cm.
Includes bibliographical references and index.
ISBN 978-0-393-07215-0 (hardcover)
1. Cruelty in art. 2. Art—Moral and ethical aspects. I. Title. II. Title: Reckoning.
N8217.C792N45 2011
700'.453—dc22

2011001828

ISBN 978-0-393-34314-4 pbk.

W. W. Norton & Company, Inc.
500 Fifth Avenue, New York, N.Y. 10110
www.wwnorton.com

W. W. Norton & Company Ltd.
15 Carlisle Street, London W1D 3BS

1 2 3 4 5 6 7 8 9 0

For Annie Dillard, who advises otherwise.

CONTENTS

THE ART OF CRUELTY

STYLES OF IMPRISONMENT

ONE SHOULD open one's eyes and take a new look at cruelty,"
Friedrich Nietzsche exhorted in *Beyond Good and Evil* (1886),
in which Nietzsche famously attempts to lay waste to traditional
notions of morality, especially those associated with Christianity.
Nietzsche hoped that, in catapulting beyond the poles of good and
evil, kindness and cruelty, the true energy and strength of mankind
would be liberated: in art as in life, this energy—which Nietzsche
termed our "will to power"—would pour forth; it would dance; it
would shine.

The next century—with its unthinkable wars, premeditated
and spontaneous genocides, rapacious exploitation of resources,
environmental catastrophes, and systemic injustices of all kinds—
provided ample opportunity to take this new look. Many of the
century's art movements (Futurism, Dada, Surrealism, Viennese
Actionism, the Black Arts Movement, and so on) made complicated contributions to this conversation, in that many artists associated with them hoped to mount a forceful protest against such
cruelties, while they also derived much of their inspiration, rhetoric, and strategy from a bellicose avant-garde tradition with thinkers such as Nietzsche at its root. To complicate matters further, the
twentieth century brought an explosion in the human capacity to

create and circulate images, via technological inventions such as film, television, Internet, digital photography, and countless other means. Given brutality's particularly fraught relationship with representation, twentieth-century art that concerned itself with its depiction or activation often found itself in turbulent ethical and aesthetic waters.

By now, it is something of a commonplace to say that twentieth-century art movements were veritably obsessed with diagnosing injustice and alienation, and prescribing various "shock and awe" treatments to cure us of them—a method Austrian filmmaker Michael Haneke usefully, if revoltingly, described in a 2007 interview as "raping the viewer into independence." (Art critic Grant Kester has described this approach more gently, calling it the "orthopedic aesthetic.") In short, the idea is that there's something wrong with us, from the get-go—be it the mark of original sin (or, conversely, as Nietzsche would have it, adherence to the "slave morality" of Christianity), alienation from our labor, a fatal rift with Nature, being lost in a forest of simulations, being deformed by systems such as capitalism and patriarchy, Westernization, not enough Westernization, or simply "an epistemological lack," as Kester has put it—that requires forceful (i.e., orthopedic) intervention to correct.

This premise is so ubiquitous that it allows phony wagers such as Haneke's to go largely unchallenged, in both artistic and political arenas. It isn't that many serious thinkers loudly profess to believe in them anymore, but rather that the habits of thought which have accrued around them remain largely intact, even when their core has been roundly disavowed. As anarchist anthropologist David Graeber puts it in an excellent short essay, "The Twilight of Vanguardism," "Revolutionary thinkers have been declaring the age of vanguardism over for most of a century now. Outside a handful of tiny sectarian groups, it's almost impossible to find radical intellectuals who seriously believe that their role should be to determine the correct historical analysis of the world situation, so as to lead the masses along in the one true revolutionary direction. But (rather like the idea of progress, to which it's obviously connected), it seems much easier to renounce the principle than to shake the accompanying habits of thought." This book attempts such a shaking.

There are, of course, major trends in contemporary art that have set themselves explicitly apart from the vanguardist, shock-and-awe strategies just described. Indeed, while writing, I have been often haunted by the fact that much, if not most of the art surrounding me at present follows a different trajectory altogether—one that goes by the name of relational aesthetics (or conversational art, or social practice, or community-based art, or littoral art, or as Kester—one of this work's most articulate champions—prefers, "dialogical" art). For Kester and others, these out-of-the-gallery projects, typically based on community engagement and interactive dialogue, offer the freshest, most viable response to what Kester calls "the most pressing questions facing us in the twentieth century: How do we reduce the violence and hatred that have so often marked human social interactions? How do we, in short, lead a 'non-fascist' life?" There is much to admire here, as well as much to question. But in the end, such projects remain outside this book's purview, if only for the simple reason that they are most always predicated on the desire to lessen the amount of cruelty and miscommunication in the world, rather than to explore or express it.

This book asks different questions. It asks whether there are certain aspects or instances of the so-called art of cruelty—as famously imagined by French dramatist and madman Antonin

Artaud—that are still wild and worthwhile, now that we purportedly inhabit a political and entertainment landscape increasingly glutted with images—and actualities—of torture, sadism, and endless warfare. It asks when and whether Artaud's distinction between a coarse sort of cruelty, based in sadism and bloodshed, and his notion of a "pure cruelty, without bodily laceration" can be productively made, and to what end. "From the point of view of the mind," Artaud wrote, "cruelty signifies rigor, implacable intention and decision, irreversible and absolute determination."

I am attracted to this precision, this sharpness, this rigor. Why Artaud and so many others have muddled it up with cruelty, I do not know. That is another of this book's questions. In his interviews with David Sylvester, painter Francis Bacon, one of this book's recurring subjects, put it this way: "Who today has been able to record anything that comes across to us as a fact without causing deep injury to the image?" Bacon, being fairly convinced of this formula, did not expect an answer. I do. I want to know whether he is truly onto something about the relationship between injury and fact, clarity and cruelty—or whether he is simply illuminating his own vision, justifying his own practice or predilections. Bacon's suggestion that an image can sustain (or cause) injury will also come up for debate; this book will consider the question vis-à-vis literature and words as well as visual art. Throughout, the aim is to attend closely to the different excitements and effects of this "pure cruelty" (such as precision, transgression, purgation, productive unease, abjectness, radical exposure, uncanniness, unnerving frankness, acknowledged sadism and masochism, a sense of clearing or clarity), while also staying keenly attuned to the various sophistries and self-justifications that so often attend its valorization.

—

MANY HAVE expressed concern about the ethical or even spiritual effects of meditating on such questions. I count myself among them. "It is possible that the contemplation of cruelty will not make us humane but cruel; that the reiteration of the badness of our spiritual condition will make us consent to it," wrote Lionel Trilling. Generally speaking, I think Trilling is right. The Buddha thought so too, which is why he advised his followers to meditate on compassion, which causes "any cruelty [to be] abandoned." Contemporary Buddhist figures like Thich Nhat Hanh advise against taking in or meditating on cruelties and violent spectacles at all, as to do so, Hanh says, only sows seeds of aggression, thereby increasing the presence of aggression in our minds, our relationships, and the world.

Generally speaking, I believe all that to be true. I believe that the obsessive contemplation of our inhumanities can end up convincing us of the inevitability of our badness, and that we likely do ourselves a grave disservice by staying riveted by top-of-the-hour, ad nauseam "proof" that humans always have steadily pursued (and, the spurious logic goes, thus always will pursue) the bloody businesses of genocide, state-sponsored war, terrorism, and individual acts of sadism across space and time. I agree that if we don't turn our attention away—or at least broaden our focus—we run the risk of floating further and further into the state described by Walter Benjamin as "an alienation that has reached such a degree that [mankind] can experience its own destruction as an aesthetic pleasure of the first order." I agree with Benjamin when he argued that this state better enables us to sweep ourselves along the road to brutal forms of self-organization, such as fascism. Or forget fascism—a term whose historical and ontological specificity is being erased daily, as Fox News searches for adequately incendiary terms to superimpose across images of Barack Obama. Why not face the brutal form of self-organization we've already got—capitalism—described by Rosa Luxemburg in her 1915 *Junius Pamphlet* in terms still applicable today: "shamed, dishonoured, wading in blood and dripping with filth, thus capitalist society stands."

Why, then, would I want to spend so much time thinking about cruelty?

It is possible that its contemplation will make us more cruel, said Trilling. He didn't say for sure.

Cruelty, as the Buddhists see it, is the far enemy of compassion. Compassion also has a near enemy—that is, an enemy that so closely resembles it that it can be difficult, albeit utterly crucial, to differentiate between them. This near enemy is called idiot compassion. I would like to understand more about compassion, and I am gambling that one way of doing so is to get to know its enemies, near and far. I realize that this approach risks looking, for a time, at our condition through the wrong end of the telescope, albeit the more commonly used one.

But perhaps I'm fooling myself. Perhaps I'm not really all that interested in compassion. Certainly it has less grip than conflict, as screenwriters everywhere preach. Certainly it doesn't "return us to life more violently," as Bacon so often named the singular goal of his art. Would it be a relief to give up, as Bacon did, on the idea of compassion altogether? "I'm not upset by the fact that people do suffer," said Bacon, "because I think the suffering of people and the differences between people are what have made great art, and not egalitarianism."

Welcome to Bacon's bracing allure (which resembles that of Artaud, and of Nietzsche), which posits this "violent return to life" as a way to restore us, or deliver us anew, to an unalienated, unmediated flow of existence characterized by a more authentic relation to the so-called real. Unlike so many avant-gardists and revolutionaries, however, Bacon does not think or hope that this restored vitality will bring about the subsequent waning of inequalities, injustices, or radical forms of suffering. Quite the contrary: for Bacon (as for Nietzsche), some people were put on the planet to dominate and some to be dominated, and that's exactly as it should be. Rather than purport that this "violent return to life" is somehow in keeping with the goals of social justice, Bacon prefers the brutal whirlwind in and of itself, with all its attendant cruelties.

In any case, one thing seems clear: whether or not one intends for one's art to express or stir compassion, to address or rectify forms of social injustice, to celebrate or relieve suffering, may end up irrelevant to its actual effects. Some of the most good-intentioned, activist, "compassionate" art out there can end up being patronizing, ineffective, or exploitative. And, of course, vice versa: much of the work that has no designs on eliciting compassion or bringing about emancipation can be the most salutary, the most liberating. This paradox is central to this book's enterprise. For not only do our work and words speak beyond our intentions and controls, but compassion is not necessarily found where we presume it to be, nor is it always what we presume it to be, nor is it experienced or accessed by everyone in the same way, nor is it found in the same place in the same way over time. The same might be said of cruelty.

One of this book's charges, then, is to figure out how one might differentiate between works of art whose employment of cruelty seems to me worthwhile (for lack of a better word), and those that strike me as redundant, in bad faith, or simply despicable. For obvious reasons, I plan to focus more on the former than the latter. But the boundaries between the two can be difficult to police or track, sometimes within the same work. Sometimes it's as simple as the difference between a piece of good art and a piece of bad art. Sometimes it's a gut feeling—one of those notorious I-know-it-when-I-see-it type of things—that arrives when I behold brutality being used as a bluff, or a bludgeon. Cruelty bears an intimate relationship to stupidity as well as to intelligence, and I am not interested in stupid cruelty, of which the world is overfull. (This includes most cruelties brought about via conformism, especially conformism to misogynistic, homophobic, xenophobic, or racist norms. It also eliminates from consideration works that strike me as fatally sophomoric or weak-minded, such as the plays of Neil LaBute.) At other times, the differentiation is more complicated—more flickering, more undecidable. This is especially so when one is watching an eminently good artist, such as Paul McCarthy, Ana Mendieta, Sylvia Plath, or Brian Evenson, slide in and out of various types of cruelty, often to uneven effect, or lurching between them, bumper-car style. Staying onboard for such a ride can generate a good amount of ambivalence, volatility, attraction, and repulsion. Some of this, I enjoy. Much—perhaps most—I do not. Nonetheless, I persist. This book is also about that persistence.

Freud—or at least the Freud of "Beyond the Pleasure Principle"—might have understood this persistence as the natural engine of a certain kind of art-making and art-viewing. Freud generally held to Aristotle's art-as-catharsis theory: that art (or, for Aristotle, tragedy in particular) is a place where spectators can come to experience pain as both enjoyable and purgative. Aristotle focused on pity and fear as the two emotions aroused, and subsequently subjected to catharsis, by tragedy; Freud expanded the idea to account for emotional responses beyond pity and fear, as well as to works not classically defined as tragedies. Freud argued that our enjoyment stems from art's ability to offer—perhaps to viewer and creator alike—retroactive mastery of traumatic experiences that one's defenses failed to deflect adequately from the organism at the time of original impact or injury. The "compulsion to repeat" the trauma—be it in art, nightmare, or waking life—is the organism's attempt to master the surplus anxiety that the original incursion produced. Of course, these attempts typically fail, often to catastrophic effect—in which case art can be seen as a relatively innocuous arena in which to showcase the failure—to enjoy, as Slovenian philosopher Slavoj Žižek has put it, our symptoms.

Freud's theory offers some real explanatory power. Nonetheless, it accounts only in part for many of the artworks, experiences, and impulses that this book chronicles. For here I am less interested in—and less convinced by—art's capacity (or desire, be it fulfilled or unfulfilled) to purge or master, and more interested in and convinced by its capacity to offer unpredictable insight into what some Buddhists have called "styles of imprisonment": the sometimes simple, sometimes intricate ways in which humans imprison themselves and their others, thereby causing suffering rather than alleviating it. This book therefore focuses primarily on works that give clear pictures of these knots or binds, rather than on those that hope to offer a map out of them.

Such a focus owes much to Scottish anti-psychiatrist R. D. Laing, whose 1970 book *Knots* sketches out the various looping, self-imprisoning patterns of thought that he observed in his patients' psyches. By spatializing, on the page, the language, shape, and circulation of each particular "web of maya," *Knots* makes clear that these knots hold compelling formal as well as psychological interest. They have, as Laing puts it, "a formal elegance." This book shares such an appreciation.

This focus is not cynical. Rather, it stems from my belief in the paradoxical yet sage statement once made by the poet Fanny Howe, that "the point of art is to show people that life is worth living by showing that it isn't." This focus does elide, however—unforgivably, perhaps, for some—works whose principal goal it is to impugn the causes or agents of the cruelties at hand. For this reason, anyone looking for a book that champions art whose main point is either an outraged "Never again should this terribly cruel thing be allowed to occur," or, conversely, a resigned "Ah, isn't life always and inevitably this way," should probably put this one down. For what I'm calling "art of cruelty" is specifically *not* art that expressly aims to protest, ameliorate, make meaningful, cast blame, or intervene in instances of brutality. To the contrary: much of the art considered here could be fairly charged with adding more cruelties—both real and represented—to an already contemptible heap.

Sometimes, as we shall see, the cruelty stays within the confines of the page or the gallery wall, which makes it slightly easier to talk about or defend. Other times, the cruelty seeps out to the viewer more directly, further troubling the ethical waters. This book diagrams a wide range of such charged instances in recent art and culture, and takes a new look at what is found there. It does not offer what, to my mind, can only be false or moralistic solutions to intractable ethical and aesthetic problems.

Many of this book's subjects are American, though by no means all—indeed, part of its point is to range widely and idiosyncratically, with no pretension toward the exhaustive. And while it isn't about American art or politics per se, it's clear to me now—and will likely be clear to the reader—that its concerns were shaped by the context in which it was initially conceived: the final years of the second administration of George W. Bush, a time in which there was no shortage of cruelties to contemplate. This was also a time in which the notion of "moral complexity" came to be defined—at least by proponents of the so-called war on terror—as a willingness to be "intolerant in order to defend tolerance, or unkind in order to defend kindness, or hateful in order to protect what we love," as one 2008 *Wall Street Journal* editorial (by conservative commentator Andrew Klavan) urged, without a shred of irony. Such a formulation struck me then, as it does now, as a cruelty of the highest order—one worthy of our analysis, and, I hope, our refusal.

Contrary to the miserable, self-justifying proclamations of Klavan's editorial, true moral complexity is rarely found in simple reversals. More often it is found by wading into the swamp, getting intimate with discomfort, and developing an appetite for nuance. "Make no mistake: this is not about more intellectual sophistication," writes Roland Barthes in *The Neutral*. "What I am looking for . . . is an introduction to living, a guide to life (ethical project): I want to live according to nuance. Now there is a teacher of nuance, literature; try to live according to the nuances that literature teaches me." Such a project generally gets a bad rap in our culture: nuance is all well and good for the ivory tower, people say, but in the "real" world, what *position* are you going to take? Whose side are you on? Where will you land at the end of the day, or at the end of days?

This book does not shrink from expressing strong opinions, from "taking sides," when it feels the need to do so. But at the end of the day, its greater aspiration is Barthes's: to live according to nuance. By definition, there is no master sketch for what such a thing might look like. It can only be an experiment.

THEATERS OF CRUELTY

Antonin Artaud coined the term "theater of cruelty" in his crackling volume of manifestos from the 1930s, *The Theater and Its Double*. *The Theater and Its Double* aimed to annihilate Western theater, and re-create it from the ashes in accordance with Artaud's principle of cruelty. "Everything that acts is a cruelty," he wrote. "It is upon this idea of extreme action, pushed beyond all limits, that theater must be rebuilt."

From the start, Artaud was anxious to differentiate his concept of cruelty from that of simple sadism, violence, or bloodshed. *His* cruelty, he insisted, meant something quite different: "the appetite for life, a cosmic rigor and implacable necessity, in the gnostic sense of a living whirlwind that devours the darkness, in the sense of that pain apart from whose ineluctable necessity life could not continue."

Despite his repeated, manic attempts at clarification, however, Artaud still thought his concept was virulently and consistently misunderstood. Indeed, for a madman who lived infamously far beyond the constraints of societal mores, he spent an inordinate amount of time defending his use of the term. "With this mania we all have for depreciating everything, as soon as I have said 'cruelty,' everybody will at once take it to mean 'blood,' " he wrote in

1933, in a sort of preemptive strike. "But *'theater of cruelty'* means a theater difficult and cruel for myself first of all." (As if self-cruelty canceled out its other effects: take note—this will recur, and ought to arouse our suspicions.)

It didn't help Artaud's case that even as he protested vociferously against the literal interpretation of his cruelty, when the time came to get theatrically specific, his examples of potential subjects were tales of literalized bloodshed: "the story of Bluebeard, reconstructed according to the historical records and with a new idea of eroticism and cruelty"; "a tale by the Marquis de Sade, in which the eroticism will be transposed, allegorically mounted and figured, to create a violent exteriorization of cruelty"; "an extract from the *Zohar: The Story of Rabbi Simeon*, which has the ever present violence and force of a conflagration," and so on.

Artaud wanted his cruelty to speak, as it were, for itself. "The person who has an idea of what this language is will be able to understand us," he wrote. "We write only for him." But the concept doesn't speak for itself. In fact, the very use of the word "cruelty" in relation to the kind of life force venerated by Artaud can at times seem a regrettable lexical error, perhaps of the Western, or Manichean variety—a distortion akin to the histrionic skewing of *shunyata*, the Buddhist concept of emptiness, entertainingly accomplished by philosophers such as Arthur Schopenhauer, who spun the notion out of fundamental neutrality and into negativity and nihilism. Artaud was looking to give a name to the "living whirlwind that devours the darkness . . . the pain apart from whose ineluctable necessity life could not continue." He had already renamed God, shit; he called this whirlwind, cruelty. "And I claim, in doing this, the right to break with the usual sense of language, to crack the armature once and for all, to get the iron collar off its neck." In short, cruelty meant whatever Artaud wanted it to mean. This makes the term, as passed down through him, somewhat difficult to work with.

But his use of the term, and his unwillingness to give it up, were no semantic accidents. Like Nietzsche before him, Artaud insisted on cruelty because cruelty is associated not only with implacability, but also with evil. And both men considered the riotous reclamation of evil something of a necessary pit stop on the way to dancing with cosmic forces which have no truck with normative, especially religious, conceptions of morality. In other words, embracing cruelty is a step—a sort of hazing, or threshold—on the path to moving beyond cruelty, a space valorized by Artaud (as well as by the Marquis de Sade, Georges Bataille, Camille Paglia, and countless others) as a more elemental, more animal, more "natural" realm than that of the civilized world, with the latter's internalized psychic limits, fretting over ethics, hypocritical moralizing, tedious social contracts and policy debates. "We sail straight over morality and *past* it, we flatten, we crush perhaps what is left of our own morality by venturing to voyage thither," Nietzsche wrote, rallying the invisible troops.

Here Nietzsche echoes the great Marquis de Sade, from whose name the word "sadism" derives. In the eighteenth century, Sade inverted Jean-Jacques Rousseau's more benevolent view of man-in-the-wild, and wickedly venerated the cruelty of Nature as a model for human affairs. As Simone de Beauvoir summarized in her 1955 essay, "Must We Burn Sade?" if Rousseau held that "Nature is good; let us follow her," and Thomas Hobbes held that "Nature is evil; let us *not* follow her," Sade held that "Nature is evil; let us follow her." "Cruelty is simply the energy in a man civilization has not yet altogether corrupted," Sade wrote in 1795's *Philosophy in the*

Bedroom. "Therefore [cruelty] is a virtue, not a vice." Two hundred years hence, Artaud pushed this notion of cruelty as fundamental, uncorrupted energy further still, into the realm of the mystical, the metaphysic: "It is cruelty that cements matter together, cruelty that molds the features of the created world," he wrote.

It was, of course, of little concern to Sade, or Nietzsche, or Artaud what kind of world, or what amount of suffering, the exaltation of such principles might bring about. Or, rather, they may have cared, but they had, as they say, different priorities—ones more in line with the attitude expressed earlier by Bacon (i.e., that suffering and difference make great art, not egalitarianism).

———

SINCE ARTAUD'S death in 1948, there have been many sincere and often laudable attempts to apply his theories to the theater. But any time an audience remains intact enough to shuffle out murmuring *how powerful* before deciding where to have its pie and Schnapps, Artaud's dream of "crushing and hypnotizing the spectator," perhaps to the point of no return, has died. Despite all his work as an actor, director, and playwright, Artaud's most enduring legacy has not lived on in the theater, but rather in more experiential, physically immersive spheres of expression, such as punk rock, radical performance art, carnivals, butoh, "happenings," festivals such as Burning Man, and so on. (During his lifetime, Artaud's major attempt to apply his principles to the stage was 1935's *The Cenci*, which was a messy flop; Artaud abandoned the theater shortly thereafter.) Like Dada, which, by definition, cannot produce a masterpiece (though it has, and plenty), Artaud's theater of cruelty cannot be understood as a means by which one might achieve aesthetic mastery. It aims instead to torch aesthetic mastery itself, and leave a "passionate and convulsive conception of life" in its place.

This call to dismantle or destroy the mediating object—be it the objet d'art, the theater experience, or the book-in-hand—in order to reveal this "convulsive conception of life" is so persistent in avant-garde rhetoric that one sometimes wonders why any of its pushers bothered with art at all. "The simplest Surrealist act consists of dashing down the street, pistol in hand, and firing blindly, as fast as you can pull the trigger, into the crowd," proclaimed André Breton, the so-called Pope of Surrealism, in 1930.

This desire to break down the barriers between life and art—and further, to have this breakdown be marked by violence and rupture—has characterized avant-garde operations at least since the Italian Futurists. The Futurists—whom many consider the first avant-garde—took aim at revolutionizing not only painting, music, sculpture, theater, and architecture, but also fashion, morals, manners, religion, and politics. They aimed to do so in the spirit of "The Founding and Manifesto of Futurism," published in 1909 by ringleader F. T. Marinetti, which infamously declares that art "can be nothing but violence, cruelty, and injustice," and promises "to glorify war—the world's only hygiene," along with "militarism, patriotism, the destructive gesture of freedom-bringers, beautiful ideas worth dying for, and scorn for woman." As much of a failure or an aborted mission as some say Futurism was (World War I, the war the Futurists agitated tirelessly to bring about, deprived the movement of much of its steam, not to mention many of its leading figures), one must also admit that much of the twentieth century, in both art and politics, unfolded in its image.

By the 1960s, proponents of abolishing the line between art and life were not nearly so fixated on violent rupture—think of John

Lennon and Yoko Ono's peace-loving "Bed-In" of 1969, or of the happily mundane art/life scores of Allan Kaprow and Fluxus, or of the advent of intentionally monotonous, endurance-based performance art, epitomized by pieces such as Linda Montano's and Tehching Hsieh's *Art/Life* (1983–84), in which Montano and Hsieh agreed to remain tied together by an eight-foot rope, without touching each other, for a year. Other artists, however—such as the Austrian artists known as the Viennese Actionists—upheld the more violent, aggressive line. "It is the assignment of the artist to destroy art and come closer to reality," Actionist Otto Muehl declared. With some measure of pathos, Muehl later explained his response to this assignment as follows: "Because I knew no other way than art to get to reality, I intensified my actions to extremely aggressive undertakings."

Why the desire to "restore us to our senses" or "get to reality" has so often leapt straight to "extremely aggressive undertakings," epitomized by bloody shock—even when the artist is well aware, as was Artaud, of the flattening effects of such a literalization— remains an open question. (Francis Bacon also judged himself quite harshly whenever he used explicitly violent subject matter, especially that which had the potential to introduce the boredoms of narrative or morality onto the canvas: a bullfight, a Nazi armband, and so on. Nonetheless, Bacon remains known for his splayed meat carcasses, crucifixions, screaming faces, scenes of unexplained but haunting bloodshed, injured heads, and imploding bodies.)

Consider, for example, the work of Actionist Hermann Nitsch, who cites Artaud as a primary influence ("his Theater of Cruelty was very deep in me. . . . I would say he was my brother"). The pinnacle of Nitsch's career was something called the *Six-Day Play*, for which Nitsch prepared over decades, and which was finally performed over six days on the castle grounds of Prinzendorf, Austria, in 1997. Nitsch describes but a snippet of the play as follows: "GRAPES, FRUIT and TOMATOES, ANIMAL LUNGS, FLESH and INTESTINES are trampled on in ecstasy. People trample in SLAUGHTERED ANIMAL CARCASSES FILLED WITH INTESTINES, in troughs full of blood and wine. Extreme noise from the orchestras. Slaughtering of the bull, slaughtering of two pigs. Disembowelment."

Nitsch may be after Dionysian revelry rather than apocalyptic terror, but the presumption that bloodshed, however ritualized, is the ultimate means of giving participants and audience a "feast of the senses," of "returning them to life," remains the same. (Whether bloodshed need always signify violence is also something of an open question, as is the definition of violence itself: think, for example, of the varying uses of the word at issue in phenomena such as "symbolic violence," "divine violence," "domestic violence," "the violence of capital," "abortion as violence," "violent language," and so on. Another open question: whether an act of so-called violence must always be characterized or accompanied by cruelty: the killing of animals for food, some instances of suicide, assisted suicide, or mercy killing, ritualized body mortifications, and so on, all offer ready sites for debate.)

It could be argued that there is, quite simply, no substitute for the visceral unease provoked by such bloodshed, either in representation or in reality, or in any smash-up of the two. It's nearly impossible, for example, to remain physically unaffected by many of the Actionist films from the 1960s, which feature multiple forms of mutilation, beatings, penetrations, and bloodletting. (The same likely goes for the more recent bloodletting work of performance artists such as Ron Athey, Franco B, and others, though their work differs profoundly in both tone and motivation.) Despite the culture's professed fatigue with transgressive body art, these Actionist films have not lost much of their visceral punch—I've yet to meet anyone who doesn't find them, at least upon first viewing, provoking, exciting, repulsive, or some combination thereof.

But however ecstatic the communion, or however viscerally startling the transgression, this emphasis on bloodshed as a jump-start into reality can be wearying. Indeed, whenever I read an articulate excoriation of the Viennese Actionists—such as those written by artist Carolee Schneemann or feminist Germaine Greer—the work can seem quickly ridiculous, a witless testament to a ludicrous white-boy repression, Austrian-style, literally trying to whip itself up to Wagnerian proportions. "Soll niemand mein Schwanz steif machen?"—"Is no one going to make my dick hard?"—a flaccid Otto Muehl reportedly yelled during a 1971 performance, a performance at which Muehl's sacrificial goose was seized (by the British poet Heathcote Williams, urged on by Greer) before it could meet its fate. Goose-less, Muehl ended up shitting on the stage instead.

In any case, whether the call is to create a Dionysian orgy (a la Nitsch), to mobilize a "hygienic violence" to cleanse society of its gangrenous elements (a la the Futurists), or simply an injunction to "free your mind" (a la Oko and Lennon), the anxiety over the relationship between art and life remains quite high; the mandate to break down the barriers between them, acute.

This anxiety and urgency—often posed as a conflict between spectatorship and action, or between the simulated, or mediated, and the real—is literally ancient. Plato famously thought mimesis (i.e., imitation, but also representation in a much broader sense) drew people away from truth, and therefore had a deleterious effect on the citizenry; it was for this reason that poets were to be banished from his ideal state of the republic. Aristotle had more of a social-control stance, arguing, via his theory of catharsis, that beholding evocative representations with the proper distance (such as going to see tragic theater) could provide a healthful outlet for impulses and ideas that might otherwise be disruptive to the social fabric.

This latter theory arrives in an endlessly debated passage in Aristotle's *Poetics*, in which Aristotle defines tragedy as an imitation of an action "with incidents arousing pity and fear, wherewith to accomplish its catharsis of such emotions." The confusion derives in part from the original Greek, which leaves not only the process itself a bit murky, but also its proper object. *Katharsis* arrives in English virtually untranslated, as "catharsis," which derives from *katharos*—"pure." But the word has stretched to signify or entail a wide variety of processes, including clarification, enlightenment, purgation, elimination, transubstantiation, sublimation, release, satisfaction, homeopathic cure, or some combination thereof. Second, the phrasing of Aristotle's original sentence leaves it unclear whether "catharsis" applies to *incidents* or to *emotions*—that is, whether the action takes place inside an individual, outside of her, or somewhere in between. Here, for example, are two plausible, but totally distinct, translations of Aristotle's sentence: "[Tragedy] achieves, through the representation of pitiable and fearful incidents, the catharsis of such pitiable and fearful incidents" (Leon Golden); "By means of pity and fear, [tragedy] contrives to purify the emotions of pity and fear" (J. L. Creed/A. E. Wardman).

In the twentieth century, dramatists Artaud and Bertolt Brecht each staged a savage reckoning with this set of problems. Both accepted Plato's premise—that there was something inherently nefarious about *mimesis*—but neither embraced Aristotle's attempted rescue of it. Brecht wrote explicitly against Aristotle's theory of catharsis, aiming to replace projective identification and emotional cathexsis—both of which he thought rendered audiences complacent and politically impotent—with strategic forms of alienation that would provoke the audience into dialectical thinking, decision-making, a desire for further knowledge, and action. Artaud—who, unlike Brecht, was no Marxist or seeker of social justice—was more concerned with resurrecting the magic and rawness that he thought spectatorship stamped out of daily life. "If our life lacks brimstone, i.e., a constant magic, it is because we choose to observe our acts and lose ourselves in considerations of their imagined form instead of being impelled by their force," Artaud wrote.

The problem is, of course, that art typically requires an audience, which loops us right back to the problem of observing actions and losing ourselves in consideration of their imagined form. (Kaprow, coiner of the term "happenings," agreed that the most persistent problem he faced in his attempts to blur art and life was the presence of the audience—a problem he spent nearly sixty years trying to solve via a more benign method he called "un-arting.") In *The Emancipated Spectator* (2009), French philosopher Jacques Rancière calls this "the paradox of the spectator," which he succinctly describes as follows: "There is no theater without spectators. But spectatorship is a bad thing. Being a spectator means looking at a spectacle. And looking is a bad thing, for two reasons. First, looking is the opposite of knowing. . . . Second, looking is deemed the opposite of acting." While Brecht and Artaud share the same set of premises, they offer opposite solutions: Brecht demands that the spectator become more aware, via a forced self-consciousness, of his or her complicity; Artaud strives to collapse the distance between looking and acting entirely, leaving the spectator subsumed, possessed, dissolved.

One can see a coarse, au courant torsion of the Brechtian approach in Austrian filmmaker Michael Haneke's notorious film *Funny Games*. *Funny Games*, which Haneke originally made in 1997, and then remade for an American audience in 2007, is the story of two torturers who terrorize and mutilate a bourgeois family over the course of the film's 108 minutes. As they go about their bloody business, the torturers periodically turn to the camera to impugn the viewer, saying things like, "You really think it's enough?" or "You want a proper ending, don't you?" This is about as crude a means of drawing attention to a viewer's complicity as you can get, which is likely why A. O. Scott, in his review of the remake, described the technique as one that "might have seemed audacious to an undergraduate literary theory class in 1985," but that today comes off as a fraud. (I might also add that while directly addressing the audience is indeed a Brechtian technique, directly indicting the nature of its attention was not; Brecht did not presume the worst about what an audience was feeling or desiring, as does Haneke here. The presumption to know collapses an important space—a space of great importance to Brecht, as he thought it allowed for the development of agency.)

It may simply be that the time for the efficacy of such an enterprise has passed—not because our complicity (in you-name-it) has lessened or grown any less toxic, but because the enormity of certain geopolitical crises has made a viewer's complicity in the presumed evils of spectatorship seem like small potatoes. (Yes, we like to watch, but so what?) Brecht himself was already onto this: at least in his early years, his curiosity was bent toward investigating the ways in which one might entertain and instruct simultaneously—to allow entertainment and instruction to stand together "in open hostility"—rather than toward advocating the abolishment or villainization of entertainment itself.

More to the point, it may be that the fast-moving pace of the so-called image regime under which many of us now live offers so little opportunity for slow looking, reflection, and contemplation that the indictment of a viewer's prolonged attention these days seems like a waste of an increasingly rare resource. Consider, for example, Chilean artist Alfredo Jaar's installation *Untitled (Newsweek)* (1994), which consists of seventeen digitally reproduced covers of *Newsweek* magazine, hung in chronological order, covering the five-month period of April 6 to August 1, 1994. The last of the covers features the Rwandan genocide, which began roughly five months earlier; below each cover is a card with printed text conveying choice details of what was happening in Rwanda on the date of the issue. The juxtaposition is meant to highlight what the United States (or the United States as represented by *Newsweek* magazine) was focusing on (the legacy of Jackie O, the O. J. Simpson trial, the World Cup, the future of North Korea, and so on) while it could have been—that is, should have been—turning its attention toward the ghastly, large-scale slaughter underway in Africa.

Jaar has a perfectly valid—if not obvious—point to make about what mainstream American media chooses to make newsworthy and what it opts to ignore. But since the artist has already predetermined what it is, exactly, that we should have been looking at—and, by extension, what is frivolous or wrong to look at in its place—what is the use of our looking at all? The artist, buoyed by good conscience, has simply replaced the hierarchy of *Newsweek*'s attention with his own.

In 2007, Jaar gave a lecture at Wesleyan University in concert with this work. The lecture was titled "It is Difficult" in reference to the ways in which Jaar's works "force us to look at events we would rather not see." But who is the "we" here? And how does the artist know in advance what we would rather not see, or how difficult the looking may be? And is it really the looking that's so hard? Or is it all the work that looking at atrocity *doesn't* do— namely, as Susan Sontag has it, repairing our ignorance about the history and causes of suffering, and charting a course of action in response, tasks that may fall fairly and squarely *outside* the realm of art? Even groups such as ACT UP (the AIDS Coalition to Unleash Power), which fought relentlessly for the radical politicization of art, sometimes found themselves landing on a similar point: think, for example, of the ACT UP flier produced in protest of a 1988 Nicholas Nixon show at the Museum of Modern Art, a show that included several photographs of people devastated by AIDS. "STOP LOOKING AT US; START LISTENING TO US," the flier read.

—

THE OTHER day, a friend hoping to gain some insight into my current project asked me to describe Artaud's theater of cruelty to him; I opened up to a weathered page of *The Theater and Its Double* and read aloud to him how it concentrates on "famous personages, atrocious crimes, and superhuman devotions," with a special appeal to the forces of "cruelty and terror." "Sounds a lot like Hollywood," my friend shrugged, before returning to his book, unmoved. And so it does. In the end, the irony of Artaud's theater of cruelty may not lie in its legendary inapplicability, but rather in the fact that our age may have given the lie to its dream of the destructive, regenerative, revolutionary power of the spectacle.

This isn't because, as some have said, there is no longer any "reality" beyond the spectacle. Nor is it because some privileged people have the luxury of "patronizing reality," while the more unfortunate—who are presumably mired in the so-called real at every moment—do not (see Sontag). Rather, it is because the whole notion that art, or a more fundamental form of representation (such as language, vision, or consciousness itself), obscures or distorts an otherwise coherent, transcendental reality is not, to my mind, a particularly compelling or productive formulation. Much more interesting, I think, are the capacities of particular works to expand, invent, explode, or adumbrate what we mean when we say "reality." Another way of putting this would be to use Rancière's term, the "redistribution of the sensible." To focus on this redistribution is to celebrate the bounty of representational and perceptual possibilities available to us, and to get excited about art as but one site for such possibilities—one means of changing, quite literally, what we are able to sense.

For this reason, however much Artaud may have desired a theater that would "break through language to touch life," I find him most moving and inspiring when he is analyzing, excavating, and making strange the very acts of thinking, articulation, and representation themselves. See, for example, 1925's "The Nerve Meter," in which Artaud reports from the void: "Words halfway to intelligence. This possibility of thinking in reverse and of suddenly reviling one's thought. This dialogue in thought. The ingestion, the breaking off of everything. And all at once this trickle of water on a volcano, the thin, slow falling of the mind."

It is a testament to Artaud's intensity—and perhaps to his madness—that the deadening aspects of his theatrical vision never seem to have occurred to him. He dreaded literalization and misunderstanding, yes, but his proposals to "get us out of our marasmus, instead of continuing to complain about it, and about the boredom, inertia, and stupidity of everything," always called for *more* intensity, *more* spectacle, *more* bloodshed, *more* shock, *more* immersion, *more* obscenity. He was, after all, a man who persisted—if just barely—in a harrowing state of near constant agony, ecstasy, trance, withdrawal, or psychosis that few others would choose or be able to suffer. He did not live to see the piece in *Le Monde* published shortly after 9/11, in which French philosopher Jean Baudrillard called the terrorist attack that brought down the Twin Towers "our theatre of cruelty, the only one left to us." Nor did he live in the age of, say, beheadings available for casual viewing on YouTube. Nor, thankfully, did he live to see the results of my Google search this morning under "theater of cruelty": up first, a piece from the *Nation* that describes the acts of torture committed by Americans at Abu Ghraib—and the circulation of the photographs of those acts—as a "Theater of Cruelty"; next, a *USA Today* blog inviting readers everywhere to weigh in on the question, "Are '[American] Idol' auditions a 'Theater of Cruelty'?"

Perhaps this is why Artaud's writing now seems to me best encountered in silence, in solitude, and—despite what he might have wanted—on the page. Its crackle is still audible, it still scorches. But there it does not rely on the decimation of thought that Artaud at times imagined as a purification, but which the anti-intellectualism of contemporary American culture has repurposed into something utterly stultifying.

For the mainstream thrust of anti-intellectualism, as it stands today, characterizes *thinking itself* as an elitist activity. And even if one were to get excited about leaving the contortions of mental effort behind, today's anti-intellectualism makes no corollary call for us to return our fingers to blood and dirt, to discover orgiastic bliss, to become more autonomous in our ability to fulfill our basic, most primal needs, or to become one with the awe-inspiring forces of the cosmos. It does not demand, as did Thoreau, "Give me a Wildness whose glance no civilization can endure,—as if we lived on the marrow of koodoos devoured raw." It does not invite us to "throw ourselves like pride-ripened fruit into the wide, contorted mouth of the wind," as did F. T. Marinetti. And needless to say, it most certainly does not imagine, a la Carolee Schneemann, that the liberated power of female erotic pleasure could gain us entrance to an ecstatic experience of our bodies no longer defined in opposition to intellectual inquiry. Instead, it promotes something more like an idiocracy, in which low-grade pleasures (such as the capacity to buy cheap goods, pay low or no taxes, carry guns into Starbucks, and maintain the right *not* to help one another) displace all other forms of freedom, even those of the most transformative and profound variety.

"Don't think, say the stupid, says the vulgar herd, *why try to think?*" wrote Artaud, who often experienced thinking as a sort of bodily agony. "As if without [thinking] it were possible to live."

GREAT TO WATCH

——————

IN HER moving, influential anti–capital punishment memoir, *Dead Man Walking*, Sister Helen Prejean asserts, "I know that it is not a question of malice or ill will or meanness of spirit that prompts our citizens to support executions. It is, quite simply, that people don't know the truth of what is going on." Prejean is convinced that if executions were made public, "the torture and violence would be unmasked, and we would be shamed into abolishing executions."

Alas, if only it were so. For if the bad news from Abu Ghraib made anything clear in recent years, it is that this model of shaming-us-into-action-by-unmasking-the-truth-of-our-actions cannot hold a candle to our capacity to assimilate horrific images, and to justify or shrug off horrific behavior. Not to mention the fact that the United States has a long history—as do many countries and individuals—of reveling in the spectacle of public executions and gruesome torture. (On this account, I unhappily recommend to you the 2000 book of documentary photography *Without Sanctuary: Lynching Photography in America*.)

Prejean's conviction that it is simple, blameless ignorance that prompts so many Americans to support executions (or the torture of detainees in the so-called war on terror, and so on) may be good-hearted. But unfortunately it leaves us but one option: know the truth, and ye shall be redeemed. But "knowing the truth" does not come with redemption as a guarantee, nor does a feeling of redemption guarantee an end to a cycle of wrongdoing. Some would even say it is key to maintaining it, insofar as it can work as a reset button—a purge that cleans the slate, without any guarantee of change at the root. Placing all one's eggs in "the logic of exposure," as Eve Kosofsky Sedgwick has put it (in *Touching Feeling*), may also simply further the logic of paranoia. "Paranoia places its faith in exposure," Sedgwick observes—which is to say that the exposure of a disturbing fact or situation does not necessarily alter it, but in fact may further the circular conviction that *one can never be paranoid enough*.

Prejean's logic relies on the hope that shame, guilt, and even simple embarrassment are still operative principles in American cultural and political life—and that such principles can fairly trump the forces of desensitization and self-justification. Such a presumption is sorely challenged by the seeming unembarrassability of the military, the government, corporate CEOs, and others repetitively caught in monstrous acts of irresponsibility and malfeasance. This unembarrassability has proved difficult to contend with, as it has had a literally stunning effect on the citizenry. *They ought to be ashamed of themselves!* we cry, over and over again, to no avail. But they are not ashamed, and they are not going to become so.

Also difficult to contend with: the fact that we ourselves have ample and wily reserves of malice, power-mongering, self-centeredness, fear, sadism, or simple meanness of spirit that we ourselves, our loved ones, our enemies, skillful preachers, politicians, and rhetoricians of all stripes can whip into a hysterical, destructive froth at any given moment, if we allow for it.

To this list, one should surely add television producers. In 1982, Stephen King published a sci-fi novel called *The Running Man*, set in the not-so-distant future. In the novel, "The Running Man" is the country's most popular TV game show, and features a contestant who agrees to run for his life while being trailed by a group of "Hunters" charged with killing him. The network engages the populace by paying civilians for confirmed sightings of the runner, which it then passes along to the Hunters. If the runner survives for thirty days, he gets a billion dollars. If he is caught, he is killed by the Hunters on live TV.

As others have noted, the dystopic plot of *The Running Man* turned out to be more prophetic than dissuasive. So-called reality television has been foraying into this territory for over a decade now, churning out show after show that draws on some combination of surveillance; self-surveillance; "interactivity" with the home audience; techniques associated with torture, interrogation, or incarceration; and rituals of humiliation, sadism, and masochism (of the I'll-do-anything-for-fame-or-money variety, not the I-do-this-because-it-gives-me-pleasure variety: outing one's pleasures, it seems, remains more taboo than outing one's ambition or avarice).

The international craze for reality programming has, to date, given us shows such as the United Kingdom's *Shattered* (2004), in which contestants are deprived of sleep for many days in a row, and *Unbreakable* (2008), in which contestants undergo various forms of torture (including being waterboarded, buried alive, or made to cross the Sahara Desert while wearing suffocating gas masks), and whose motto is "Pain Is Glory, Pain Is Pride, Pain Is Great to Watch." In the United States, reality TV has at times joined forces with soft-core journalism and law enforcement to produce shows like Dateline/NBC's *To Catch a Predator. To*

Catch a Predator—which operates in questionable legal conjunction with not only the police but also a vigilante "anti-predator" group called "Perverted Justice"—hires decoys who pretend to be underage teens. These decoys attempt to entice adults into online sex chats; if and when one of the adults agrees to meet his online pen pal at the "decoy house," he (and it is always a he) is there greeted by the show's host, Chris Hansen, who first verbally humiliates him by reading him the most tawdry excerpts of his online sex chatter, then turns him over to the police, who are waiting nearby with handcuffs.

The legal, ethical, and psychological ramifications of such shows have occasioned quite a bit of debate, as these effects have often proved unmanageable. On November 5, 2006, for example, after a SWAT team trailed by TV cameras forced its way into the home of Louis Conradt Jr., a longtime county prosecutor in Murphy, Texas, Conradt said, "I'm not going to hurt anybody," before firing a single bullet from a semiautomatic handgun into his brain, thereby ending his life. (There had been no pressing reason to break into Conradt's home—Conradt had, in fact, refused to meet the decoy at the decoy house—but the show's producers were anxious to capture the arrest of a prominent public figure on tape, as it promised to make compelling TV. In the end, Dateline refrained from airing the death itself, but it did run a segment on the case.) As one newspaper columnist writing about the incident acidly put it, "When a TV show makes you feel sorry for potential child rapists, you know it's doing something wrong." (Or right, depending on your point of view; *To Catch a Predator* was one of NBC's hit shows for some time.)

As if a test were needed of how much sadism reality television participants, audiences, and producers are willing to indulge, on March 17, 2010, French TV broadcast something called *Le jeu de la mort*, or *The Game of Death*, a faux game show which re-performed the Milgram experiment on eighty unknowing contestants. The contestants had been told that they were taking part in a game-show pilot, in which they were to administer electric shocks to other contestants when they answered questions incorrectly. A smiling host and vociferous studio audience, rather than a taciturn guy in a lab coat (as was the case in Stanley Milgram's experiment), urged the behavior on, but the results were remarkably similar: sixty-four of the eighty contestants were willing to deliver shocks that could have killed their recipients, had there been any actual receivers.

But beyond prime time, which the digital age may be rendering a quaint outpost, more literal renditions of the Running Man scenario—and ones that offer their viewers slightly more participation than that of armchair schadenfreude—are now available via a few strokes of your computer keyboard. Consider, for example, the Texas Virtual Border Watch Program, in which "The Texas Border Sheriff's Coalition (TBSC) has joined BlueServo℠ in a public-private partnership to deploy the Virtual Community Watch, an innovative real-time surveillance program designed to empower the public to proactively participate in fighting border crime." In other words, the TBSC has placed cameras along the U.S.-Mexican border in Texas at so-called high-threat spots for border crossing or drug trafficking, and now invites the home viewer to log on, pick a spot, and start "directly monitoring suspicious criminal activity via this virtual fence℠." Viewers can watch the live feed from one of the "virtual stake outs" for as long as they like—the

New York Times recently interviewed a housewife from Rochester, New York, who reported watching for at least four hours a day.

While controversial, the BlueServo℠ project should come as no surprise to anyone familiar with the Minutemen and its off-shoots, whose volunteers have been (non-virtually) patrolling the U.S.-Mexican border, looking for "illegals," since 1995. "It's just like hunting," explained Chuck Stonex, a prominent member. "If you're going out hunting deer, you want to scout around and get an idea what their pattern is, what trails they use." Stonex, along with Minuteman founder Jim Gilchrist and other leading figures, has since taken a more defensive stance, after one of their principal associates, Shawna Forde, was arrested in June 2009 in connection with the murder of two members of a Hispanic family in their home in Arivaca, Arizona; one of those killed was a nine-year-old girl. But the chilling new anti-immigration law signed by Governor Jan Brewer of Arizona on April 23, 2010, which authorizes police to demand proof of any person's immigration status should "reasonable suspicion exist that the person is an alien," has breathed new life into the "hunt 'em down" mindset, in both Arizona and the nation at large.

With BlueServo℠, the condition of spectatorship is not so much abolished as it is recast as a form of empowerment: you, too, can defend the homeland, without ever having to leave your home! The project eerily combines the appeal of a spectator sport with language more typically reserved for left wing–sounding community activism: *Innovative. Proactive. Participation. Partnership. Coalition. Community. Empowerment.* (Especially poignant: "public-private partnership"—in the age of Blackwater [now called Xe] or the Tea Party, every vigilante need be prepared for a trademark!) Last time I visited the BlueServo℠ site, there were fifteen cameras rolling on scenes of bucolic calm. My favorites were Camera 5, which featured a still patch of golden weeds with the directive, "During the day watch for subjects on foot carrying large bags," and Camera 10, which featured a swiftly moving river alongside the directive, "During the day if you see four or five men in a boat report this activity. At night if you see vehicle, boat, or people movement report this activity." The static, unending nature of the footage bears a weird resemblance to the endurance-based, art house aesthetic of, say, Andy Warhol's *Empire* (1964)—a film that consists of eight hours and five minutes of continuous footage of the Empire State Building—or that of a virtual yule log, albeit one of a more sinister variety.

On the flip side of such a "if you see something, say something" policing projects lies a human rights organization such as the Hub, which describes itself as "the world's first participatory media site for human rights." I'm thinking in particular of the Hub's Witness project, whose motto is "See It, Film It, Change It," and which aims to use "video and online technologies to open the eyes of the world to human rights violations." The operation of Witness is twofold: one, to give people cameras and train them to videotape atrocities or injustices they may be suffering or witnessing; two, to invent a circuitry by which one can upload one's own videos and view those of others, presumably as a prelude to taking a form of action after viewing. For convenience, one can scroll through the videos by category (armed conflict, children's rights, discrimination, violence, women's rights, and so on), or by "most viewed" (Japanese sexual slavery during World War II has occupied this slot for some time now).

As the creators of the Hub well know, the employment of image or moving image in service of mobilizing an individual or a populace is tricky business. For this reason, the Hub aims to zero in on the little window of time between an upsurge of outrage or sympathy and the onset of apathy—to hurl an otherwise fleeting emotion into action before it dissolves. (What action consists of is a difficult, debatable question—right now the "take action" tab on the Hub's Web site links to "a growing portfolio of advocacy tools to help allies and users call for action," ranging from signing email petitions to writing members of Congress to sending money to a variety of organizations to creating "offline events.")

I mean it as no slight to the Hub when I say that I find the smorgasbord of human suffering offered on its site repellent. Not because "it is difficult to look" (though sometimes, of course, it is), but because the physical and mental activity of Web surfing, which consists of rapid image flow, the distillation of long, complex stories and situations to 2-inch-high, four-minute snippets, one-click decision-making, happenstance isolations, juxtapositions, and linkages that have an eerily leveling effect on content and context, is, in my experience, an exceptionally poor means by which to contemplate the horrors of human trafficking, child prostitution, landmines, and the like. For better or worse, one's experience of surfing the Hub is shaped by the do-I-or-don't-I-want-to-watch-this question, as in: Do I or don't I want to watch a Tibetan pilgrim being shot dead by the Chinese police at Nangpa La Pass? How about cell phone footage of a man being hung upside down and sodomized with a rod in an Egyptian prison? Or the testimony of women in Bangladesh whose faces have been disfigured by acid? Well intentioned and effective as the operation may be, scrolling through such choices makes me feel as though I've arrived at the hub of a problem rather than its solution.

—

Insofar as "image flow" isn't going away any time soon, it certainly makes sense to try to harness the powers of YouTube for all kinds of social causes as well as for entertainment. But there are also perils. And one is that in a cultural moment defined (by some, for some) by image flow, the question of what one should look at, along with attendant inquiries into the nature and effect of the images blowing by, has a creepy way of overtaking almost all other questions. This may in fact be part of the so-called image regime's raison d'etre, rather than a puzzling side effect. In any case, it can lead to cul-de-sacs, red herrings, or distractions fatal to the primary issue at hand.

For example, in a director's statement about his Abu Ghraib documentary, *Standard Operating Procedure*, filmmaker Errol Morris names the principal question posed by his film as, "Is it possible for a photograph to change the world?" But what could the answer to this question—be it in the negative or the affirmative—really mean? As Sontag puts it in *Regarding the Pain of Others*, "The image as shock and the image as cliché are two aspects of the same presence"—a notion that partially explains how the iconic image of the hooded prisoner at Abu Ghraib forced to hold a foreboding wire in each hand could literally sicken one's stomach when first viewed, then move on to become a much-parodied image (e.g., on the satirical posters that appeared throughout the New York subways not long after the Abu Ghraib story broke, posters that borrowed the distinctive design of Apple's iPod campaign, but substituted the word "iRaq" for "iPod," and featured the silhouette of the hooded man in lieu of the iPod's silhouetted dancer). It isn't that this photograph played no role in the unfolding of human events—clearly, it did. But after nearly 200 years of photography, it may be that we are closer than ever to understanding that an image—be it circulated in a newspaper, on YouTube, or in an art gallery—is an exceptionally poor platform on which to place the unending, arduous, multifaceted, and circuitous process of "changing the world."

In his April 2008 *Artforum* review of *Standard Operating Procedure*, critic Paul Arthur noted something of the same. In thinking about Morris's focus on the revelation that the man who identified himself publicly as the hooded prisoner turned out *not* to be the actual victim, Arthur writes, "Morris finds this revelation telling because it shows how massively disseminated pictures can mask their own provenance or 'attract false beliefs.' Really? I thought the images under consideration, especially when supplemented by salient verbal contexts, revealed more about policy than about epistemology, more about state-sponsored barbarity than about media deception." In other words, one need not immerse oneself in horrific images or a debate about their epistemological status in order to apprehend and protest barbarities wherever they are to be found. Nor does one need to distract oneself with rehashings of the Milgram experiment, which uselessly reiterate what we already know about our capacity to cause harm under pressure (or, as the case may be, at simple invitation).

One does, however, need to know what barbarities have taken place: there's the rub. Enter President Obama, speaking about his administration's May 2009 decision to suppress the release of a new spate of photographs that depict the abuse, rape, and torture of Afghan and Iraqi prisoners in American custody. "The most direct consequence of releasing [these photos]," Obama said, "would be to further inflame anti-American opinion and to put our troops in greater danger." Mark down one vote for the idea that images have the power to cause injury—though to warn against such a thing in this case smells pretty rotten, given that the suppressed photos presumably depict our troops injuring others.

Obama also skips over the most obvious direct consequence of releasing the photos: that Americans would see—along with the rest of the world—more evidence of the barbarities that have been committed in their name, on their supposed behalf, and on their dime. To state the obvious but oft-repressed or denied point, it isn't the act of releasing photos that inflames anti-American sentiment; it's the behavior captured by the photos. In the age of "the torturer with the Toshiba," as art historian T. J. Clark has put it, no image flow can be fully marshaled. Nor can survivors and witnesses be unilaterally silenced. If you don't want to inflame via images of the behavior, then you have to stop the behavior.

Of course, it isn't entirely clear that the United States meant to keep the news of its use of torture a secret. No regime hoping to gain power from its use of such violence (an impossibility, according to Hannah Arendt) ever has. Certainly the revelations from Abu Ghraib appeared as a mistake, a rip in the fabric; certainly the U.S. government has employed intense secrecy, censorship, and denial about everything from the Red Cross Torture Report to the exact interrogation methods used to the operations of "black sites" around the world. Certainly journalists from Seymour Hersh to Jane Mayer to Mark Danner to Scott Horton have had an enormously difficult time obtaining the information they need to inform the public about what, exactly, has gone on; certainly the CIA has classified and egregiously destroyed pivotal evidence, such as the videotapes depicting the 2002 interrogations of several terrorism suspects—tapes the CIA outrageously destroyed in 2005, in the midst of a federal investigation.

And yet. On a parallel track run the monologues of Dick Cheney, who, since leaving office, has toured the talk shows, speaking with candor and pride about his role in "The Program." Then there's the ongoing consideration of the topic in the bright glare of television and the blogosphere, in which everyone from Bill O'Reilly to Andrew Sullivan to Christopher Hitchens to Elisabeth Hasselbeck openly debates the efficacy of torture, and the effect its use has had on our country—not whether or not we have done it. The Bush/Cheney dyad of denial/justification represents two sides of a single coin: Bush spoke the voice of delusion (it never happened, it will never happen); Cheney, the voice of justification (we had to do it, we should still be doing it). The average citizen can then ricochet between these two irreconcilable, collaborative poles until desensitization sets in, and with it, a begrudging (or, for some, an enthusiastic) acceptance of the practice.

—

BACK IN 1965, Sontag declared that we live in "an age of extremity," characterized by "the continual threat of two equally fearful, but seemingly opposed destinies: unremitting banality and inconceivable terror." Much of the art produced under the influence of Artaud—such as Nitsch's—proceeds from this premise, and attempts to replace the crush of banality with some form of brutal, sensory overload. Even quieter works such as Jaar's *Untitled (Newsweek)* depend on this by-now familiar dichotomy—one that places benumbing banality on one side, and unthinkable, rupturing calamity on the other.

The moral of this dichotomy is that distraction by the banal obviates a necessary focus on the all-too-real calamitous. This equation became ubiquitous in the weeks and months after 9/11, when media commentator after commentator lamented the fact that instead of focusing on the real threat from Al Qaeda, Americans spent the summer of 2001 unforgivably obsessing over the latest incarnation of Britney Spears. But really this is a self-flagellating, essentially nonsensical diagnosis, especially in its supposition that Americans would have been better off spending more of their time worrying about an impending terrorist attack, the shape of which they could have had no foreknowledge. (The next seven years and four months of the Bush administration provided a good picture of what a populace in thrall to such anxiety might look like—and what it might tolerate from its leaders—and it wasn't pretty.)

After 9/11, Sontag's formulation would seem to have more adherents than ever, on both the right and the left. See, for example, the leftist collective RETORT's *Afflicted Powers: Capital and Spectacle in a New Age of War* (2005), which repeatedly pits the eviscerating "false depth" of consumerism (i.e., unremitting banality) against claims that "we have never been closer to hell on earth" (i.e., inconceivable terror). But is it true? Or more precisely, for whom is it true, and who presumes it to be true for others? Do we really live under the aegis of these opposing threats, or is it the very reiteration of them as our two primary ontological options (and our unthinking acquiescence to such a formulation) that acts as a truer threat to our enlivenment, to our full experience of the vast space between these two poles—a space which, after all, is where the great majority of many of our lives takes place? And if, as David Graeber has suggested, revolutionary action is "not a form of grim self-sacrifice," but rather "the defiant insistence on acting as if one is already free," what good does it do us to charge those who refuse to live under the aegis of these two grim choices with false consciousness, with not truly understanding the stakes of the age?

Compare, for example, the "troughs of blood and wine," the "extreme noise from the orchestras" of Nitsch's *Six-Day Play* with John Cage's Zen-inspired *4'33"*, first composed in 1952, in which Cage famously asks audience members to sit in complete silence for four minutes and thirty-three seconds, in order to awaken to the sounds going on around them, to hear all the ambient noise of which they would have otherwise been unaware. In light of the heightened state of perception conjured by Cage's piece—its profound capacity to "return us to our senses" via an emptying out of input rather than an overload of it—one may begin to wonder whose interests it serves to keep us believing in, and riveted by, the mythos of this "age of extremity," which focuses on knocking oneself out rather than tuning in.

Perhaps more controversially still, given our inarguable complicity in all kinds of systemic forms of global injustice: is there any space left for *not* watching, *not* focusing, *not* keeping abreast of all the events and atrocities unfolding in the world, as an ethically viable option? "Why are we watching the news, reading the news, keeping up with the news?" asks Annie Dillard in *For the Time Being*, a book that sets forth the deeply unfashionable argument that our times are not uniquely grievous—that they are, in fact, not unique at all—and further, that their vicissitudes may make no intrinsic demand on our attention, or on our conscience. That enlivenment may consist of quiet, even monastic retreat, rather than bombardment or disembowelment. "Who can bear to hear this, or who will consider it?" Dillard wonders.

In completely disparate circles—such as those of leftist political philosophy, for example—a distinct but not wholly unrelated idea of "engaged withdrawal" has also begun to hold sway. Rather than fixate on revolution, this strategy privileges orchestrated and unorchestrated acts of exodus. As Italian political philosopher Paolo Virno has put it, "Nothing is less passive than the act of fleeing, of exiting." In anarchist circles, this withdrawal bears a relationship to the idea of the "TAZ," or "temporary autonomous zones" (as elaborated by writer Hakim Bey; Graeber prefers the term "provisional autonomous zones"): ephemeral but crucial gaps in an otherwise suffocating global capitalist order, gaps that, at the very least, make other forms of social organization and perception seem momentarily possible.

In short, after decades of critical focus on the evils of spectatorship, the gaze, and the presumably passive role of the audience, an increasing chorus of critical voices is currently arguing that we have somehow gotten wildly off course by treating the condition of spectatorship as a problem, or at least as *the* problem. There's Jacques Rancière, who argues in 2009's *The Emancipated Spectator* that spectatorship is not "the passivity that has to be turned into activity," but rather "our normal situation." Then, of course, there's Sontag, whose final book, *Regarding the Pain of Others*, argues that to impugn the sense of sight for allowing us to "stand back from the aggressiveness of the world" and to free us up "for observation and for elective attention" is to impugn the function of the mind itself. Sontag concludes, "There's nothing wrong with standing back and thinking. To paraphrase several sages: 'Nobody can think and hit someone at the same time.' " In a culture obsessed with pitting thought against action (in order to privilege the latter), not to mention a culture perpetually dubious of the cash value of rumination, these are fighting words. In 2006, T. J. Clark—who is known as much for his fierce political convictions as his insights into Picasso (he is, in fact, a member of RETORT)—published *The Sight of Death*, a 242-page meditation on two works by seventeenth-century painter Nicolas Poussin, in which Clark aims to honor the slow work of "this focusing, this staying still, this allowing oneself to respond to the *picture*'s stillness—everything hidden and travestied, in short, by the current word 'gaze.' " Clark also rebukes those scholars of "visual culture" who, in his words, are "chained to their image-displacement machines like lab animals to dispensers of morphine," and whose knee-jerk response to an expansive, devoted, patient contemplation of classical painting (such as his) would be to dismiss it as nostalgic, or elitist, or "some such canting parrot-cry."

The above-mentioned writers have dedicated their lives to slow seeing, slow thinking, measured articulation, and radical dissent or defection from any *doxa* that stifles existence or adds injustice to it. I am inclined to listen to them. Rather than lambast that which mediates as our enemy, each makes a concerted effort to reclaim the value of the "third term." "In the logic of emancipation," Rancière writes, "there is always a third thing—a book or some other piece of writing—alien to both [teacher and student] and to which they can refer to verify in common what the pupil has seen, what she says about it and what she thinks about it." The emancipatory value of this third thing, as Rancière sees it, lies in the fact that no one can own it; no one can own its meaning. Its function is to mediate, but not in the sense of imitating or representing a reality from which spectators are barred. Here, "the mediate" relates people to each other, with *relation* signifying the process of being brought together and given a measure of space from each other at the same time.

This is essentially a spatial construct—a diagram, or, as Bacon might have it, a ring of action—that constructs both distance and association (or, if you like, individuality and collectivity). Its construction demarcates some sort of boundary, but it does not follow that the function of that boundary need be a constrictive or restrictive one. In fact, the function of the boundary may be wildly variable and even liberating, especially insofar as it creates sub-spaces, and guarantees that there can be a game. As philosopher Ludwig Wittgenstein puts it, "If I surround an area with a fence or a line or otherwise, the purpose may be to prevent someone from getting in or out; but it may also be part of a game and the players supposed, say, to jump over the boundary; or it may shew where the property of one man ends and that of another begins; and so on. So if I draw a boundary line that is not yet to say what I am drawing it for." Given that "breaking down boundaries" has come to act as a synonym for innovative or progressive action, be it in art, social justice, or beyond, Wittgenstein's distinctions bear some repeating. Not all boundaries or mediating forces are created equal; not all serve the same purpose. Neither politics nor art is served if and when the distinctions between them are willingly or unthinkingly smeared out.

Rancière's veneration of this third term also echoes certain remarks Hannah Arendt made over fifty years ago, in speaking about the importance of the public realm (which, Arendt makes clear, is definitively *not* the same as the social realm). "The public realm, as the common world," Arendt wrote, "gathers us together and yet prevents our falling over each other, so to speak. What makes mass society so difficult to bear is not the number of people involved, or at least not primarily, but the fact that the world between them has lost its power to gather them together, to relate and separate them. The weirdness of this situation resembles a spiritualistic séance where a number of people gathered round a table might suddenly, through some magic trick, see the table vanish from their midst, so that two persons sitting opposite each other were no longer separated but also would be entirely unrelated to each other by anything tangible."

For Arendt, this collapse signifies a deep and dangerous failure in human relations. (God only knows what she would have made of the vast social realm of the Internet, and its creation of a wholly different type of séance—one in which the table remains, but the human bodies are disappeared.) For others, this collapse serves as the gateway to ecstatic, unmediated union. Others still, seeing this fantasized union as utopian nonsense, but who are equally troubled by the forms of alienation that ostensibly prohibit it, offer up satirical or cynical dystopias in its place. And others—especially younger others—simply ignore both the promises and the perils of the whole communion/alienation dyad, as one typically ignores any binaries that no longer speak to the defining conditions and possibilities of one's time. The mind-bending work of an artist such as Ryan Trecartin offers a particularly gripping example of the latter.

Trecartin's 2007 feature-length video, *I-Be Area,* while nominally based on the concept of "virtual reality," is a riotous exploration of what kinds of space, identity, physicality, language, sexuality, and consciousness might be possible once one leaves the dichotomy of the virtual and the real behind, along with a whole host of other need-not-apply binaries (the everyday and the apocalyptic, the public and the private, the utopic and the dystopic, male and female, gay and straight, among them). The hyperactive cloning, frenetic strobing of characters, and post-identity verbiage of *I-Be*

Area make James Cameron's *Avatar* (2009) or the Internet game Second Life look like relics from the Stone Age. "I love the idea of technology and culture moving faster than the understanding of those mediums by people," Trecartin has said, and his works aim to immerse viewers in this failed-to-upload state. The disorientation of this state is not that of grandpa befuddled by a fistful of printer cables, but rather the sort of psychological and physiological stupefaction more often associated with acid overdoses and schizoid breakdowns.

I-Be Area takes incapacity—to absorb, to make sense, to cohere, to sort, to concentrate—as its starting point. ("It's like the jumper being jumped before the onset of 'jump,'" Trecartin explains, both helpfully and unhelpfully.) Then it amplifies this incapacity by turning up the speed, the color, the hysteria, the flicker. Image or speech overflow is no longer a problem, and certainly not one that art could or should aid in solving. It is where we live, at least while watching Trecartin; it is our "abstract plot of now," as he calls it. Trecartin's ability to sustain us here for some real time often feels like a miracle, in that such an ability seems as if it should be, by definition, also beyond the artist. That is to say, the art often feels as if it is moving faster than Trecartin himself could be—which is likely why his films, when combined with his youth (*I-Be Area* was finished when he was twenty-six), have had something of an awe-inducing effect on the art world. "All I can do is generalize about this world and point to it with a yearning, stumped pleasure," writes Wayne Koestenbaum about Trecartin's work. "My pointing finger is the gesture of an outsider, a tourist, gawking at a radioactive carnival I can't domesticate or quarantine."

Koestenbaum notes that Trecartin's work is about radical distraction—that dreaded, proliferate state that leads to dazzlingly high numbers of cell phone–related car crashes each day, or that leads otherwise progressive professors to shake their heads in despair as their students text each other under the classroom table. But Trecartin's brand of distraction doesn't rely on any simple use of the imitative fallacy—that is, "contemporary life is mind-scrambling, fragmented, and distracted, so my art must be mind-scrambling, fragmented, and distracted, too." It is too tightly orchestrated for that—too layered, too well performed, too purposefully edited, too intelligently perverse. However bawdy and hysterical, Trecartin's videos draw tight rings of action: they are condensed, fast-moving world creations that make an intense demand on our attention. And the animating paradox of this world, as Koestenbaum has put it, is that "*Trecartin's characters concentrate on distraction.*" However frenetic *I-Be Area* may be, its distraction is not of the same order as that of, say, the idiotic pop-up balloons and crawling tickers that have become staples of the television screen. To stay with *I-Be Area* all the way through—to listen to every word, to follow every decision and cut—requires a keen effort. You'll get the most out of it if you, too, can concentrate on distraction.

Of course, you may not remember much of what happened; you may not remember any of the characters; you may not even be left with an image. If your experience resembles mine, you'll be left with something far more amorphous—a kind of vibrating memory of the unnerving psychic state the work induced, or captured, or invented (and, perhaps, a notebook full of scrawled lines that sounded great at the time, such as, "My personal really concise pussy is developing a very inner monologue which I will not reveal to you as I become dynamic"). In his lucid, compelling book on craft, *Unbalancing Acts: Foundations for a Theater*, famed avant-garde dramatist Richard Foreman articulates this aesthetic-of-amnesia quite well: "The image of the Marlboro man riding his horse and smoking his cigarette has stuck with me for many years—and so what? It's garbage. It's kitsch. All it means is that the image seduced me, that it pushed a button that was ready to be pushed, and I responded. It didn't widen my sensibilities, compassion, or intuition. Whereas an art that affects you in the moment, but which you then find hard to remember, is straining to bring you to another level. It offers images or ideas from that other level, that other way of being, which is why you find them hard to remember. But it has opened you to the possibility of growing into what you are not yet, which is exactly what art should do."

Foreman is a bit more sanguine about the possibility of "growing into what you are not yet" than Trecartin, whose enthusiasm about new technologies and their relationship to human consciousness has a decidedly who-cares-where-we're-headed-let's-party vibe. I don't think, for example, that Trecartin is explicitly setting out to make work that offers his viewers "artistic structures—models of consciousness—that might evolve into a new kind of lucidity and self-possession, which would enable us to navigate the rapids of our times," as Foreman says he has been trying to do for upward of forty years now. In short, critics and viewers who look to Trecartin as an idiot savant emissary from the next generation who has come to answer the question *Are we going to be alright?* are not likely to feel reassured.

But in the end, it may not matter. Both Foreman and Trecartin work from a conception of the human, or the "real," borne out of contradiction, fluctuation, incoherence, and perversity; both offer immersion in their vision without rehashing the avant-garde fetish of terrorizing the audience or the mainstream one of chaperoning it. "We abide by cultural directives that urge us: clarify each thought, each experience, so you can cull from them their single, dominant meaning and, in the process, become a responsible adult who knows what he or she thinks," Foreman has said. "But what I try to show is the opposite: how at every moment, the world presents us with a composition in which a multitude of meanings and realities are available, and you are able to swim, lucid and self-contained, in that turbulent sea of multiplicity." After an hour or so of watching *I-Be Area*, or of watching a Foreman play, you start to swim in such a sea. The experience seems to me at least a start on a worthwhile sense of human freedom.

CAPTIVITY, CATHARSIS

I n *Unbalancing Acts*, Richard Foreman writes that reactionary
critics are correct to worry that subversive forms of contemporary art might undermine Western culture. "But they shouldn't
worry," he counsels calmly. "Something better is coming."

For better or worse, no one seems so worried anymore. After all,
why bother picking on Andres Serrano's *Piss Christ* or Robert Map-
plethorpe's photograph of a fist up someone's ass when queers can
get legally married in six states and counting? Surely there are reac-
tionaries out there who remain periodically or perpetually preoc-
cupied by the filth and degeneracy of modern art (God bless them).
But since the culture wars of the late 1980s and early '90s—that
is, the ones that swirled around funding for the National Endowment for the Arts, and culminated with the Supreme Court case
National Endowment for the Arts et al. vs. Finley et al. (1998)—the
question of whether images can lead to injury (moral or otherwise)
has been posed and tested most literally (and most hysterically, and
most litigiously) in relation to art's trashy cousin, mass media.

Not that the change of venue has changed the preoccupations
of the family-values crowd very much. Consider, for example, the
American Family Association, whose mission statement says the
organization's purpose is "to promote traditional family values,

focusing primarily on the influence of television and other media on our society." A quick trip to the AFA's Web site reveals the main gist of its concerns regarding television and media: its homepage today (February 21, 2010) showcases a boycott of PepsiCo, on account of its running of a "non-neutral" ad about homosexuality—all part and parcel of PepsiCo's (reprehensible) effort to become "the gay cola." Then there's the featured article on the site titled "News Just Keeps Getting Worse for Homosexuality," which contains this reassurance: "Pro-family groups are the ones who are accused of lacking compassion. But note this: we are not calling for homosexuals to be put to death. We're calling for them to get help."

Should the likes of the AFA become one's bedfellows, it's hard to feel much appetite to join in a debate about "the influence of television and other media on our society." With a handful of exceptions, this is a debate populated by moralists and marketers, who can appear in the bright light of C-SPAN as opponents, but who regularly work together to promote the conjoined forces of the so-called free market and so-called family values, even when the alliance frays into conceptual incoherence.

At this point, it would be naive to express surprise at the fact that of the twenty-two items listed under the AFA's heading of "television indecency," only one is concerned with violence. (The rest, unsurprisingly, have to do with sex.) Countless other organizations, however—from the Federal Communications Commission to the American Academy of Pediatrics to Parents Against Media Violence—have taken a different tack, and have placed representations of violence at the forefront of their concerns. This conversation typically heats up in the wake of a Columbine- or a Virginia Tech–type massacre, even though school shootings (which, as of February 12, 2010, must sadly now include those by professors in faculty meetings) have become a frequent enough staple of American life to ensure a near continuous—and perhaps increasingly futile—discourse in their wake.

By this point I have read countless studies, editorials, congressional transcripts, and book-length investigations of media violence. In doing so, I have been consistently struck by the fact that the one question that seems to gain the most traction with anyone—including the American Civil Liberties Union—is the most literal one: does viewing TV, comic-book, movie, or video-game violence increase the chances of people—usually boys or men—hurting other people? I respect the pragmatism of that question—even if the morass of statistics that constitutes its answer seems to me an inadequate response to much larger questions about what kind of reality-making we, as a culture, and as a species, might want to put our efforts and imagination into. (A culture that spends an enormous amount of its time glutting itself on, say, ultraviolent, misogynistic video games, but that maintains miraculously low rates of rape and murder—perhaps because so many people remain narcotically affixed to their devices—still does not strike me as one I would want to live in.) At any rate, while I am disinclined to see prohibition as a solution, I have come to believe that the larger questions deserve our attention, even if they do not lend themselves as easily to measure.

—

On March 13, 2007, I awoke to find my neighborhood blanketed by an ad campaign for a movie titled *Captivity*. The first round of advertisements, which consisted of 30 billboards in Los Angeles, and 1,400 taxi-cab tops in New York City, was divided into four panels, each charting a woman's progress through four possible stages of being: "abduction," "confinement," "torture," and "termination." The abduction panel showed a black man's hand or a black-gloved hand (the difference blurred, so as to provoke racial panic while shrugging off the trick) over her mouth. The confinement panel showed a close-up of her face, smeared with dirt and mascara, pressed up against a chain-link fence. The torture panel featured her face bandaged up like a mummy's, a tube shoved up its nose, with dark red blood draining out of the tube, then out of the frame. The termination panel showed her mostly disrobed body splayed over a table, its dead head dangling toward the ground, its dead breasts facing up toward the heavens, another sacrifice to God-knows-what.

After a public outcry, which Reuters said came in the form of "a flood of e-mails and phone calls from angry parents and offended women," the confinement panel was the only one that remained. And remain it did, everywhere, for four months. Sometimes I'd find myself standing in front of a poster for the movie at a bus stop, then I'd look up and see a billboard on the western horizon, then I'd turn around and see one on the eastern horizon. On the street level, it often appeared alongside advertisements for two other movies to be released concurrently—Eli Roth's *Hostel: Part II*, which featured a menacing man in a blood-spattered butcher's apron, ready to perform the torture-killing of three female college students on vacation in Europe, and Gregory Hoblit's *Fracture*, which featured a close-up of everyone's favorite movie monster, Anthony Hopkins, with the bragging slogan "I SHOT MY WIFE" in huge red letters floating over his face. It was a real you've-come-a-long-way-baby trio.

Or that's at least how Courtney Solomon, CEO of After Dark, the marketer behind the *Captivity* billboard campaign, pretended to see it. "The movie is certainly a horror movie and it's about abduction, but it's also about female empowerment," Solomon said. He was trying to explain that he, too, had been upset about the abduction-to-termination billboards—not because of their graphic nature or their glorification of sexualized torture, but because they were "misleading" about the arc of the film. He explained that after many test screenings and focus groups, they had reshot the ending "so the main character ends up in as much of a positive situation as the situation would allow." This is, I suppose, one version of female empowerment—the kind you might see looking through a pinhole, angled toward hell.

———

IT ISN'T much fun to analyze American pop culture anymore. In the 1980s and '90s academics went to town on it—what scandalous fun to bring all the fierce powers of one's mind to bear on Madonna or *The Matrix* or Spike Lee or *The X-Files* or, more recently, *The L Word* or *24*. I'm not saying there's no fun or value or necessity in this work anymore; maybe there's more than ever. I'm just saying that for me, personally, it feels like a dead end. The cultural products now seem designed to analyze themselves, and to make a spectacle of their essentially consumable perversity. "They really let me showcase my creativity!" the writers say, while churning out more crap. And there, as Slavoj Žižek explains (in *The Ticklish Subject*), lies "the unbearable paradox of this postmodern 'disalienation': the tension is no longer between my innermost creative impulses and the Institution that does not appreciate them or wants to crush them in order to 'normalize' me." Instead, according to Žižek, postmodern corporations (such as Microsoft) work in a more Foucauldian fashion: rather than be threatened by our idiosyncratic creativity, they depend on putting it into service on their own behalf. As Žižek puts it, one becomes useless for them the moment one starts losing one's "imp of perversity."

This paradox makes commenting on the "kinda-hegemonic, kinda-subversive" operations (to use Eve Kosofsky Sedgwick's wonderful phrase) of so much popular culture feel like a bore— like planting a flag on the moon after forty countries have landed there before you, or on a moon whose sole purpose it is to host flags. Lionsgate/After Dark puts up a round of billboards—unapproved by the Motion Picture Association of America—depicting sickening torture; you call to complain, disliking the sound of your Tipper-Gore-esque voice. You hang up and start worrying about the free-speech implications of your protest, so you turn to Noam Chomsky and ponder hard questions about manufactured consent and the meaning of free speech in an everything-is-owned-or-for-sale world, then to Jürgen Habermas, to ponder the meaning of public space in an everything-is-owned-or-for-sale world. "The world fashioned by the mass media is a public sphere in appearance only," writes Habermas, and so it is. And (to paraphrase Theodor Adorno) it is crucial to remember that while this world may appear to emanate *from* society as a whole, it is, in fact, *directed at* society as a whole.

So you wonder how to tell what emanates from where, and how you might balance your visceral outrage against the *Captivity* emanations with your deep veneration of writers from Sade to Jean Genet to Dennis Cooper to Heather Lewis to Pat Califia to Benjamin Weissman, and ask yourself if you can keep resting on some quasi-nostalgic and most certainly elitist (but not-wholly-without-significance) distinction between high and low art, or the value of the complex and essentially private written word versus that of the mass-marketed, in-your-face media image. Then you hear a voice saying, *That's the problem with liberals today, they think too much, they're too interested in complexity to effect any real change*, and you say back, *So be it—a life devoted to complexity is the life I want to live*. Then you rejoice when the *Captivity* ads are pulled and all the executives momentarily look like fools as they are forced to make all kinds of artificial apologies and excuses—like Peter Wilkes at Lionsgate, who swore that his company "had no involvement with the ads," or Solomon, who said in one breath, "Personally, I wasn't going to go with this campaign. I thought it was OTP (over the top)," and in another that the ads were an "accident," that "the wrong files were sent to the printer." But then the billboards come down and overnight are replaced with the scrawl "Captivity Was Here" and a new release date, and you realize it was all part of the plan, the plan to create controversy by pushing the envelope, the plan to make anyone who protested the first round out to be schoolmarms, scolds, "angry parents and offended women"—you know, those who go into the lifeboat first—and the movie gains in publicity because people hear about the controversy and wonder what other forms of torture they weren't allowed to see, and more people get ready to pony up their ten dollars to see the pretty blonde lady get tortured to death, or if not to death, then into "as much of a positive situation as the situation would allow," which I would imagine, in this case, means her stumbling naked out of a cellar with about a quarter of her internal organs intact. And then, when the movie finally comes out, Solomon throws a release party in West Hollywood at a club made over into a torture chamber, draped with the original "OTP" advertisements and serviced by the Suicide Girls, and calls the event "[his] little personal tribute to [the women's groups]," and later tries to bait groups like the

National Organization for Women into having "a town-hall style debate" about the film (which, for obvious reasons, NOW declines to do). And the wheel keeps on turning.

—

BUT WHY am I spending so much time thinking about the movies, or, odder still, getting worked up over movie ratings or ad campaigns? Who cares about the movies anyway, especially about these kinds of movies? "For the audience [*Captivity*] is made for, it's satisfying to that audience. I'm sure that's not the same audience that's complaining about the billboards," Solomon asserted. In my case, he is most certainly right. (Though it must be said that this statement smears out the distinction between billboards, which are visible by everyone, without their consent, and films, which are not.) In any case, I know countless people who love these torture-porn movies—some of them shrewd feminist, Marxist, queer, anarchist, anti-globalist, you-name-it academics and writers who offer up such good-humored, campy, intelligent readings of these films (especially Eli Roth's *Hostel* series, which has attracted a fair amount of laudatory academic attention) that I feel ashamed in their presence of my squeamishness, the shrillness of my moral compass, the obviousness of my critique.

I suppose that one partial answer is that the face of the *Captivity* lady (which is that of actress Elisha Cuthbert, who has made a quick, miniature splash for herself by specializing in victimization; she played Jack Bauer's daughter on *24*) served, throughout some of the darkest days of the George W. Bush administration, as an outsized, daily reminder of the cultural and political forces working overtime to normalize—or in this case, make sexy—that which would have been unthinkable in (publicly acknowledged) American policy not so long ago: namely, torture, especially sexualized torture. ("Torture is hot, period," an anonymous blogger wrote in support of the *Captivity* ad campaign.) And so when I saw Cuthbert's face I saw not just the airbrushed image of another blonde actress pretending to be held in captivity and tortured and potentially terminated, but the nameless bodies of all the real brown people being held in captivity and tortured and potentially terminated, and this huge, sexed-up, Aryan, crying face standing in the way, like some gigantic porno scrim.

There was no billboard of Manadel al-Jamadi, for example, who was tortured in American custody at Abu Ghraib, and who died after being subjected to a form of torture known as a "Palestinian hanging." (In a Palestinian hanging—one of the many "enhanced interrogation techniques" approved by the Bush administration— one has one's arms shackled behind one's back, then affixed far above the torso so that one's body hangs down in a form of crucifixion. After being beaten, Jamadi was hung this way with a green plastic sandbag over his head. When CIA interrogators finally removed his hood and lowered his body to the ground, "blood came gushing out of his nose and mouth, as if a faucet had been turned on.")

One form of self-deception: to offer reversals that have rhetorical impact but crumble when pressed for meaning. So, to revise: I am not really convinced that a billboard of Jamadi would have "done" anything, even if it made us feel sadness or confusion or anger or shame or outrage. As Sontag has justly observed—and I think it bears repeating—focusing on the question of whether or not an image retains the capacity to produce a strong emotion sidesteps the problem that having a strong emotion is not the same thing as having an understanding, and neither is the same thing as taking an action. "You do not necessarily *feel* [compassion]," Buddhist teacher Chögyam Trungpa once warned a student who was worrying about how to act compassionately without feeling it first. "You *are* it."

—

IN HIS creepily committed polemic, "The Media Violence Myth," historian-turned-media-violence-defender Richard Rhodes makes the claim that ultraviolent media actually does the public a service by "taking the psychic garbage out." How, exactly, this evacuation-via-proliferation works, however—not to mention whose psychic garbage a movie such as *Captivity* is (or on whom it gets dumped)— is never really explained. For there is no evidence that the torture portrayed in TV shows like *24* or in movies such as *Captivity* takes the garbage out, unless "catharsis" now means "tune in next week."

Indeed, the whole psychoanalytic notion of catharsis-as-cure has been somewhat put to the test by market-driven ventures that profit from egging on particular desires rather than freeing anyone from them. Freud himself eventually abandoned the idea of catharsis-as-cure, but the notion has stayed alive and kicking throughout twentieth-century psychology, present in everything from primal scream therapy to high colonics to rolfing. At present there remain profound differences of opinion about how one might best manage unmanageable, potentially destructive emotions, such as anger: many Western therapists encourage angry adults and children to "let it all out" by beating, say, a pillow; whereas Buddhists such as Thich Nhat Hanh—author of *Anger: Wisdom for Cooling the Flames*—gently but firmly discourage such methods, believing that they only rehearse and reinscribe destructiveness, in their suggestion that pummeling something—even if that something be, for the moment, an insentient object—is a useful and appropriate response to anger.

And, again, it all depends on what meaning of "catharsis" one is employing. Here is Rush Limbaugh's, for example, in reference to the treatment of Iraqi prisoners at Abu Ghraib: "This is no different than what happens at the Skull and Bones initiation, and we're going to ruin people's lives over it, and we're going to hamper our military effort, and then we are going to really hammer them because they had a good time. You know, these people are being fired at every day. I'm talking about people having a good time, these people, you ever heard of emotional release? You [ever] heard of need to blow some steam off?"

When Aristotle used the term "catharsis," he was talking about Greek tragedies, which are, without a doubt, violent, often gruesomely so (although a tragedy, by one definition, has the most violent acts take place off-stage). What was at stake for Artistotle, vis-à-vis catharsis, were the emotions of "pity and terror" aroused by the play, not the ability to hold down one's lunch while watching a woman being forced to drink internal organs that have been ground up in a blender (which is apparently one of the things that happens to the heroine of *Captivity*). For these reasons and more, this classical type of tragedy is not easily analogous to mass-marketed media spectacle that shoves images of torture porn down our throats, especially at a time when our country has slipped into making use of actual sexualized torture.

There is, however, evidence to suggest that the advent of glorified torture in popular entertainment serves a political function, insofar as it creates a network of identifications through which people find themselves warming to torture and torturers at a time when our government has begun to permit and utilize torture.

(Limbaugh knows this well, and clearly angles his remarks to provide this service.) During the run-up to the 2008 presidential election, for example, the nice woman who runs the cash register at my school cafeteria started wearing a button on her lapel that read "Jack Bauer for President" (Jack Bauer being the "whatever it takes" counterterrorist agent, played by Kiefer Sutherland, on *24*, who tortures both the so-called innocent and guilty alike with regularity). She thought it was funny, and she was also completely serious. Her ideal candidate for president had become The Man Who Most Closely Resembles Jack Bauer, Torturer, which is probably why the field of Republican presidential candidates duked it out in the 2008 pre-primary debates to out-Bauer one another. Conservative talk-radio host Laura Ingraham summarized this ethos on September 13, 2006, when she told Bill O'Reilly on FOX News: "The average American out there loves the show *24*. OK? They love Jack Bauer. They love *24*. In my mind, that's as close to a national referendum that it's OK to use tough tactics against high-level Al Qaeda operatives as we're going to get."

Such proclamations do not coexist easily with the refrain, also frequently made by Limbaugh and company, that *24* is "just a television show! Get a grip." In the case of *24*, the fact is that the popularity of the show (which aired its final episode in May 2010) created a great deal of on-the-ground trouble for the military— so much so that in November 2006, U.S. Army Brigadier General Patrick Finnegan, the dean of the United States Military Academy at West Point, along with a team of military and FBI interrogators, flew to Los Angeles to meet with the show's creators. The military delegation hoped to convey the severe, adverse effects they felt the show's depiction of torture was having on American soldiers, who seemed to be increasingly seduced by Bauer's "whatever it takes" motto, and decreasingly inclined to take seriously the importance of adhering to international and military law. In her February 19, 2007, *New Yorker* article on the subject, Jane Mayer reported that *24*'s creative team was not particularly interested in hearing or responding to this news. As Gary Solis, a retired law professor who designed and taught the law of war for commanders at West Point, and who was one of the members of the military team at the meeting, later told Mayer, trying to get the producers to alter their tack was "like trying to stomp out an anthill."

EVERYTHING IS NICE

"For those who believe that violence in cinema consists either of harmless action spectacles or Martin Scorsese masterpieces, I might suggest heading down to the local multiplex and taking a look at some of the grotesque, morbid creations being projected on the walls," filmmaker Mike White wrote in an Op-Ed that appeared shortly after the 2007 shooting at Virginia Tech—a shooting that prompted new rounds of offensive and defensive posturing in regard to the role media violence plays or does not play in real-life killings. "To defend mindless exercises in sadism like 'The Hills Have Eyes II' by citing 'Macbeth' is almost like using 'Romeo and Juliet' to justify child pornography," White wrote.

I respected White's Op-Ed, because it came from someone in the industry who wasn't calling for censorship or increased legislation or shame or sanitization, but rather for filmmakers simply to pause, stop screaming that "movies don't kill people, lunatics kill people," ask a few mindful questions about the propensity to do anything for big money, and admit that movies have an enormous capacity to "shape our thinking and inform our choices," which is why, White suggests, most people who work in the industry were drawn to do so in the first place.

Beyond that, I respected White's Op-Ed because the examples he used from his own life shed some light, whether intentionally or not, on the gendered nature of the problem. He remarked that as a kid, movies most certainly influenced the way he and his friends talked to their girlfriends, and that while no one got shot in the face in his backyard, there were plenty of acts of "male bravado," which "ranged from stupid to cruel."

I wish I could have written, or that someone could have written, an Op-Ed that shed some light on how certain movies influence female behavior in the backyard, but as we still so often can see female behavior only in reaction to male behavior, it would be difficult to know where to start.

One (local) place to start might be my bookshelf, from which I make a list of recent and contemporary female writers known for violent or cruel writing (there is a difference, I know). Here is my short list: Kathy Acker, Dorothy Allison, Octavia Butler, Angela Carter, Ivy Compton-Burnett, Virginie Despentes, Mary Gaitskill, Patricia Highsmith, Shirley Jackson, Elfriede Jelinek, Sarah Kane, Natsuo Kirino, Heather Lewis, Joyce Mansour, Susannah Moore, Joyce Carol Oates, Flannery O'Connor, Sylvia Plath, Pauline Réage, Sapphire, Valerie Solanas, and Christina Stead. Does it come as any surprise that most, if not all, of these writers are known for writing in relation to—and often explicit protest against—male violence, misogyny, or patriarchy? Is that one of the injustices of "phallocentrism" itself—that is, its suggestion that there's nothing else imaginable under the sun—not even a form of female aggression or rage or darkness—not shaped by or tethered to the male? "*Let woman find once more her cruelty and her violence that make her attack the vanquished because they are vanquished,* to the point of mutilating them," cries Valentine de Saint-Point in her 1914 "Manifesto of Futurist Woman," in which she calls on women to act like the "Furies, Amazons, Semiramis, Joans of Arc, Jeanne Hachettes, Judith and Charlotte Cordays, Cleopatras, and Messalinas" that they essentially are or can be. *Woman, become sublimely injust once more, like all the forces of nature!*"

In an attempt to cover up al-Jamadi's murder at Abu Ghraib, CIA personnel packed him in a body bag filled with ice to slow his decomposition, which is how he came to be known as "the Ice Man." His iced corpse was then immortalized in snapshots taken by Specialists Charles Graner and Sabrina Harman, who posed for each other next to his battered body. The most famous of these snapshots shows Harman giving a green-gloved thumb's up in front of Jamadi's face, one of whose eyes appears to have been nearly bludgeoned out of its socket. Valentine de Saint-Point would have been proud.

For the many others for whom a female reclamation of sadism provides no reason to rejoice, the photographs from Abu Ghraib depicting Specialist Megan Ambuhl, Private First Class Lynndie England, and Specialist Sabrina Harman engaged in brutal acts of torture and sexual abuse were devastating. Writer Barbara Ehrenreich went so far as to claim that "a certain kind of feminism, or perhaps I should say a certain kind of feminist naiveté, died in Abu Ghraib." The feminist naiveté she is referring to is the kind that "saw men as perpetual perpetrators, women as the perpetual victims, and male sexual violence as the root of all injustice," and presumed that women were morally superior to men due to their "lesser inclination toward cruelty and violence." All that was before, Ehrenreich says, "we had seen female sexual sadism in action."

The existence of something that could be called female sexual sadism did not and does not come as a surprise to me. (Nor would it have come as a surprise to the Marquis de Sade, whose *Philosophy in the Bedroom* puts forth the rather strange argument that "female cruelty [is] always more active than male, by reason of the excessive sensibility of women's organs." For more on this account, see Angela Carter's brilliant act of disobedience and resistance, *The Sadeian Woman*.) Nor would I think any more or any less of my purported sex should such sexual sadism be a part of it. We are, after all, human beings (are we not?). Nonetheless, it is a mistake to read the role played by women in the photographs from Abu Ghraib primarily as evidence of such a phenomenon. My response to the pictures had more in common with that of Angela Davis, who saw in them a reiteration of the tragic but familiar historical fact that "people in power, regardless of gender or race, have equal opportunity to inflict racist and sexist violence on others." Alas, and also: but of course.

I did fear, however, that those who might have thinkingly or unthinkingly relegated kindness and compassion to the feminine realm (as Ehrenreich admits to doing, as Western thought has generally done, at least since the Victorian period—and, I admit, as I have also found myself doing from time to time) would now have cause to shrug and say—with varying degrees of cynicism, sadness, or wickedness—*Look, even the girls are doing it—it must really be the rotten core of human nature! Welcome to the dark side, one and all!*

Should the rest of the photographs from Abu Ghraib ever be released, the presence of women throughout will likely give us a fuller—albeit more distressing—sense of the various roles they played at the prison. Not only are there likely to be more abuses committed by female soldiers, but also there are allegedly photographs depicting the rape of both female and male Iraqis by American soldiers, along with the sexualized abuse of children, some allegedly as young as ten years old. (As recently as May 2009, the Pentagon fiercely denied that such photos exist, or that such acts occurred; General Antonio Mario Taguba, the official responsible for conducting a full investigation of the abuses committed by Americans at the prison, has gone on record as saying that he has seen such photos, and that such acts did occur.)

Taken together, these two sets of photos may serve as a forceful reminder of something that an isolated meditation on Lynndie England and her leashed detainee may lead us to forget: that whether the perpetrators be male or female, the strategies used remain rooted in an all-too-familiar, age-old mash-up of misogynistic and homophobic violence, racist dehumanization, and militarized conquest—an operation that has not exactly had, and still does not have, something called "female sexual sadism" as its driving force.

Davis argues that the photos of women soldiers at Abu Ghraib call for a form of feminist analysis that "challenges prevailing assumptions that the only possible relationship between women and violence requires women to be the victims." Certainly the long history of relations between white women and black men and women in this country—from slavery through the Civil Rights era, at least—has already presented an immediate and formidable challenge to such an assumption. This form of feminist analysis is utterly crucial, and thankfully now quite prevalent, largely due to the efforts of feminists such as Davis, who have justly and relentlessly insisted that myriad forms of oppression be understood and confronted together (as in Davis's 1982 classic, *Women, Race, and Class*).

The problem remains, however: given the patriarchal structure of most societies on earth, and given that our most ancient, archetypal examples of female behavior and expression—from Antigone to Medea to Judith—are, in some sense, inextricable from the social structures that birthed (and often authored) them—it remains unclear if and how these relationships can be disentangled from the circumstances from which they emerged. Likely such an exploration has elements of a fool's errand, as do most efforts to isolate nature from nurture—as if any life has ever been lived under the aegis of one or the other, rather than in a complex brew of both.

But if the possible relationships between women and cruelty or violence seem inevitably shaped or even generated by the misogynistic and/or patriarchal social structures from which they emanate, then the same must hold true for those of men. There's no reason, for example, why work by Paul McCarthy, Brian Evenson, Chris Burden, Michael Haneke, Martin McDonagh, Otto Muehl, and countless others cannot be, indeed should not be analyzed in this light. (Indeed, much of it has been—McCarthy's work is famous for raking masculinity and imperialism over the coals; Evenson has explicitly named fascist patriarchy and the misogyny of the Mormon Church as among his subjects; the work of the Viennese Actionists is, in many respects, an aggressive exploration of sexual power relations and taboos, not to mention deeply linked to the various post-Nazi psychoses plaguing postwar Austria, and so on.)

In other words, if, when it comes to the subject of cruelty and women, it turns out that one cannot disentangle contingency from essence, then there is no reason why such a disentanglement should suddenly become possible when it comes to men. Unless, of course, women cannot properly be said to share in the human condition—a recurring assertion in religious and philosophical circles over the past few millennia, as well as an ongoing legal and political conundrum. (For the former, see the satirical, oft-reproduced Renaissance text, *Disputatio nova contra mulieres, qua probatur eas homines non esse* ["A new argument against women, in which it is demonstrated that they are not human beings"]; for the latter, see Catharine MacKinnon's 2006 international study of women's human rights, 500 years hence, titled *Are Women Human?*)

Further, despite their desire to catapult us into a cosmological sphere in which forces such as Artaud's "living whirlwind that devours the darkness" reign supreme, many male thinkers and artists evidence an obsessiveness with gender that can be difficult, if not impossible, to ignore, even if one is trying hard to board their post-gender, transcendental train. Nietzsche and Bataille rely relentlessly on gendered terms in their attempts to access this "living whirlwind": in Nietzsche, this plays itself out via a multitude of misogynistic asides, and endless metaphors pertaining to women, pregnancy, castration, effeminacy, maternity, impotence, rape, and so on; Bataille's philosophy of transgressive erotism often depends on the alignment of virility and violence, frequently made manifest in the stereotypical dyad of male assailant and female victim. Compared with these two comrades-in-cruelty, Artaud's preference for the anal, or the fecal, over the genital, comes as a welcome relief. I'll take Artaud's "God is shit" over Nietzsche's "Suppose truth is a woman" any day.

—

I AM not at all convinced, for the reasons named above (among others), that this question is a good one, but I'm posing it anyway: are there specific forms of cruelty—beyond a willingness to partake in the varying forms of racist and sexist violence that surround us—that women have seemed to excel at, in "representation" if not "reality"?

There is, of course, the "rape and revenge" model, used as the premise for any number of dramas, from the notorious *I Spit on Your Grave* (1978) to its more mainstream offshoots, from *The Burning Bed* (1984) to *Thelma and Louise* (1991). The rape-and-revenge scenario is closely related to the potentially-justifiable-self-defense-morphing-into-unforgiveable-psychosis model, most recently brought to the fore by *Monster*, the 2003 film based on the real-life story of female serial killer Aileen Wuornos, or the French film *Baise-Moi*, based on the book by Virginie Despentes. (I should note that Despentes, who codirected the film, disputes its assignation to any bad-girl ghetto: "Forget the tits and cunts, for one second. The key words here should be: gun, death, fake blood. Not 'pussy pussy pussy.' . . . I don't care those two characters have cunts. They are archetypes: violent outcasts. Should not be always defined by them having cunts.") For a more enigmatic, understated spin on a similar theme, there's Chantal Akerman's 1975 classic, *Jeanne Dielman, 23 Quai du Commerce, 1080 Bruxelles*, a film that placidly follows the daily activities, over a three-day period, of a single mother who occasionally supports herself as a prostitute. After three hours and thirty-five minutes, the film reaches an unexpected, violent conclusion when Jeanne stabs one of her male clients to death by scissoring him in the neck.

Haunting each of these scenarios is the notion of excess—the sense that while the emotions behind the violence might be understandable, the act itself—unless imminently tied to an act of self-defense necessary to preserve a life—is always in excess, out of scale, hysterical, monstrous. In 1987, Toni Morrison provided the world with one of its most indelible, most morally profound dramatizations of this saga in her novel *Beloved*, with its multivalent portrayal of Sethe, a mother who attempts to kill her children so that they would not have to live in slavery. In her attempt "to put [her] babies somewhere they would be safe," Sethe ends up successfully killing only her eldest, whose throat she slits with a handsaw. This child's ghost—called Beloved, after the sole word on her tombstone—subsequently haunts the surviving family in unpredictable and suffocating ways.

Part of *Beloved*'s brilliance lies in its narrative elaboration of the relationship between what Žižek has termed "subjective violence" (i.e., the readily apparent eruptions of violence in everyday life, with discernible agents and victims) and "objective violence" (i.e., the systemic or symbolic violence, often as invisible as dark matter, that underlies and mobilizes the structure of capitalism itself). In his 2008 book *Violence*, Žižek argues that one must always read explosions of subjective violence against this structural or objective violence, rather than remaining transfixed by the former, as we so often are. Without such perspective, acts of subjective violence (such as murder, terrorism, and war) will nearly always seem in excess, monstrous, inexplicable, and—perhaps most dangerously, according to Žižek—more horrifying than the structural violence that is their truer and more heinous cause.

Most obviously, however, and arguably most commonly, there is self-vanquishing, sometimes to the point of mutilation. "Girls are cruelest to themselves," observes Anne Carson in "The Glass Essay," her brilliant long poem about the ravages of female anger, loneliness, grief, and desire, giving us as poetic adage what any number of other fields give us as statistic. But girls can be very good at something else. They can be good at exposing the cruelties of others. And one disturbing subset of this talent involves the creation of scenarios that give others the option, or the opportunity, to behave cruelly.

———

THE HISTORIC "WACK: Art and the Feminist Revolution" exhibit, which opened at the Museum of Contemporary Art in Los Angeles on March 4, 2007—just a few days before the *Captivity* posters saturated the city—offered a dense forest of these overlapping forms of cruelty. There was Nancy Spero's *Torture of Women* (1976), enormous paper panels pairing fragmented, documentary accounts from Amnesty International about torture experienced by women around the globe with snippets from various mythologies that depend on the dismemberment and mutilation of women. There was Annette Messager's *Les tortures volontaires* (1972), eighty-six framed photographs from newspapers and magazines, all of which depict women undergoing beautification processes whose bandages, electrodes, blindfolds, incisions, compressions, pumps, tubes, and restraints resemble torture. There was Orlan, the performance artist who has undergone many such "beautification processes" as a particularly unsettling form of feminist theater, dismantling and reconstructing her face in repeated surgeries, which attempt to make her resemble icons of female beauty, such as the Mona Lisa and Venus de Milo.

Perhaps most unsettling, however, were the works that provided platforms for new cruelties, or at least the potential for them. Most simple and subtle of these is Yoko Ono's *Cut Piece* (1964), in which Ono sits impassively on the stage with a pair of scissors beside her, and allows audience members to approach her, one at a time, and cut off pieces of her clothing. For the first several minutes of her 1965 performance of this piece at Carnegie Hall, most of the audience members were content with a playful single snip. But it isn't long before an aggressive young man comes along and sets to some more serious cutting. As he works on dismantling her, Ono twitches, seemingly struggling to maintain her still posture. The pleasure the man takes in snipping through her bra straps feels childish—a small, dim cruelty. Yet the whole point of the piece is that Ono has invited this violation. She didn't lay out a feather or a jar of cream; she laid out a pair of scissors and named the piece *Cut Piece*. The result is deeply unnerving. Also unnerving: how erotic the performance is. I long to see Oko's clothes fall, to see her breasts bared. Yet I also feel a mounting sense of alarm, empathy, and injustice in watching her body be made vulnerable. I feel the urge to protect her, to chase off the smirking assholes who hog the scissors and come back for more. The surplus of contradictory emotions builds in slow motion toward the unbearable. Cut tape.

Now fast-forward ten years to 1974, to the Galleria Studio Morra in Naples, Italy, where Serbian artist Marina Abramović is performing her infamous *Rhythm 0*, which makes Ono's *Cut Piece* seem like a paragon of modesty and restraint. *Rhythm 0*, which Abramović performed only once, has the artist stand motionless for six hours, with seventy-two objects laid out on a nearby table for the audience members to use on her body in any way they see fit; the first item on the list is "Gun." (Other items: a needle, a scalpel, a knife, plus others whose relative benevolence has kept them out of legend: a rose, olive oil, a feather, and so on.) As with *Cut Piece*, the violations to Abramović's body begin slowly, then pick up speed. By the end of the performance, her clothes have been cut off, her body burned, sliced, and decorated. Eventually a man holds the loaded gun to her head and tries to make her fire it, at which point some audience members intervene to stop him.

In her 1999 treatise *On Beauty and Being Just*, Elaine Scarry argues that "far from damaging our capacity to attend to the problems of injustice, [beauty] instead intensifies the pressure we feel to repair existing injuries." Scarry wants to base an ethics on "the fact that something is perceived as beautiful is bound up with an urge to protect it, or act on its behalf." In six short hours, Abramović's *Rhythm 0* razes this notion to the ground, and reveals it to be the wishful claptrap that it is. Who needs the academic formalities of the Milgram experiment to demonstrate how quickly humans can slide into harming one another when a gorgeous Serbian artist can prove it to you simply by standing naked and motionless for six hours next to a table of sundry tools? Scarry is right that we often feel the urge to protect and worship beautiful things or people. But it is dangerous folly to ignore the fact that often we also feel the urge to injure or destroy them. With ethics, as with psychology, you cannot just lop off the negative or contradictory impulses and hope for the best.

The genius of Abramović's early pieces lies in their ability to dramatize, using her body as a stage, what happens when these impulses collide. Or implode—see, for example, her 1975 piece *Art Must Be Beautiful, Artist Must Be Beautiful*, in which the artist, armed with a hairbrush in one hand and a comb in another, maniacally reprimands herself with the command of her title while whacking her beautiful head and face with her grooming tools for an hour straight, to the point of drawing blood from her scalp. "At that time, I thought that art should be disturbing rather than beautiful," Abramović commented in a 1999 *Art Journal* interview. "But at my age now, I have started thinking that beauty is not so bad. My life is full of such contradictions." As is her art—a fact that was recently made clear throughout her 2010 retrospective at New York's Museum of Modern Art, the museum's first retrospective ever devoted to a performance artist.

———

ONE OF the most chilling pieces in the WACK show was, to my mind, one of the smallest: a tiny still from the documentation of Ana Mendieta's *Rape Scene* (1973), a performance piece in which Mendieta meticulously re-created the aftermath of a rape and murder that took place at the University of Iowa, then invited students over to her apartment to stumble, without warning, upon her "corpse." Naked, tied up, her underwear around her ankles, her body smeared with blood and dirt and bent over a table, Mendieta peers over her shoulder at the camera like a ghost risen from mud. (Mendieta had previously done an outdoor version of the same, 1972's *Rape Piece*, in which she re-created the murder scene in a wooded area near campus, and invited friends to discover her there.)

I imagine that Mendieta thought her politics here were sound—that she was drawing attention, via horror, to a horror that had been inadequately attended to. But her compulsion to re-enact the scene (not once but twice!) and to terrorize an unwitting audience (not once but twice!) complicates any simple look-at-how-bad-rape-and-murder-is feminist gesture. To my mind, that complication is part of what makes Mendieta's work so interesting, so formidable, so unsettling. You can't toss it into the ghetto of feminist protest art and ignore its more aggressive, borderline sadistic motivations and effects. Nor can you easily partition the *Rape* pieces off from her more shamanistic works involving blood, many of which were made that same year—*Untitled (Self-Portrait with Blood)* (1973), *Sweating Blood* (1973), *Mutilated Body on Landscape* (1973), *Blood Signs I and II* (1974), and so on.

Blood, for Mendieta, often signified violence, especially sexual violence—as in 1973's *Blood Writing*, in which Mendieta dips her hands in a bucket of blood and writes the ominous report, "SHE GOT LOVE," on a white gallery wall. But just as often, blood meant otherwise, or additionally. (About working with blood, Mendieta— who was deeply interested in ritualistic Santeria practices from her native Cuba—once said, "It's a very powerful magic thing. I don't see it as a negative force.") Mendieta's audacity—which is echoed throughout the work of artists such as Carolee Schneemann, Abramović, and French performance artist Gina Pane—was to claim this multivalence repeatedly and without apology, regardless of the culture's capacity to apprehend it.

The cruelty of pieces such as *Rape Scene* (or *Rhythm 0*, or *Cut Piece*) may start with a certain cruelty to the self, but that cruelty quickly leaks out to the viewer. The artists are not content to stare at the camera and ask, "Why are you still looking?" Instead, they ask, "How will you participate in this?"

Mendieta's *People Looking at Blood, Moffitt* (1973) poses this question in a particularly oblique, disturbing manner. In this piece, Mendieta spilled a large amount of what appeared to be chunky blood over a doorway and sidewalk on an Iowa City street. Then she removed herself from the scene and, from a distance, photographed the reactions of various passersby. (The piece ended when a storekeeper took it upon himself to clean up the mess.) At the WACK show, *People Looking at Blood* appeared in the form of twenty-four slides placed on a light board. To look at them, you had to bend over the board and use a magnifying lens, adding another layer of voyeurism to a work already laden with it.

Standing in front of *People Looking at Blood* and *Rape Scene*, which appeared side by side at the exhibit, it occurred to me that *People Looking at Blood* is the crueler, albeit the more abstract, of the two. It intimates to passersby that a grievous and dramatic injury has taken place, but it gives no explanation and, more important, no recourse to action. It may incite horror, concern, compassion, and revulsion—in short, pity and fear—but it doesn't offer anywhere for these feelings to go. Certainly it does not subject them to any catharsis. Each pedestrian's only real choice is to walk on by, which looks from the outside—and likely felt, on the inside—like an uncaring abandonment, even if of an indeterminate or imaginary entity. And now, almost forty years later, we peer in at the whole mess, likely with as little idea what to make of it as a pedestrian had stepping over it that day. And somewhere out of sight lurks Mendieta, a voyeur of each passerby's involuntary voyeurism. Mendieta's *Rape Scene* says, *Look at what someone did. People Looking at Blood* says, *Look at this pile of carnage, with no clear story, source, assailant, or victim. Just look at it. Now look at others looking at it. (And I will be looking at you looking.)*

—

IN A February 28, 2010, piece in the *New York Times* titled "Violence That Art Didn't See Coming," editor Sam Tanenhaus sets forth the argument that art—especially art made by women—utterly failed to predict the kind of violence by a woman that occurred on February 12, 2010, when Professor Amy Bishop opened fire on her colleagues in a faculty meeting at the University of Alabama. Despite coming up with a number of works along the way that would seem to disprove or at least complicate his titular thesis, Tanenhaus argues that "the topic of women and violence—especially as represented by women—remains more or less in a time warp, bound by the themes of sexual or domestic trauma." He thinks that this fixation on trauma (read: victim art) has blinded women artists to the shifting social landscape that formed the conditions of possibility of Bishop's shooting spree. (His list of these conditions: girls outdoing boys in the classroom, women making up "the majority of undergraduates at many prestigious colleges," women outnumbering men in the workforce, and women becoming "in thousands of cases, their family's principal breadwinner.")

Never mind, for the moment, how one measures the effects of these social conditions on Bishop's murderous actions (the fact that Bishop fatally shot her younger brother twenty-four years earlier, before these trends had come to pass, certainly complicates the issue). Put aside, too, the odd supposition that art's utility lies in its capacity to forecast the actions of a particular individual on any given day. Tanenhaus's point is that even though "these conditions have been developing for some years now . . . the most advanced narratives of female violence seem uninterested in them."

And what are these "advanced narratives"? Here Tanenhaus singles out the work of artists Abramović and Karen Finley, whose work he deems "stimulating in its way," but "curiously outmoded." In a populist gesture that doesn't quite ring true (few do, these days), Tanenhaus pits high art against low art, using Abramović and Finley as representatives of the "advanced," or highbrow, wing, which compares negatively to "popular, even pulpish art," which includes (surprise!) a whole raft of "crowd-pleasing movies" directed primarily by men (Bob Rafelson's *Black Widow*, Jonathan Demme's *Silence of the Lambs*, Quentin Tarantino's *Kill Bill*, and so on). Somehow these films "got" what the women artists missed, and therefore offer "the most useful glosses on Dr. Bishop." And what, exactly, did they get? That "women can be just as violent as men." Equality achieved; conversation closed—but not without pausing to put one more laurel in Tarantino's cap, while suggesting that the bulk of work made by "advanced" female artists over the past half century or so has been culturally irrelevant.

The claim that "women can be just as violent as men" not only runs into serious trouble on the statistical level (99 percent of rapes and 90 percent of homicides are committed by men), but also hardly comes as a news flash to the multitudes of artists, writers, critics, and activists—self-identified as feminists or otherwise—who have labored for decades, if not centuries, to explore the complexities of women's relations to violence, aggression, and structures of psychic, economic, social, and political power. If one really wants to step out of this dead-end dichotomy, which poses a regrettable equality ("women can be just as violent as men") on the one side, and an equally regrettable difference ("women are essentially victims and men are essentially aggressors") on the other, one has to develop a sharper ear for dissonance, for artistic instances and tonal nuances that do not derive their charge from making pit stops at well-trod narrative stations.

—

ONE OF the strangest and spikiest of such instances that I've come across is Jane Bowles's short story "Plain Pleasures," from 1946. One should go in fear of such a title, for in this quietly brutal, fourteen-page masterpiece, there are few pleasures, and certainly none that are plain (save the pleasure of Bowles's plain prose, which is immense).

In "Plain Pleasures," we are introduced to Mrs. Alva Perry, a widow of eleven years who now lives in a grumpy, structured solitude. One day this solitude gets pierced by a certain John Drake, a delivery man who also lives in her tenement. Mr. Drake offers to help her carry a bag of potatoes up the stairs. Later that night, they end up having a potato bake together in their desolate backyard. Excited by this encounter, the equally lonely and reserved Mr. Drake invites Mrs. Perry out to dinner the following evening, an invitation she warily accepts. In spite of her avowed dedication to only "plain pleasures"—that is, "ones that come without crowds or fancy foods"—Mrs. Perry finds it in her to get gussied up for the date, and she awaits Mr. Drake at the restaurant wearing a newly altered lavender dress and a string of her sister's beads. Mr. Drake is late, however, and the resentment Mrs. Perry develops while waiting for him proves insurmountable. After he arrives, she gets drunk on sweet wine, lays her beads in her gravy, says some harsh words to him, then wanders off to an empty room above the restaurant/hotel, where she weeps until she passes out.

The quick souring of their encounter, and the needless dashing of the high (if heretofore repressed) hopes of these two isolated souls, would be cruel enough. But Bowles adds another twist, in the form of the proprietor of the restaurant/hotel. The proprietor quickly ascertains how drunk Mrs. Perry is, and judges that "in her present drunken state it would be easy to sneak a kiss from her and perhaps even more." He follows Mrs. Perry upstairs when she wanders off, and notices with malevolent glee that the room she has accidentally passed out in is his own. He then lies to Mr. Drake about her whereabouts, assures him that she will be well taken care of, and encourages him to go home.

When Mrs. Perry awakens the following morning, she is alone but naked, and the reader is put in the discomfiting position of surmising that she has been raped. To complicate matters further, Mrs. Perry wakes up in an inexplicably good mood, although she cannot remember a thing about her evening. The blacked-out lacuna at this story's navel is one of literature's most understated slivers of cruelty. But cruelty to whom? Indeed, one of the most remarkable things about Bowles's stories is that more often than not they leave the reader not knowing how to feel. Should we pity Mrs. Perry? Or should we allow her her good feeling? Who are we to call her good morning mood false consciousness? Bowles here allows herself the freedom to make a queasy satire out of a possible rape—a move that constitutes its own form of disobedience in a world obsessed with the big-deal-ness of female defilement. In such a context, the story's title, "Plain Pleasures," starts to seem as wicked as it is multivalent.

"Everything is nice," says a chorus of Moslem women in another of Bowles's razor-edged stories, which bears this ludicrous maxim as its title. For in "Everything Is Nice," as in Bowles's world at large, very little—if anything—is "nice." In fact much of Bowles's wit stems from putting such truisms in the mouths of her characters in order to reveal them as meaningless, erroneous, or delusional. It isn't so much that Bowles is out to tell us that the world is a cruel and cold place, and isn't it a pity. Like many artists of cruelty, she is no philosopher. She is roaming a world of balloons, armed with a pin.

—

THIS SLY debunking, accompanied by an unnerving inscrutability, is often a sign that something new is happening. It is the dissonant sound of a new territory being entered, a new story being told. It isn't feminist in the sense of serving some predetermined aim of empowerment or equality; certainly if there were a litmus test of such, "Plain Pleasures" would fail. But the story's presentation of a world in which a blackout signifies a sweet triumph, rape is not soul murder, and liberation consists of laying down one's necklace in gravy and pronouncing, "I am not a mashed-potato masher," is utterly refreshing. Nothing here is nice, but the story's cool combination of the flat-footed sublunary and the irremediably distressing produces a quietly ecstatic effect.

These dissonant chords may be difficult for a writer or artist to chime; they can be even harder for the culture to hear. The impulse to assimilate them by rendering them self-deluding, farcical, or even criminal can be quick and severe. Take, for example, the case of Karen Finley. Certainly some of Karen Finley's work could be characterized as "victim art" (the phrase coined by Arlene Croce in her infamous non-review of Bill T. Jones's 1995 dance production *Still/Here*). But now that twenty years has passed since Jesse Helms and company pilloried Finley as "that chocolate-smeared woman"—and twenty years after Finley became a feminist hero to artists of my generation (and, as often is the case with heroes, someone to push against, differentiate oneself from, sometimes to the point of rejection or mockery)—there is space to hear her monologues with a different ear.

I challenge anyone to read pieces from Finley's *I'm an Ass Man* (1984), such as "Yams Up My Granny's Ass," or *The Constant State of Desire* (1986), such as "The Father in All of Us," and maintain some rote notion of Finley as a victim artist, or even as a woman speaking a nasty male script solely in order to critique it. Here is the speaker of "The Father in All of Us," for example, discussing his fetish for women with babies, and describing getting turned on by a lady in a Laundromat: "Oh, gets me going, seeing a woman's body vibrate against a machine. I just take that mama and push her against the washer—then I take her baby, a bald-headed baby, put Downy fabric softener on baby's head—strap that baby around my waist til it's a baby dildo. Then I take that baby, that baby dildo, and fuck its own mama—CAUSE I'M NOTHING BUT A MOTHER-FUCKER!" And here is the speaker of "Yams Up My Granny's Ass," explaining that "when things get real bad, real bad dad, I take a can of yams and smear it in my granny's ass. She's such a fine granny to humiliate, she's such a fine granny to torture, because she's a mute granny. Doesn't make a sound. Her eyes stick out like blue raisins on a rabbit, some furry little animal. I'm smearing her all over with the candied, sugared yams. And I turn her over on her back so the candied syrup yam juice runs down her back, along her spine."

The desires here expressed are too weird, too lyrical, too length-ily formulated, too unsettling, to serve any one nameable, digestible purpose. Such monologues continue to present us with complex, disturbing acts of reclamation, aggression, excoriation, abjection, and identification, the likes of which continue to be rare, even as the culture professes to have absorbed or "moved on" from them.

Indeed, in the face of the suggestion that such acts have become "curiously outmoded," I cannot help but think of the summary Eve Kosofsky Sedgwick offers (in *Epistemology of the Closet*) of the preemptive dismissal of inquiry into queer issues: "Stop asking here, stop asking just now; we know in advance the kind of difference that would be made by the invocation of *this* difference; it makes no difference; it doesn't mean." I also think of the college freshman I once had in a poetry workshop who announced, after we read the poem "In Celebration of My Uterus" by Anne Sexton, that he'd rather die than read yet another poem about a woman's uterus or period. Dear God, I thought, has something radically changed in high school education? Are the youth now inundated with such poems by the time they get to college? Or—more likely, to my mind—was it that a handful of poems on the topic (or, more likely still, this single one) made him feel as though he'd already had enough?

In short, purporting to know in advance what difference a difference might make—or purporting to be sick and tired of it before it has elaborated itself—is one fast way of being rid of it. Often, to experience the dissonance—especially in art—one has to take the time, and leave open the divine possibility of being taken by surprise. When someone first told me, for example, about a 1992 piece by performance artist Nao Bustamante called *Indig/urrito*, in which Bustamante invites white men from the audience to join her on stage, get down on their knees in penance for 500 years of white-male oppression of indigenous peoples, and take an absolving bite of the burrito she is wielding as a strap-on, I think I spouted off some lazy dismissal of the venture, citing a disinterest in collective guilt, identity politics, audience humiliation, and dominatrix chic. After watching a fifteen-minute performance of the piece (filmed at Theater Artaud in San Francisco, and available for viewing on the artist's Web site), I realized I couldn't have been more wrong. Largely due to Bustamante's quick-witted humor and benevolently sarcastic persona, the piece transforms political cliché into absurdist theater, opening up space for comedy, unpredictability, titillation, and an unlikely camaraderie. The indictment made by the piece, if there is any, is multivalent: Bustamante begins by poking fun at a (nameless) arts organization that has offered to fund artists of color whose work "addresses the past 500 years of oppression of indigenous peoples," and introduces this piece as her response. She then invites "any white man who would like to take the burden of the past 500 years of guilt" to report to the stage. After no one ascends, she moves on to invite "anyone with any inner white men," then "anyone who is hungry," then "anyone who knows a white man who is hungry," and so on. The concept of collective guilt—along with that of unswerving identity—receives all the complication it deserves, swiftly and hilariously.

Eventually a hodgepodge of white men amble up to the stage and get down on their knees behind her, and Bustamante revels in their pitifulness. (About one particularly scrawny, bald, and hunch-shouldered volunteer, she coos, "Aw, I think he's going to take it for a lot of people, don't you?") At the same time, she lauds them as heroes and martyrs, as those willing to bear the guilt and shame that the more cowardly white men out there are unwilling to face. The unpredictability of the performance arrives when she asks each man to state his name into a microphone (fixed at knee height), and make a statement before taking an absolving bite of her burrito.

As everyone from Ono to Abramović to Lynn Breedlove (lead singer of the queercore band Tribe 8, who often invited male audience members to come onstage and suck her dick) knows, even men who have volunteered to take part in such ventures can behave volatilely. The feeling of suddenly being in the spotlight with a woman indisputably running the show is, for many, an intolerable reversal (albeit one that many men have a taste for, behind closed doors). For this reason, part of the deep pleasure of *Indig/urrito* lies in watching Bustamante's commanding grace, power, and wit as she banters with each man's self-introduction and apologia, as well as with the occasionally over-theatrical fellating of her burrito by the hammier of them. There's also plenty of edgy flirtation: after a handsome "Justin" says, "I'm male, I'm white, and I'm sorry," with more coquettishness than penitence, Bustamante responds, "I'm not sorry, Justin, I'm not sorry at all," and rolls her eyes in ecstasy at his bite. As the bald gentleman—who introduces himself as "Allan"—takes his bite, Bustamante squeals, "He's so pitiful!" and holds his head against her rocking pelvis. By the time the last biter, a slim, short-haired figure in a suit, announces into the mic, "I'm a girl, I'm Hispanic, and I'm prepared," and attempts to unroll a condom against the mess hanging from Bustamante's harness, all facile premises have disintegrated (as has the burrito).

Before the biting of *Indig/urrito* begins, Bustamante asks the members of the audience to yell a congratulatory "Amen" at the moment that each man's teeth enter her burrito, and to think, at that moment, of any white man they know who needs absolving, so that "we can all just *move on*." The audience at Theater Artaud responds to this call with a loud cheer. Obviously, Bustamante and her audience know that "moving on" from 500 years of exploitation and racism isn't that easy. But neither her call nor the audience's spontaneous response comes off as a total joke. *Indig/urrito* provides fifteen minutes of what a different kind of "moving on" might feel like—one not based in denial, abdication, derision, or preemptive dismissal, but in discomfiting role reversals, fraught but consensual confrontations, humor that rides the edge of contempt and anger without collapsing into their force, and a dedication to seeing what happens next, to seeing how individual humans might comport themselves in a politically and sexually charged situation they have been invited to address rather than repress. "Anyone who is offended by this," Bustamante warns before the ritual begins, "I really encourage you to leave your body."

THEY'RE ONLY DOLLS

IF WE'RE going to listen to what a slew of newspaper editors, social scientists, CEOs, politicians, historians, concerned parents, university presidents, and statisticians have to say about the role that representations of violence may play in "real" life, it seems also right to listen to artists or works of art that explicitly take up the question. A scissor of a play such as Martin McDonagh's *The Pillowman* (2003), for example, has plenty to say on this account, even if what it has to say may not please a soul.

The Pillowman takes place in a police interrogation room in an unnamed totalitarian country. Two policemen—Ariel and Tupolski—are interrogating and torturing a writer, Karturian, in an attempt to figure out the relationship between Karturian's short stories—many of which feature the horrific torture and murder of children—and three recent, "real-life" torture-killings, the details of which closely resemble those in Karturian's stories. The interrogation reveals a complicated knot of "real" and invented brutalities: we learn that Karturian has a slightly retarded brother, Michal, who spent the first seven years of his life being tortured by their parents in a room next to Karturian's; that Karturian eventually liberated Michal from the torture, then smothered their parents to death in retribution; that, as an adult, Karturian lived with brother Michal, and read him all of his stories; and that one day, brother Michal took it upon himself to murder three children in the ingeniously gruesome ways imagined by Karturian in his tales.

Before Karturian learns what his brother has done, he thinks that it is solely his writing that is at issue with the state. He asks his interrogators, "Do you think I'm trying to say, 'Go out and murder children?' . . . Are you trying to say I shouldn't write stories with child-killings in them because in the real world there are child-killings?" To which Ariel responds, "He wants us to think that he thinks that all we've got against him is a disagreement with his fucking prose style." Of course, they have more against him than that, as brother Michal turns out to be in custody next door and has already confessed to the crimes. Later, however, after some confusion arises as to Michal's culpability, the policemen make it clear that whichever of the two brothers actually killed the children, Karturian's writing alone would still make him guilty. "You know what? I would torture you to death just for *writing* a story like that, let alone acting it out," Ariel says, as he removes an electrode-torture-device from a cabinet and readies it for use.

The intelligence of *The Pillowman* (which, I might add, I have no interest in seeing on stage, where the visual dramatization of its cruelties seems to me as needless as it is inevitable) is that it shows, via the injustice of Karturian's torture and eventual execution, how cruel it is to insist that "life" and "art" have some kind of direct, one-to-one relationship, while at the same time showing how preposterous it is to insist that they have nothing to do with each other. After all, Karturian's ghastly stories are clearly revisitations and restagings of the trauma of his and his brother's youth, just as his brother's acting out of the stories is part and parcel of his own damage. Eventually we even get the "problem childhood" backstory of torturer Ariel, a childhood that Tupolski shorthands as a "'fucked by your dad' childhood." The two torturers end up giving voice to two equally reasonable positions vis-à-vis the crimes (including their own) at hand: "I'm just tired of everybody around here using their shitty childhoods to justify their own shitty behaviour," Tupolski says, whereas Ariel tells Karturian, "I know all this isn't your fault . . . and I'm sorry for you, I'm really sorry for you," moments before he pulls the black execution hood over Karturian's head so that Tupolski can shoot him dead.

—

"To RENDER a violent act in language is not at all the same as committing a violent act," argues writer Brian Evenson. "The writing itself is not violent, but rather precise. If you've ever been involved in real acts of violence, you can see how profound the difference is." True enough. It would be an utterly egregious, essentially totalitarian mistake to conflate McDonagh's writing—or Evenson's, or anyone's, for that matter—with the commitment of a violent act. (Evenson—once a high priest in the Mormon Church, now a professor at Brown University—has had reason to note the difference: in 1996, a controversy over his first collection of stories, *Altmann's Tongue*, cost him his job at Brigham Young University, precipitated the dissolution of his first marriage, and led to his eventual departure from the Mormon Church.)

Still, I don't entirely buy Evenson's sleight of hand, by which representations of violence in literature slide into being simply "precise." There are, after all, many other forms of precision (are there not?). Is violence simply the sharpest, the fastest, the most immediately or physiologically affecting? As A. O. Scott—who has been writing articles in the *New York Times* for some time now about the escalating brutality in mainstream cinema—put it in his review of Quentin Tarantino's *Inglourious Basterds* (2009), "All you have to do is scalp someone—as happens with loving graphicness—to put the audience on edge."

Clearly violence is not always a shortcut, nor do I mean to imply that one could or should substitute it with some sort of nonfat equivalent. My point is simply that it isn't quite right to say that McDonagh's slow revelation of the fates of the murdered children in *The Pillowman*—one little boy bleeds to death after having all five toes of one foot chopped off, one little girl dies from eating apples laced with razor blades, and one little girl is literally crucified by her foster parents, then buried alive to see if she will rise again (she doesn't)—is just "precise." It is cruel—as is much in Evenson's work. And part of *The Pillowman*'s cruelty is that we, like Michal, have now internalized these sickening tales (not to mention another—that of the play *The Pillowman* itself). The question of what effect they might have on us—on our psyches, our souls, our social landscape, and our deeds—has become our burden to bear.

"In life," Evenson says, "violence happens to you. In literature, you make the choice to pick up the book and read, and to continue reading." He is right—consent is absolutely key. The feeling that we have been violated by a work of art is compounded—and perhaps made tolerable—by the fact that we chose to experience it, come what may. But that doesn't render the apprehension that a cruelty has taken place entirely invalid. In this sense, the Brigham Young student who wrote the anonymous letter intended to "alert the authorities" to the nature of Evenson's writing may have been onto something. In reading *Altmann's Tongue*, the aggrieved student wrote, "I feel like someone who has eaten something poisonous and is desperate to get rid of it."

Now, to whom, exactly, a play like McDonagh's *The Pillowman* might be cruel, and what the nature of that cruelty is, I cannot say. If I could say, Simulated cruelty performs no cruelty at all, then there would be no discomfort. I could relax—even if it meant denying my felt experience of many works of art, or—and this is harder— ignoring the full-fledged assault on the barriers between art and life that much twentieth-century art worked so hard to perform. I could draw my line in the sand each time, and rest comfortably on the "art" side—just as those who regularly root on the humiliations of reality TV are accustomed to dissolving whatever guilt or reservations they might otherwise have about the treatment of their fellow humans by resting on the "TV" part of the equation. (At least, that is what I typically do: this woman signed up to be encased in a coffin full of biting rats for an hour; this cruelty therefore does not count as a "real" cruelty; it need make no claim on my conscience.) And certainly some suffering—such as that experienced by the handful of journalists who have been voluntarily waterboarded, for example, so that they might weigh in on whether the procedure is "really" torture—cannot easily be categorized as a cruelty at all.

Conversely, if I could say, Simulated cruelty does perform a sort of cruelty, and if one is "against" cruelty in all its guises, whatever that might mean, then one should also be "against" cruel simulations, whatever that might mean—then there would also be no discomfort—then I could join the ranks of those working overtime to criminalize and prosecute anime depicting the rape of prepubescents, for example, or just partake in a good old-fashioned book-burning at my local library, tossing everything from *Lolita* to *The Pillowman* on the pyre.

In a 2003 piece in *The Believer* called "The Bad Mormon," writer Ben Ehrenreich chronicles how, in response to his accusers at Brigham Young, Evenson wrote a thirteen-page apologia in which he argued that his work was, in fact, "uncompromisingly moral," insofar as it attempted "'to paint violence in its true colors and to let it reveal for itself how terrible it is.'" (See Michael Haneke: "Violence in my films is shown as it really is. . . . That's why the films are often experienced as painful.")

Ehrenreich notes—correctly, I think—that while Evenson's attackers may have sounded unsophisticated, Evenson's remarks seemed disingenuous. First, even when art produces the sensation of having presented something "as it really is," it does so by means of focus and artifice—or, rather, by a complicated procedure one could describe as using artifice to strip artifice of artifice. In other words, it is still and always an act of invention, transformation, and selection. Second, as Ehrenreich notes, "there is far too much humor in [Evenson's] stories, too much aesthetic delight in the syntax of even the most gruesome episodes, for Evenson to pass himself off as a simple pedant." Not only are humor and aesthetic delight crucial aspects of Evenson's genius, but it is foolhardy to take any artist at face value when he or she purports to use violence in only a moral way. To be frank, I don't believe such a thing is possible—not because of any failure on the part of the artist, but because of the unmanageable natures of violence, sadism, and voyeurism themselves.

In the well-known opening sequence of David Lynch's 1986 film, *Blue Velvet*, the camera zooms in on a severed ear nestled in the grass of a picture-perfect, suburban American lawn, thereby intimating the world of submerged cruelties into which the film's protagonist, Jeffrey, will soon descend. In contemplating this scene in his book *A Good War Is Hard to Find: The Art of Violence in Amer-*

ica, David Griffith writes, "The severed ear in the vacant lot invites us to enter, with Jeffrey, the underworld. We think we'll return uncorrupted, even wiser. But violence doesn't enlighten; it taints. We can't be both pervert and detective."

Griffith is right that violence or cruelty does not enlighten. He may also be right that it taints (though the hygienic paranoia embedded in the word seems unnecessary—better, I think, to stick with our aggrieved student, who feels like she has "eaten something poisonous and is desperate to get rid of it": the imbibing of cruelty or violence thereby turns from a moral dilemma into a metabolic one). But Griffith is not right that we cannot be both pervert and detective. More often than not, that is exactly what we are. Well-intentioned moralists such as Griffith may wish that it weren't so. (Perhaps for him, it isn't.) But if one is to take Jacques Rancière's principle of emancipation seriously—that "an art is emancipated and emancipating . . . when [it] stops wanting to emancipate us"— then no artist can or should pretend to patrol the borders.

But perhaps Griffith simply means to return the burden to us. Perhaps he means to say that we—as audience members, spectators, readers, participants, consumers—cannot hope to ferret out injustices, protest certain forms of injury, violence, and violation, while also deriving pleasure or excitation from representations of them (much less from the things themselves: super verboten!). I disagree. It does not help to wish the complexity of our responses away, to punish ourselves for them, to fail to make distinctions between them, or to dream of coming back uncorrupted from them. "It is very unhappy, but too late to be helped, the discovery we have made that we exist," wrote Ralph Waldo Emerson. "That discovery is called the Fall of Man." Or—if we'd rather leave the lapsarian saga behind (and I would), artist Joseph Beuys gives us the sentiment with an activist twist: "A lifetime is not so long," he wrote. "You cannot wait for a tool without blood on it."

———

RICHER AND raunchier than *The Pillowman*—which is, at the end of the day, a pretty conventional "issue play," albeit with an ingenious Chinese box structure and some rough material—is the work of artist Paul McCarthy, which customarily offers more gratuitous—and more nuanced—opportunities for meditating on our responses to disturbing representations. I'm thinking in particular of the 1987 video *Family Tyranny*, made with Mike Kelley, which manages, in just eight minutes, using a polystyrene ball, a funnel, and what appears to be a very runny mayonnaise, to produce an unrivalled amount of tension, revulsion, and bewilderment about the functioning of cruelty.

On an Astroturf stage set, McCarthy's shirtless, hairy Dad character uses his hand to stuff the mayonnaise-cum-substance down a funnel that has been stuck into the polystyrene ball. The ball has been made to look minimally like a head, by means of a tin hat and an opening where the mouth would be. As the Father repeatedly rams his greased-up fist into the funnel, causing mayonnaise-cum-juice to smear and spill all over, he repeats, with the sing-song lilt of an instructional abuser, "Daddy come home from work today," and "My daddy did this to me; you can do this to your son, too" and "Do it slowly, let them feel it, do it slowly—let 'em get used to it." Later in the video, a Son character (played by Kelley) appears, whimpering and futilely attempting escape. But for whatever reason, it isn't until another coarse simulation of rape—this time with the Son cowering and screaming under a table, and the Father mercilessly, rhythmically jamming a baseball bat into a red pitcher on the table's top—that the effect of a nearly unwatchable cruelty is once again achieved.

How can ramming mayonnaise down an opening in a polystyrene ball, or banging a baseball bat into a pitcher, make a viewer feel so profoundly, almost unmanageably, ill at ease? As Arthur Danto once said in response to *Family Tyranny*, " 'They're only dolls' helps about as much as 'It's only art.' " Or, as critic Bruce Hainley put it in a 2001 piece in *Frieze*, "McCarthy has reiterated that 'there's a big difference between ketchup and blood.' Of course, there's just as big a difference between a dummy, mannequin or doll, and a human being. But how and why does one invoke the other and can the referential impact be throttled? In a media-saturated society can anything be or remain only what it is?" This latter isn't a question that can be easily answered—which is likely why Hainley sagely doesn't try. Things do and do not remain "only what they are": that is the slippery space from which work like McCarthy's derives so much of its power.

"What you have to do is *emotionally* get this to him," the Father in *Family Tyranny* insists, offering another clue as to the short video's potency. To get it to him, or to us, *emotionally* (rather than physically, or "actually"), simulation and artifice are key. One obvious layer of simulation involves McCarthy's celebrated use of easily recognizable food substances (chocolate, catsup, mayonnaise, and so on) in lieu of actual body fluids (a tack which, as many have noted, differentiates his work from that of the Actionists, whose work McCarthy's both references and transforms). Another is that McCarthy does not cast the audience as voyeurs on a discrete scene unfolding in the privacy of a home. Rather, the Father character is already re-performing these operations on his Son—parodically, pedagogically—for the viewer's benefit, on a stage set, at one point even counseling, "Try this at home!" On the one hand, this transparent attitude toward fakery makes the work bearable to watch (and, in my case—only after repeated viewings—a species of funny). On the other, the obvious artifice also makes the piece more insidious, as it liberates the abuse from the burden of believable representation, and places a crystallized version of its effects on display.

Now, whatever echo of psychological discomfort we may feel after viewing *Family Tyranny* clearly pales in comparison to the psychological harm experienced by the actual sufferer of such an assault. We are having uncomfortable and complicated feelings while watching a video, which is to be distinguished from undergoing involuntary psychic and physical damage. And yet McCarthy's emphasis on psychological haunting is unnerving, insofar as psychological haunting is precisely where the action of both art and trauma occur. "Don't worry, they'll remember it," the Father coos throughout—as if the point of the violation lay less in the momentary discharge of malignant psychosexual energies, and more in the abuser's capacity to leave a debilitating psychic scar.

After all, "Don't worry, they'll remember it" is the direct, negating promise that trauma makes to catharsis. And it is a mantra that may hold true for the viewer as well, as he or she may end up remembering the video with a disconcerting sense of anxiety and unease for some time. Reenactments of sexual trauma that aim for abreaction are one thing; reenactments that explicitly aim to make the trauma contagious and lasting—both to the Son and to us, the viewers—are another. In lieu of purgation or sublimation, *Family Tyranny* promises that there will be recurrence. There will be legacy. There will be mess.

Given that I, too, felt like "someone who has eaten something poisonous and is desperate to get rid of it" after my first viewing of *Family Tyranny*, the question remains: why bother? Why inhabit this mess, even if temporarily? (This question was, in fact, once posed by a student in tears after an in-class screening of this piece.) I am not sure I have a good answer. By this point in my life, I would support anyone's desire *not* to bother—a stance that can make the pedagogical ethics of presenting such material a bit difficult to negotiate.

What I can say, however, is that I have gotten something different out of *Family Tyranny* each time I've watched it, and that the video has provided me with an exceptionally unpleasant but uncannily productive platform from which to think about representation, trauma, humor, improvisation, and the nastiest aspects of patriarchy and sexual violence. I can also say that I much prefer its poison over the grandiose, mythopoetic renditions of such as explored by, say, Hermann Nitsch's Orgies-Mysteries Theatre, which happily takes as its "mythical leitmotif" a roster of phallocentric, patriarchal, and/or literally Oedipal acts of violence (i.e., the crucifixion of Jesus Christ, the rending of Dionysos, the blinding of Oedipus, the murder of Orpheus, the murder of Adonis, the castration of Attis, ritual regicide, and something Nitsch calls, likely after Bataille, "the sado-masochistic primal excess"). My preference remains even though—or perhaps precisely because—Nitsch aims to emancipate; McCarthy, to impart claustrophobic dread. For if Rancière is right that an art is emancipated and emancipating when it stops wanting to emancipate us, there may be no mystery to my preference at all.

Nitsch's work explicitly depends on the idea that there exists such a thing as sacred or sacrificial violence, and that this type of violence can provide a beneficial, cathartic outlet that diminishes rather than augments the proliferation of violence within any given society or group. French anthropologist-philosopher René Girard set forth this theory in *Violence and the Sacred* (1977), in which Girard argues that sacrificial violence, or scapegoating, acts as a necessary, foundational "safety valve" in human society. The ritual elimination of a chosen, often arbitrary Other serves to appease otherwise diffuse violent urges in individuals, and to unify the group against the chosen scapegoat. (Girard does not spend much time contemplating the victims of such sacrifices, who are often presumed to be either willing, engaged in a deep projective identification with their sacrificers, or simply inconsequential. Historically speaking, however, it bears noting that these chosen Others have most often been non-consenting animals, criminals, poor people, prisoners of war, women, adolescents, people from a different race, nation, or tribe, or anyone else whose agency has been sufficiently compromised or deemed irrelevant.) According to Girard, we repress the scapegoating mechanism at our peril, as "our society's obligatory compassion authorizes new forms of cruelty."

If and when society, in thrall to this Pollyanna-like "obligatory compassion," ceases to provide platforms for such natural, restorative, and cathartic sacrificial activity (the reasoning of an artist such as Nitsch goes), then art must step up to provide the altar. If one finds this employment of the scapegoat mechanism—in art or in life—a toxic proposition generally not worth its risks, then McCarthy's work—which, as he has said, is more about being a clown than a shaman—can act as a bracing and desirable tonic.

Here one could say that I am simply noting the difference between a mystic and an ironist, and that I—typical of my generation—would naturally prefer the ironist. As critic Tom Moody put it in a 1999 review of younger artists Sue de Beer and

Laura Parnes's video *Heidi 2* (1999), an "unauthorized sequel" to McCarthy and Kelley's *Heidi* (a 1992 video even more notorious than *Family Tyranny* in regard to its violation of dolls), "This immersion in media and popular culture sets Parnes and de Beer apart from an older generation of performance artists (McCarthy, Schneemann, Nitsch), who seek to heal a split between a 'repressed, cultural' self and an 'authentic, natural' self through ritualistic acts of transgression (fecal smearing, orgiastic sex, and so on). In de Beer's and Parnes' view, no split exists because everything is mediated: the most extreme acts can be found on tape at the corner video store and 'real' experience is suspect. Rejecting the superior vantage point of the artist/shaman, the artists use pop culture tropes without apology; expressing the most 'primal' events—childbirth, orgasm, incestuous rape—in the idiom of sitcoms, video games, and splatter films."

Moody has a point. But to me, the most interesting works of art are those that gum up this either-or equation, with its dependence on a whole host of by-now familiar dualisms—repressed/authentic, primal/synthetic, real/mediated—or sidestep it entirely. German filmmaker Rainer Werner Fassbinder lived and breathed in this discomfiting, riveting space, somehow managing to conjure literally dozens of cerebral, melodramatic masterpieces from it before his death at the age of thirty-seven. More recently, video and performance artist Kalup Linzy has emerged as one of the wiliest, most compelling navigators of this territory, with his raunchy, lo-fi, weirdly tender renditions of soap operas, such as his *All My Churen* series (2003, 2005), which chronicles the trials and tribulations of a dysfunctional African-American family, the Braswells, in the rural South, with Linzy playing all the parts with an ecstatic charisma.

Indeed, camp has had a corner on this market for years. One

need look no further than drag queen Divine's infamous shit-eating scene at the end of *Pink Flamingos* to see how it's done. As Divine struts and prepares to eat a poodle's still-warm shit, the voice-over says, "Watch as Divine proves that not only is she the filthiest person in the world, she's also the filthiest actress in the world!" The layers here are multiple: not only do person and actress meld together in the act of eating dog shit, but also Divine herself is already at least three people—a man born Harris Glenn Milstead, a drag queen named Divine, and an actor/actress playing a character named Divine. Together, "real person," persona, character, actress, and actor really do eat shit. But they don't do so to get primal. Divine, containing all her multitudes, is getting filthy, and it is gross, hilarious, and ecstatic to behold.

THE GOLDEN RULE

ARISTOTLE'S THEORY of catharsis has been very useful to artists who believe that humans have a certain measure of bloodlust that must be given controlled discharge, or who insist that their work is not injecting anything foreign into any viewer's bloodstream—that everything nasty that exists (violent incest, for example, in the case of *Family Tyranny*; the desire to torture and murder children, in the case of *The Pillowman*) also already exists in some form in the viewer, and that the depiction of it therefore gives the viewer the chance to confront his or her fears, or desires, in relation to it. (Or, if he or she doesn't have a sense of it already, then that's the fault of his or her naiveté, which deserves to be crushed.) As Evenson once put it in an interview, "I disturb nobody—I only give them an occasion for disturbing themselves. . . . [My readers] have externalized their fears in me, but what they really fear is what they see of themselves in the stories."

I find it an enormous relief, in the face of such arguments, to hear Mike Kelley's flat assertion: "I make art in order to give other people my problems." Such a statement lies at the polar end of the spectrum to the (equally refreshing) attitude of someone like John Cage, who spent his life developing an open-ended system of music based on the opposite conviction: "My feelings belong, as it were, to me, and I should not impose them on others." In service of this conviction, Cage spent his long career aiming to discover forms of "waking people up" that privilege making space around them rather than violating their boundaries.

"I do not disturb your center, nor you mine": such was Cage's emancipatory credo. This is obviously not the credo of *Family Tyranny*, which takes as it subject not only the smearing of sadistic feeling and action down through generations, successively dismantling psychological "centers," but also the uncanny ability of hyper-simulated representation to smear potent and unpleasant sensations onto viewers, disrupting, even if for a brief spell, theirs.

And yet. Hoping to "give other people your problems" dovetails with Cage's approach in an important respect. Namely, it agrees with the first part of Cage's statement—"My feelings belong, as it were, to me"—and makes a simple reversal of the second—"I should not impose them on others." In all the work of McCarthy and Kelley I've seen, no matter how disturbing, I've never felt from them the bossy conviction I feel from so many other artists, to admit that my problems are actually their problems—to admit that they are actually Our Problems. Instead, they inhabit their obsessions so thoroughly, with so blessedly little concern for my well-being, as they catapult their feelings, problems, and obsessions into the public sphere, that some space is created.

This space exists when an artist may hope to give other people his or her problems, but also knows that the transmission cannot be surely made, and that the fallout is likely to be unpredictable, disorderly. Rather than stake everything on a projective identification that has been mapped out for the viewer in advance, the artist doesn't care, and the not-caring makes space. (After all, even if the transmission goes through, all one gets is the experience of new feelings or problems, not a set of solutions.) In that space, even if I'm surrounded by multiple giant screens showing images of hyper-simulated, over-the-top butchery and plunder for over an hour (as was the case during my viewing of McCarthy's gore-fest, *Caribbean Pirates*, made with his son, Damon), I can feel a species of freedom.

At this screening, this sensation derived in part from the layout of the exhibition: the screens at the theater—the REDCAT theater in downtown Los Angeles—were hung in a semicircle around both stage and risers, thereby surrounding the viewer with sight and sound. But as the stage itself remained open and empty, many descended to it and watched the film sitting or lying down there. I stayed in the risers, but when I tired of watching the gore on the walls, I'd turn my gaze to the people lolling around on the stage floor. I watched their interest, their discomfort, and their sleepiness; I watched them come and go, sometimes returning, sometimes not. For all the work's relentless assault, my actual experience of it was memorably spacey.

Space is distinct from alienation. It is fundamentally about volume, rather than about distance. Space also defies the vertical logic of revelation, which insists there is something beneath the surface of our every day—be it ultimate meaning, the face of God, our fundamental nature, a final terror, ecstasy, or judgment, or some combo of the above—that will be revealed when the veil is finally lifted. In lieu of this logic, space offers a horizontal spreading, the possibility of expansion into dimensions no one yet thoroughly understands. Space is also intrinsic to the creation of freedom. As Arendt once put it in a very different context (in 1953's "Ideology and Terror"), "The one essential prerequisite of all freedom . . . is simply the capacity of motion which cannot exist without space."

—

FREEDOM, CONSENT, alienation, boundary, and incursion: the early works of Chris Burden dramatize the play between them by means of some of the simplest yet most notorious episodes in the history of performance art. Most famous of these is *Shoot* (1971), in which Burden invited a small audience to a gallery in Santa Ana, California, to watch a friend standing about fifteen feet away shoot him in the upper part of his left arm with a .22 rifle. Unlike Haneke's taunting, "Why are you watching this?" in the middle of a simulated bloodbath he would presumably prefer that we keep watching, Burden constructed a "real" situation available for viewing by a very small, invited public. (*Shoot* now exists solely by means of oral and art history, lo-fi documentation, and physical relic.)

In 1971—in the middle of the Vietnam War—the principal questions raised by *Shoot* seemed to be, what kind of person would orchestrate and undergo such a self-inflicted thing in the midst of an outrageously cruel and unjust war, and what kind of audience would allow it to proceed? Almost forty years later, the outrage has dimmed, but questions still abound. Here are some of mine, jotted down after watching Burden's grainy Super-8 documentation of *Shoot*: Would I have attended such an event at the time? Why do I still feel morally uncomfortable about watching this now? What are the differences—ethical, sensory, aesthetic—between being present for such a thing and watching a recording of it? What about between watching and listening? What are the differences between beholding—or enacting—self-harm versus other forms of harm? What's the difference between shooting yourself and asking someone to shoot you? How did the shooter feel? Where is he now? Who took the greater (legal, ethical) risk—Burden or the shooter? What forms or contexts of inflicting harm, on one-self or others, should be allowed (S/M, suicide or assisted suicide, performance art, any other consensual scenario, and so on), and which should be discouraged or prohibited? Who defines harm? On whose behalf? Who has the power, authority, right, duty, and/or audacity, to intervene on behalf of another's body, especially a body that is doing what it says it wants to do? When and how (if ever) is it anyone's business to mandate what we do with our bodies in our lifetimes? Does anyone "have" the power, or is it always a means of asserting it, seizing it, inventing it? In what sense, under what conditions, can we say that a body knows what it wants?

The tension is monochromatic but pulsing. Burden's friend asks him if he's ready; Burden answers, Yes, go ahead. The pacing, save for the gunshot itself, is glacial. It's two of the longest minutes I know, with reverb.

An interviewer once asked Burden why he wanted to be shot; Burden responded, "Well, it's something to experience. How do you know what it feels like to be shot if you don't experience it?" Fair enough, I'd say—even if the average citizen might think him a complete moron. I'd much rather the artist be thinking about his or her own experience than trying to micromanage mine. As for Burden's somewhat singular desire to be shot, I think of Cage's sage remarks: "I think the Golden Rule, which is often thought of as the center, really, of Christianity, is a mistake: 'Do unto others as *you* would be done by.' I think this is a mistaken thought. We should do unto others as *they* would be done by." This, to me, has the ring of emancipation to it—which isn't to say that it resolves any of the above questions about the nature of desire, consent, or interven-tion. Those questions are ours to contend with, as we struggle to know and name what we want, to hear what others want from us, to imagine and enact fulfillment, and to live with the inevitable missteps, taboos, crossed signals, and impossibilities.

———

THERE ARE those who think that to ask an audience to stand back and watch someone be shot, no matter what the intent behind the event, is in itself a form of cruelty, insofar as it invites people to behave as passive spectators to an act of violence (even if the use of the word may be, once again, complicated by the event's suspension between gratified self-wounding, assisted self-wounding, and unpredictable wounding by another). But to place this work of Burden's too quickly under the rubric, or even in the vicinity, of "cruelty" seems wrongheaded. Insofar as some of Burden's early performance pieces could be deemed masochistic (such as *Trans-Fixed*, in which a friend crucifies Burden to the front hood of a Volkswagen bug), such a designation may eventually serve as but an occasion to reflect on how distant the operations of masochism and sadism really are—a distance that can make the oft-circulated dyad "sadomasochism" appear as "one of those misbegotten names, a semiological howler," as French philosopher Gilles Deleuze once put it. What's more, in contrast to other artists whose work seems to embrace the clinical definition of a masochist—"one who derives sexual gratification from pain" ("super masochist" Bob Flanagan comes to mind, for example)—Burden has always seemed aloofly adrift from carnal pleasure, and more devoted to the formal creation of abstract, minimalist, intensely charged spaces.

This is literally so in *220*, also from 1971. In *220*, Burden lined the F Space gallery in Santa Ana, California, with black plastic, set up four wooden ladders, flooded the gallery with twelve inches of water, and climbed up the ladders with three other participants (one ladder per person). After everyone had perched atop their ladders, Burden dropped a 220-volt electrical wire into the water. The four participants then stayed in their perches from about midnight to six o'clock in the morning, at which point sculptor Nancy Rubins, Burden's wife, shut off the electricity, and the participants climbed down.

While *Shoot* evokes a species of horror akin to that of a snuff film, *220* offers a more unusual, more unnameable species of dread. For this reason, I find it vastly more intriguing. The documentation of the piece consists of another grainy Super-8 video, this time depicting four shadowy, mostly immobile shapes perched atop ladders above a murky floor. The figures stare bemusedly at the water, as if waiting for its danger to become manifest. At times, they appear to be asleep, their arms hooked in the rungs. Their stillness and nonchalance make for an utterly chilling contrast with the life-or-death stakes of the situation. It's like a silent version of *Waiting for Godot*, performed by slackers, suspended over an actual abyss.

On the face of it, *220* is a contained experiment, posing serious risks only to the participants. But the primary elements of the piece—water and electricity—bespeak spillage, circulation. Moment by agonizing moment, the situation threatens to become unmanageable, to spread, to transfer its risk to others. Watching the piece now, it seems a miracle that no one was hurt. If the piece had spilled out to injure nonparticipants (such as facilitators of the piece, or people in adjacent studios or buildings; there was no audience), the results would have been tragic, unforgivable. Had it injured Burden and company, the tragedy would have been limned by their utter jackass-ness. Indeed, some of Burden's pieces seem but a more self-serious precursor to the Jackass industry (i.e., the movies, video games, and spin-off groups derived from MTV's

2000–2002 hit TV show *Jackass*, in which the stars perform a series of self-injuring stunts, such as piercing their butt cheeks together, firing a bean bag rifle into their stomachs, snorting wasabi to the point of vomiting, and so on). In *Deadman* (1972), for example, Burden lay down on a busy street in Los Angeles (La Cienega Boulevard), placed two flares around his body, covered himself with a tarp, and waited to see what would happen next. (What happened: The police arrived on the scene and asked him what he was doing. Burden responded, "Making a piece of sculpture." They arrested him for creating a false emergency; later, Burden settled the matter in court, still angry with the cops for "wrecking his piece.")

Pieces like *Deadman*, with their wager that one man's sculpture is another man's crime, are meant to put Evenson's distinction between "life" and "art" to the test. But to be more exact, the distinction Evenson makes is between "life" and "literature": "In life, violence happens to you. In literature, you make the choice to pick up the book and read, and to continue reading." Insofar as it consists of words printed on a page rather than a body under a tarp that you swerve to avoid hitting on your drive home, literature typically makes such distinctions easier to draw. Not only that, but the written word doesn't have the animal presence or basic unpredictability of performance, nor the bossiness of a visual image, especially a moving image. Unlike much contemporary media, which aims, asymptotically, for a total takeover of the senses, reading doesn't make demands on more than one sense at a time. Consequently, while one is reading, one's agency and physical autonomy remain front and center: The feeling of a page-turner is partly so exciting because *you still have to turn the page*. You can put down a book and start it up again without missing anything—there's no imperative to sit through it simply because you paid the price of admission, your date is digging it, and you bought a seven-dollar tub of popcorn.

This freedom is important. It allows for a dance; it allows you to see yourself dancing in reaction. There's information there. Your choice to keep going can itself become a cause of puzzlement. Or, if you choose to abandon ship, you can then ponder the classic question, did I fail the work, or did it fail me? When, or what, was the tipping point, and why?

In my experience, when people talk about disturbing images from art that have stayed with them—images they often wish they hadn't seen—they are almost always talking about images from movies (and sometimes photographs) rather than images from books. This seems to me a function of the fact that one beholds an image all at once, which leaves the organism more vulnerable to assault, as well as to the fact that an image created by words requires the aid of one's own mind in its construction—it is not entirely given. As classic literary ghost stories such as Henry James's *The Turn of the Screw* (1898) have made clear, it is precisely this sense of collusion between reader and text that can make the reading experience so guilt-inducing, so uncomfortable, so deeply wicked.

As much ink as has been spilled on the operations of the visual and verbal, the truth is that both modes remain something of a mystery. As David Levi Strauss has put it (in "Take as Needed," a 1994 essay that refreshingly takes up the subject of the *therapeutic* potential of images), "Very little is known at this point about the actual physiological effects of images. What happens to the automatic nervous system, to neurotransmitters and hormones, when a person is moved by an image?" Think, for example, about the fact (noted by Alexander Theroux in *The Primary Colors*) that "upon merely seeing the color red, the metabolic rate of a human being supposedly increases by 13.4%." Does this quickening have any relationship to words that conjure red in our minds? What sense, exactly, gets engaged when we read? We typically (though not always) use our eyes to see words, but the images our brain creates in response have little to do with black-and-white type, or with the shimmering appearance of words on a screen (or, for the blind, with the raised letters of Braille). "It's a very, very close and difficult thing to know why some paint comes across directly onto the nervous system and other paint tells you the story in a long diatribe through the brain," Francis Bacon once observed. The same could surely be said of words.

—

As FAR as Burden's stance toward his audience goes, it runs the gamut, from invitation to intervention to ambush. The most hilarious and beautiful of the interventions may be *TV Ad* (1973), which came out of Burden's long-standing desire to be on television. To fulfill the desire, Burden purchased as long a time slot as he could afford—ten seconds—and submitted a snippet of 16-millimeter footage from *Through the Night Softly*, a 1973 performance piece in which Burden crawls on his stomach, his hands tied behind his back, through fifty feet of broken glass on Main Street, Los Angeles, wearing only his underwear. (The underwear is a crucial mitigator, though it's hard to say why—I'll just admit that I'm grateful, each time I watch, to see the Speedo-like apparatus come into view as Burden slithers toward the camera.) Sandwiched between a psychedelic ad for a compilation record called *Good Vibrations* and a dopey, unwittingly homoerotic ad for deodorant soap, Burden's agonized body appears like a skinny worm come up from the underworld. The tag of masochism that may have haunted *Through the*

Night Softly on its own is here obliterated: next to the shiny, happy, sudsy people on TV, Burden's shredded, dogged worm seems but their inevitable, shadowy counterpart, their tragicomic relief.

As brilliant as *TV Ad* is, Burden's *TV Hijack*, from the previous year, is stupid. Burden describes *TV Hijack* as follows: "On January 14 I was asked to do a piece on a local television station by Phyllis Lutjeans. After several proposals were censored by the station or by Phyllis, I agreed to an interview situation. I arrived at the station with my own video crew so that I could have my own tape. While the taping was in progress, I requested that the show be transmitted live. Since the station was not broadcasting at the time, they complied. In the course of the interview, Phyllis asked me to talk about some of the pieces I had thought of doing. I demonstrated a T.V. Hijack. Holding a knife at her throat, I threatened her life if the station stopped live transmission. I told her that I had planned to make her perform obscene acts."

Some have since argued for the piece's merits by saying things like "*T.V. Hijack* was ultimately about who is in control over what's presented through the media" (curator Irene Hofmann), or "Burden's simulation of televised violence references also the mediation of real bloodshed that was occurring at the time, not only in Vietnam, but also at Kent State (May 4, 1970) and Attica Prison (September 1971)" (academic Sami Siegelbaum). Maybe so, but it's not enough. For it wasn't simulated violence for Lutjeans—she had a knife held to her throat by a man speaking threatening obscenities, felt terrified, and feared for her life. Any desire of Burden's to stage an incisive intervention about media control ends up vastly overshadowed by the unimaginative cruelty of using a woman's mind and body, without her consent, as disposable backdrops. Burden's primary achievement here was to marry the spectacle of such cruelty (already a staple of TV and movies) to the actuality of it (already a staple of so many women's lives). The result is a redundancy that stands as a regrettable low point in Burden's early career.

One of Burden's more recent gestures makes a fitting counterpoint to *TV Hijack*, perhaps setting it right (or standing in hypocritical relation to it, depending on your point of view). I'm thinking of his controversial resignation from UCLA's art department in 2004, over the university's failure to expel a student who performed a frightening staged shooting in a class being taught by guest Ron Athey. (Nancy Rubins resigned as well.) In a 1975 interview, Burden famously defined art as "a free spot in society, where you can do anything." In his 2004 resignation letter to UCLA, he insisted on a "cardinal difference between an act performed in an art space for an audience that had been warned and one sprung on students in a classroom." Likely it's obvious by now that I think the 2004 Burden had it right.

I think this partly for ethical reasons and partly for aesthetic ones. Consent and warning are not acquiescences to arbitrary, repressive notions of decorum or authority. Rather, they are space-makers, and they allow for the very possibility of voluntary submission or emancipation. The desire to catch an audience unawares and ambush it is a fundamentally terrorizing, Messianic approach to art-making, one that underestimates the capacities and intelligence of most viewers, and overestimates that of most artists. "They always want to hear *about;* they want an objective conference on 'The Theater and the Plague,' and I want to give them the experience itself, the plague itself, so they will be terrified, and awaken," Artaud reportedly told Anaïs Nin, in explanation of his notorious performance of his essay "The Theater and the Plague" at the Sorbonne in 1933, during which he dispensed with his planned lecture and acted out the delirium and death throes of the plague itself. "They do not realize *they are dead*," Artaud insisted.

I can't speak to Artaud's audience that evening, which may well have been full of easily offended, bourgeois putzes. But in my own life, I know I generally feel very alive and emancipated when I choose to walk out of something. After all, you walk out when you realize that whatever it is that you're watching, for whatever reason, simply isn't worth it. Walking out reminds you that while submission can at times be a pleasure, a risk worth taking, you don't have to manufacture consent whenever or wherever it is nominally in demand. (I know countless people—mostly women—who refuse to watch movies with gratuitous rape scenes. And many of these people believe—and I count myself among them—that there is an excellent argument to be made that any rape scene, at this point in cinematic history, is gratuitous. Here, the refusal to manufacture consent to watch bears a strong, albeit metaphorical relationship to the refusal to manufacture consent to tolerate unwanted sexual incursions.) The fact that the exit door isn't barred, the feel of the fresh air on your face when you open it—all of this serves to remind you of how good it feels to angle the full force of your body and attention toward that which seems to you a good use of your short time on the planet, and to practice aversion toward that which does not. These are freedoms that life does not always grant; God help us if we would prefer an art that further whittled down the choices.

"The principle of emancipation is the dissociation of cause and effect," Rancière has said, in his argument for something he calls "aesthetic efficacy"—that is, the paradoxical kind of efficacy that art has to offer, one that "escapes the dilemma of representational mediation and ethical immediacy." One could hear this argument as yet another stodgy affirmation of art's need to stand at a distance from instrumentality, for it to retain that "purposeless purposiveness" that Kant famously assigned to it (a distance and purposelessness that many artist-activists have fiercely refused). But I think Rancière is saying more than that. He is saying that no one can do our waking up for us. You can't rape someone into independence any more than you can deliver democracy at the tip of a gun. Charging others with false consciousness—"They do not realize *they are dead*"—rarely helps, either. The door has to stay open.

Of course one does not always know, nor does one's body always know, when to venture forth, and when to turn away. When to abide, when to refuse; when to accept, when to intervene. For better or worse, some trial and error is required, as is the case for most worthwhile forms of self-knowledge.

NOBODY SAID NO

———————

Fast-forward now to 2007, to the so-called postfeminist age. An art student is showing a handful of faculty the film that she has been working on, called *Do You Have Time to Kill Me Today*. The film consists of a series of takes of the student—a knockout, punky blonde from Copenhagen—getting in her car and driving around a block in her sunny Southern California neighborhood. At some point during each take, a rednecky, middle-aged-to-elderly man pops up from the backseat and drags a knife across her neck, pops an obviously fake bag of blood in his fist, then falls back out of sight. The woman pretends not to notice the event and drives on unperturbed, the fake blood dripping down from the fake slash across her neck.

For the first few takes, the man is entirely quiet. Then, after about seven "kills," he starts to talk. He says things like, "Die, Bitch," before dropping out of sight.

The student tells us that this man is her neighbor, and that he was originally quite reluctant to be a part of her film. He didn't want the neighbors to see him "killing her" and get the wrong idea. But, she explains, as their work together progressed, he got more and more into it. He would even start coming over to her house on days when she wasn't planning on filming to say, Why can't we do the killing today? The talking he started doing during the scene was ad-libbed, she said, and became more frequent and spirited as the killings went on.

The film was undeniably interesting—it was funny in a complicated way, poised, as it was, between empowerment, horror, and camp, and paced with the slow fascination of a screen test. Yet as she spoke, the faculty became increasingly concerned. The student admitted that it was a bit unnerving to see this man transformed from a reluctant, soft-spoken participant into a "Die, Bitch"–yelling, overeager "killer," but it didn't seem to bother or interest her too much. One faculty member asked if his transformation was a part of the piece; she said, No, not really. Another advised her that for her neighbor's sake, she should probably just work with the footage she already had, and tell him the exercise was over. "He'll be disappointed," the student said. (The student, Stine Marie Jacobsen, later went public with the piece, which she now describes as a "social horror project with my American neighbor, Kirk Douglas Sample, whom I train to be a killer.")

Was the unintentional wager of her project that every reluctant, soft-spoken neighbor has a "Die, Bitch" script lurking inside him? Maybe so. But even if he does, I wouldn't necessarily take it as proof that every man carries within him a deep, pent-up misogyny just waiting for the opportunity to express itself in a controlled or uncontrolled manner. I might be more inclined to chalk it up to the fact that we've heard and seen this script so many times that its words are there for us as soon as we dip into it. The words of this particular script are "Die, Bitch." I could dip into any number of other scripts and start spewing, but I won't bother. You already know the words.

—

EVENTUALLY, THE film student was put on ethical warning, as was a dance student who was choreographing a piece in which several female dancers danced blindfolded while he threw items such as buckets of water and phonebooks at their bodies from the wings. Why not just acknowledge that the piece has an element of cruelty to it, I asked him, and take it from there? "Because it *isn't* cruel," he argued. "The dancers have signed release forms, and they are choosing to be in it." That makes it *legal*, I told him—it doesn't absolve it of cruelty, or at least the evocation of it.

"Evil is in the eye of the beholder," Hegel wrote. But is cruelty? Does there exist such a thing as a *mirage* of cruelty? Or is the apprehension of cruelty one of those things that we should definitively *not* try to talk ourselves, or each other, out of? The first time I taught an undergraduate seminar titled "The Art of Cruelty," my students often ended up arguing with each other as to whether they felt a particular piece of art was cruel or not. These conversations—which sometimes slid into an "is too!/is not!" type of debate—always felt off base to me. I knew it was my job to lead us out of this dead-end forest—especially as I had unintentionally led us into it—but how?

Often I found myself reminding them that the piece at hand wasn't on trial—that absolving it of cruelty wasn't giving it a stamp of approval, and, conversely, that finding aspects of it guilty of such didn't sink it. After all, the implicit reasoning behind such arguments is that art has more value if its creator or its ultimate "message" can be somehow neutralized into the benevolent, or at least be interpreted as critical of the cruel—or if its creator could be satisfactorily proved to be uncontaminated by any sadistic or narcissistic urges. Not only would this standard of judgment disqualify much of the world's most interesting art, but also, at the end of the day, it is as fundamentally arbitrary as any other standard ("art should serve beauty," "art should intensify human consciousness," "art should revolutionize society," "art should make the everyday strange," "art should redistribute the sensible," "art should be an axe for the frozen sea within us," and so on and so forth).

I also tried to get my students to pay attention to the variety of responses they likely had *throughout* a piece, rather than submit to the feeling that they needed to arrive at some fixed or final verdict. After all, a verdict typically gets made later, simply by virtue of time, as time alone reveals what works, or what aspects of a work, will stick with you, and which will fall away. I would guess that most people attempt to remain open and withhold judgment throughout a movie, book, or play—you know, "give it a chance"—but find their feelings inevitably congealing after the fact. (I saw the Wooster Group's 2010 production of *North Atlantic* the other day, for example, and within a matter of twenty-four hours I heard myself go from telling people that it was interesting but flawed to saying that I had completely hated it. Whence the change?)

For this reason, I find it fascinating—albeit occasionally strenuous—to return to pieces, sometimes years later, that deeply offended me upon first encounter. It is unnerving to realize how much one's compass or tastes can shift throughout a lifetime, how one's sense of "okayness" is contingent on a host of factors, including the simple question of whether one is experiencing something for the first or the second time, not to mention the twentieth. A first encounter with a harrowing work that unfolds in time (i.e., literature, film) will always be more harrowing due to the simple fact that one does not know what's coming. In such a scenario, the organism reads or watches in a state seasoned by dread and self-protective anxiety—a state that, while not without its excitements, is not necessarily the one most commensurate with critical analysis.

Live performance provides another complicating factor, in that while watching, one can never be sure of exactly what's going to happen, even if the piece is scripted. To take a Technicolor example, consider the work of choreographer Elizabeth Streb. Over the past several decades, Streb has been developing a form of movement she calls POP action, which showcases impact, velocity, and bodily risk. While watching her company, one might feel (as does Streb, and as do I) that the work is essentially about gravity, athleticism, and the limitations and possibilities of the human body as it moves through space-time, rather than violence, sadomasochism, or cruelty. "I suspect that a lot of the language thrown at my work over the last couple of decades would've been different if I were a guy," Streb said in a 2003 *Village Voice* article. "Instead of calling it 'violent' and 'sadomasochistic,' it would've been considered 'athletic' and 'rambunctious.' "

But it's also possible that, during one of Streb's pieces, you might feel a flash of something else—not that the work is cruel per se (after all, the bodily agonies of POP action pale in comparison to those of ballet or football), but that its showcasing of the hardship endured by its dancers is gimmicky. "You could call it dance-theatre of cruelty, for its chief object seems to be to make the audience wince," a grumpy reviewer for the UK's *Independent* wrote in a 1995 review. "After the initial gasp-response, this spectator tired of such extravagant assaults on the senses." Personally, I've more often felt that Streb's assaults—if one could even use the word with a straight face—aren't extravagant enough, at least not tonally speaking: the shiny spandex unitard costuming, the circus aesthetic, the primary-color palette, the reliance on dare-devil or superhero motifs, have often struck me as unnecessarily, even relentlessly, limited—strangely at odds with Streb's questing, expansive, and blessedly original approach to the predicament and possibilities of the human body.

But then, just when you're losing faith, something can happen to bring you back on board. Such was my experience upon see-ing a preview of Streb's 2003 homage to flight, *Wild Blue Yonder*, in which Streb's dancers repeatedly swan dive from a platform rigged high above a mat, landing each time, facedown, with the company's signature *thud*, before popping up and returning to the platform to dive again. (Streb often mikes the surfaces of her per-formance spaces, so as to maximize the sound of her dancers strik-ing against them.)

As chance would have it, I saw this piece in October 2003, just three days after one of my dearest friends in the world had been thrown from her bicycle while riding down a hill; upon landing, she cracked two cervical vertebrae, rendering her paralyzed. In light of my friend's accident, Streb's piece irritated me. I was not in the mood to watch potentially vertebrae-cracking disasters, how-ever controlled, and I doubted I ever would be again. In the face of the involuntary harm my friend had just suffered, the risks here taken seemed ridiculous. Life has enough suffering in it, I thought. But as the piece went on, swan dive after preposterous, glorious swan dive, my feelings changed. The perverse beauty of it all rose slowly, then triumphantly to the surface—not because there was no price to such flight, but because there could be. It ended up being one of the most moving viewing experiences I've had, in that it transported me from protesting our bodily vulnerability to accepting it, then cheering it on, come what may. (I tried to remember this feeling several years later, when I heard that deeAnn Nelson, one of Streb's dancers, broke her back during a Streb performance on May 20, 2007.)

In any event, the dance student was right about one thing: the consent of his dancers mattered. (I might here note that Streb's dancers are typically wildly devoted to the work—not despite but because of the risk and difficulty associated with it.) The *Do You Have Time to Kill Me Today* student knew that consent mattered too: as a conceptual gesture—perhaps intended as a cheeky reply to the ethical concerns voiced by her faculty—she exhibited her neighbor's consent form alongside her video in the gallery. But, alas, a framed consent form cannot shake a piece clean of its unruly effects, nor should it. The question of whether it is ever cruel to do unto someone what she would like you to do unto her—or at least what she has authorized having done unto her—remains alive.

For example, if the participants have consented, but the work still strikes the viewer as cruel, must one then charge the participants with false consciousness? Is this charge its own form of cruelty—the cruelty of condescension, in which the viewer presumes to know more about the subject than he or she knows about himself or herself? And why the condescension—why the presumption that there's anything wrong with signing up to get mistreated a little, or a lot? Who defines mistreatment, anyway?

I've sometimes found myself wondering such things while watching the seriously drug-addled performers stagger through some of Andy Warhol's tougher films. (Gerard Malanga's eventual passing out from being fed amyl nitrate poppers by the "doctor" topping him in 1965's *Vinyl*—Warhol's grim, fascinating adaptation of Anthony Burgess's *A Clockwork Orange*—comes to mind.) Warhol's films unnerve in that they showcase unfeigned activity (people really are fucking, shooting up, slapping each other, and so on) in collision with over-the-top melodrama and artifice; the collision provides the films' texture, their alienated genius. However high or hysterical the players may be, it seems likely that they would be doing what they are doing anyway, with or without his camera, with or without our gaze. As Wayne Koestenbaum notes, there exists perhaps only one player in all of Warhol's films—Ari, singer Nico's toddler son—"whom we may justly pity for his unwitting participation in a purgative ritual of cosmetic, educational psychosis." I agree. I don't pity the others, nor have I ever been tempted—as some have been—to charge Warhol with behaving evilly toward his players. To say that Warhol valued voyeurism, prurience, passivity, and performativity over reparative compassion is an understatement. But Warhol didn't transform his players into self-destructive drug addicts or suicides, nor could he necessarily have altered their fates. As he himself notes in *POPism* (in an odd echo of Al-Anon), "When people are ready to, they change. They never do it before then, and sometimes they die before they get around to it. You can't make them change if they don't want to, just like when they do want to, you can't stop them."

The problem becomes more complicated when the work at hand presents itself as documentary and features populations whose ability to consent is more contested, such as the incarcerated mentally ill. See, for example, Frederick Wiseman's 1967 documentary *Titicut Follies*, which revealed appallingly sadistic treatment of mental patients at Bridgewater State Hospital in Massachusetts. *Titicut Follies* was banned for a number of years by the State of Massachusetts, on the grounds that the film violated the privacy and dignity of the inmates; it has also been credited with directing national attention to improving conditions for the mentally ill.

Occupying something of a middle ground between campy performativity and agonizing documentary stand Diane Arbus's hypnotically creepy portraits of retarded adults, taken at various residences between 1966 and 1971—or, more recently, Jonathan Caouette's harrowing, narcissistic memoir-film *Tarnation* (2003), in which Caouette films his mentally ill mother, Renee, hanging the fragments of her psyche out on the line. This exposure becomes most uncomfortable during the scene in *Tarnation* in which Caouette films Renee dancing with a small pumpkin for an excruciatingly long period of time. Caouette's refusal to stop filming, or to edit the scene down later, begins to feel more troubling than his mother's mental illness. Elsewhere in the film, Renee begs her son to put down his camera, by which point one may feel inclined to take her side.

At such moments, it isn't the psychological motivation or agency of the participants that comes into focus, but that of the creator. Such is clearly the case with Spanish artist Santiago Sierra, whose more controversial pieces include *160 cm Line Tattooed on 4 People* (2000), in which Sierra gives four prostitutes a shot of heroin for agreeing to have a line tattooed across their backs, and *10 People Paid to Masturbate* (2000), in which Sierra offers ten poor Cuban men twenty dollars to videotape themselves masturbating, then give him the footage for exhibition. "A person without money has no dignity," Sierra explains, in service of the by-now nauseatingly familiar argument that the point of his work is simply to lay this fact bare. "The tattoo is not the problem," Sierra says of the prostitute/heroin piece. "The problem is the existence of social conditions that allow me to make this work." True enough, in a sense—but Santiago's invented equation, in which the radical problems of the world neatly erase the problems posed by his work, is quite obviously a self-serving convenience.

Even if and when Sierra's diagnoses are spot-on, the pity he has expressed toward his subjects gives me pause, and evaporates whatever interest in the work I might have otherwise been able to muster. For this pity doesn't just stand behind the scenes; it also structures the forms of the artwork at hand. As he told the BBC about *10 People Paid to Masturbate*, "Nobody said no and for me that was very tough. When I made this piece I would go to bed crying." It's one thing to set up situations that aim to alert the world—even if just the art world—to the bad news of radical exploitation, even if one feels the lamentable need to exploit others to make one's point. It's quite another to decide in advance on the terms of human dignity (i.e., that a willingness to film oneself jerking off for money signifies that you have none), set up situations which prove (to you) that someone is utterly debased, then weep over the fulfillment of your puritanical prognostication. No wonder there's not much to think about Sierra's subjects themselves—such as the ten Iraqi immigrants Sierra found on the streets of London and paid "as little as possible" to be coated beyond recognition with toxic foam in his 2004 piece, *Polyurethane Sprayed on the Backs of 10 Workers*. Their dignity—which, to my mind, the artist has the power neither to restore nor to annihilate—remains untouched.

As far as my dance student was concerned, the most I could really hope for (pedagogically speaking) was that he learn a little something about a long tradition of works in which a (typically male, but not always) ringmaster places a body (typically female, but not always) on the line, for any number of reasons, and to any number of effects. I wanted him to know about Santiago Sierra. I wanted him to know about Yves Klein's *Anthropometries* performances from the early 1960s, in which a formally dressed Klein directed naked women smeared in blue paint to roll around on sheets of paper laid out on the floor while a string quartet played nearby. I wanted him to know about Yoko Ono's *Cut Piece* and Abramović's *Rhythm 0*, as these works deconstruct the tradition of the female body marshaled by the male ringmaster by disappearing the ringmaster, leaving the artists open, sometimes at alarming risk, to whatever might happen next.

I wanted him to know about the phenomenon art historian Jane Blocker has termed "risk transfer," in which an artist becomes known as a fearless risk-taker by transferring the risk to those around him or her. (Blocker makes reference to, among others, Richard Serra, whose gigantic steel sculptures once occasioned the death of one of their installers, and Brock Enright, who has made a name for himself by setting up an abduction/torture service for people who sign up for it via his Web site.) As Blocker points out in an important essay titled "Aestheticizing Risk in Wartime: The SLA to Iraq" (2008), the term "risk transfer" (which Blocker borrows from corporate capitalism) also applies to the West's current method of waging war, in which bodily risk gets transferred to the populations of other, faraway countries; the costs, to future generations. Troubled by the ways in which the valorization of risk—and the prevalence of risk transfer—in recent and contemporary art practice rely on the same logic as that in the political realm, Blocker ends up wondering what "an artistic boycott of risk might look like, and whether our refusal to participate in that game would help productively to change its rules."

I also wanted him to know about Mendieta's minimalist, haunting *Body Tracks* (1974) in which Mendieta uses her own arms, sweat-shirted and soaked in tempera and blood, to drag her body down a wall, leaving a smeary red V. And about Carolee Schneemann's ecstatic "action painting," as in *Up To and Including Her Limits* (1976), in which Schneemann suspends herself from a rope harness, crayons on hand, and makes marks on paper as she dangles and swings. I wanted him to know about Streb, whose interest in the body happily ignores the oft-plumbed, psychologized poles of resilience and vulnerability, and focuses instead on the human animal as a robust occupier of space-time, in thrall to forces such as rebound, gravity, and centrifugal pressure. I wanted him to know all these things and more, so that he and his work could stand in confident relation to them, rather than in unconscious echo.

Such is the prototypical teacherly stance. But, of course, many young artists don't want to know all these things, or at least they don't want to be flooded by them. And they certainly don't want to be lectured about them as if receiving a scold or a warning. People need to do their own thing, make their own mistakes, work through their own psychodramas, reinvent the wheel, if they must, on their own time and in their own terms. Fair enough. Perhaps, as Rancière might have it, my impulse to give context, to inform, to "help," is but part and parcel of what he calls "the logic of the stultifying pedagogue," which presumes that "what the pupil must *learn* is what the schoolmaster must *teach* her." I don't really think so, however. Mostly I want to point to third things—unruly, inscrutable, multivalent, un-ownable third things—without knowing exactly what they have to say or teach. For when things are going well with art-making and art-viewing, art doesn't really say or teach anything. The action is elsewhere.

THE BRUTALITY OF FACT

I'VE ALWAYS hoped to put over things as directly and rawly as I possibly can, and perhaps, if a thing comes across directly, people feel that it is horrific," Bacon once said, in an attempt to explain why some people find his paintings "brutal" rather than manifestations of "the brutality of fact," which is what he thought he was after, or, when successful, revealing. "Because, if you say something very directly to someone, they're sometimes offended, although it is a fact. Because people tend to be offended by facts, or what used to be called truth."

Bacon is right, in his suggestion that today "facts" are no longer interchangeable with "truth." Unlike Bacon, however, I don't think this is necessarily a bad thing. More perturbing is the state of "facts" in a world of "truthiness." ("Truthiness" is comedian Stephen Colbert's word meaning "what I say is right, and [nothing] anyone else says could possibly be true." As Colbert sees it, truthiness has a selfish quality in addition to a delusional one: "It's not only that I *feel* it to be true, but that *I* feel it to be true.") Indeed, it has become an almost comedic phenomenon, that as mainstream news reporting in the United States continues its slide away from fact and into a partisan cesspool of spin, invective, and infotainment, news programs have started to blanket themselves with a "just the facts, ma'am" brand of sloganeering. In 2009, there was Campbell Brown's "No Bias, No Bull," FOX's knowingly duplicitous "Fair and Balanced," CNN's juvenile "Just sayin'," and so on: all bank, however disingenuously, on an offer of "straight talk"—that is, the manufactured sound of a citizen (say, a talk radio host or town hall ranter, rather than an informed journalist) telling it "like it is."

I don't know who, exactly, feels as though they're hearing truth spoken to power by watching a shellacked cable news anchor read aloud from incoming tweets, but no matter—it is characteristic of today's supposed hunger for truth that it coexists with a general repudiation of, or disinterest in, fact. The results can be dizzying: think, for example, of Representative Joe Wilson's notorious "You lie!" outburst during President Obama's September 9, 2009, address to Congress, on the subject of health care—an address in which Obama was explicitly setting out to dispel, as he put it, "fabrications that have been put out there in order to discourage people from meeting what I consider a core ethical and moral obligation, and that is that we look out for one another."

Fact-checkers quickly confirmed that Wilson's "You lie!" was technically in the wrong, but his supporters wasted no time printing up T-shirts, buttons, and bumper stickers anointing Wilson as a "truth-teller," even if the truth Wilson might have been telling was unclear. (Was it the truth of his anger? The truth of his racism? The truth of the anger or racism of others, which he was channeling on their behalf? The truth of Obama's duplicity, as he marches our great capitalism into a nefarious socialism, all under the ruse of some touchy-feely notion of "looking out for one another"?) Whatever one makes of such logic (or lack thereof), it's clear that the distance between "fact" and "truth" is an accepted, if blurry, commonplace.

This commonplace is by no means unique to cable news. Philosophers from Plato to Kant to contemporary French philosopher Alain Badiou have put in long hours attempting to differentiate "knowledge"—a category presumably containing discernible, provable facts—from "truth," which can indicate the opposite (i.e., spiritual or metaphysical knowledge that is somehow *evidence of itself*), or at least something altogether distinct (see Badiou: "Truth is first of all something new. What transmits, what repeats, we shall call knowledge. Distinguishing truth from knowledge is essential"). Theologians have been obsessed for millennia with the same, arguing that there is "truth" in its everyday sense, and then there is "Truth-truth," and it is the duty of the God-fearing to tell the difference. Pursuit of the latter may, in fact, necessitate a willful seeing past or disbelieving of the former, if and when local truths appear inconvenient or inconsistent with Truth-truth.

The idea that the visible, palpable, or present world is but a shadow of a different, "truer" world that exists elsewhere lies at the heart of the Platonic universe. It also undergirds the biblical notion that in the here and now, we must "see through a glass, darkly," but that on Judgment Day, our vision will clear. As William Blake put it in *The Marriage of Heaven and Hell* (1793), "If the doors of perception were cleansed every thing would appear to man as it is, infinite. For man has closed himself up, till he sees all things thro' narrow chinks of his cavern." Blake says man has "closed himself up"; a less pointed diagnosis might treat these "narrow chinks" as our inevitably limited senses, the apertures through which we must apprehend and construct the world, a world we presume to exist independently of us, "out there."

In Christianity, the textual paradigm for this form of seeing is typology, the teleological practice of reading the Old Testament as a set of figures or symbols that foreshadow events to come in the New Testament. And what a relief: instead of tumbling forth on a floating planet, which may or may not be an anomaly in the universe, its affairs driven by the twin whims of chance and will, we can imagine ourselves living a dress rehearsal for a foreshadowed revelation. Seen in this light, apocalypse seems less of a fear and more of a cheap ticket out of fear. What would you prefer: a bloody, climactic season finale, or the ongoing tragicomedy of inscrutable lives, inevitable deaths, and an unknowable universe?

"Wherever he looks, he sees extremists," said Hugo Chavez, president of Venezuela, in his September 20, 2006, address to the United Nations, referring, of course, to George W. Bush. Chavez went on: "And you—my brother, he looks at your color, and he says, oh, there's an extremist." In the same speech, Chavez counseled his listeners to make no mistake—Bush may have appeared in the chamber as a man, but really he was the devil, whose sulfuric stink Chavez could still smell at the podium. Amusing as Chavez's speech was, I couldn't help but notice his rhetorical flips: when Bush sees brown people who oppose his policies, Chavez argues, he mis-sees them as "extremists"; likewise, when we see Bush, we too are subject to a sort of mirage—the correct vision would behold not a man but a devil. In both cases, seeing things as they "really are" requires looking past that which is right in front of you—penetrating beyond deceptive appearances and into a reality imagined with alarming regularity as Manichean.

Putting aside, for the moment, the question of whether this mode of seeing—or not seeing, as the case may be—provides any passage to the Kingdom Come, we must admit that historically speaking (and for Americans in particular) it has birthed some astonishing cruelties. "The Puritan . . . was precluded from SEEING the Indian," writes William Carlos Williams in *In the American Grain*. "They never realized the Indian in the least save as an unformed Puritan." Williams was utterly revolted by this legacy of Puritanism—its tendency to skip over the visible world, or worse than skip over it, to *devour* it. "They should be bread for us," said Puritan founder Thomas Hooker of the Native Americans—that is, seen more correctly not as humans but as sacrament, to be consumed by the settlers with God's blessing. This is an astonishingly efficient, well-worn recipe for making use of—or dispensing with—people whose presence on the earth strikes others as an inconvenience.

Judge them as you will. But one thing is for sure: the Puritans were primed. Before their boats had even landed in the New World, they had been trained to have an intolerant, unseeing response to whatever they found here. John Winthrop's 1630 sermon, "A Model of Christian Charity," which famously lays out the imperative to found "a NEW ENGLAND"—a "city upon a hill"—no matter what stood in its way—was given to 700 settlers on the boat itself (the *Arbella*) as it tumbled across the Atlantic Ocean. Once the settlers arrived, they were mostly sick, under siege, and terrified. William Bradford, the Puritan governor of Massachusetts, described their state upon their 1620 arrival at Plymouth as follows: "what could they see but a hideous and desolate wilderness, full of wild beasts and wild men—and what multitudes of them they knew not . . . which ever way they turned their eyes (save upward to the heavens) they could have little solace or content in respect of any outward objects."

So when they turned their eyes to "outward objects," their task was to transform them as quickly and convincingly as possible into parables that might justify their terrifying mission. Listen, for example, to Winthrop's account of a skirmish between a mouse and a snake, recorded in his journal on July 5, 1632: "At Watertown there was (in view of divers witnesses) a great combat between a mouse and a snake; and, after a long fight, the mouse prevailed and killed the snake. The pastor of Boston, Mr. Wilson, a very sincere, holy man, hearing of it, gave this interpretation: That the snake was a devil; the mouse was a poor, contemptible people, which God had brought hither, which should overcome Satan here, and dispossess him of his kingdom." There might be more comedy than cruelty here, had the "poor, contemptible people" not succeeded in dispossessing Satan (i.e., the Native American) of his kingdom, and were present-day Americans not its living inheritors.

"There is a 'Puritanism'—of which you hear, of course, but you have never felt it stinking all about you," Williams wrote from New England, three centuries later. "It is an atrocious thing, a kind of mermaid with a corpse for a tail. Or it remains, a bad breath in the room. This THING, strange, inhuman, powerful, is like a relic of some died out tribe whose practices were revolting. . . . I wish to drag this THING out by itself to annihilate it." At times it seems that such an annihilation would qualify as a blow of direct, ruthless compassion.

—

IN THE publishing world, the "fact"-versus-"truth" divide came to prime time most recently vis-à-vis the controversy over James Frey's 2003 memoir, *A Million Little Pieces*. The revelation that Frey had fabricated aspects of his story drove *New York Times* book reviewer Michiko Kakutani to pen a splenetic, spasmodic piece titled "Bending the Truth in a Million Little Ways" (January 17, 2006). In this piece, Kakutani treats the Frey affair not as an instance of an individual taking liberties with the facts of his life for dramatic, mercenary, and/or psychological purposes, but rather as a referendum on "how much value contemporary culture places on the truth." Her review—which never defines "the truth," but instead takes a kind of if-you-have-to-ask-what-it-is-then-your-soul-is-already-lost attitude—lumps all kinds of purportedly malignant cultural and political phenomena together under the most purportedly malignant rubric of all: our "relativistic culture," which, according to Kakutani, has spawned everything from reality TV to academics who "argue that history depends on who is writing the history" to the hazardous lies of the George W. Bush administration to the literary genre currently going by the name of "creative nonfiction."

For Plato, it was the practice of mimesis or representation itself that was to blame for this distancing from truth—in which case "creative nonfiction" (a la Thucydides) would have been no more at fault than fiction (a la Euripides). In fact, in the *Phaedrus*, written language itself is to blame for this distancing, and must therefore also be forsaken. For Protestant theologian John Calvin, two thousand years later, the problem had become even more difficult to exorcise, as Calvin diagnosed (correctly, so it would seem) the human mind itself as a "perpetual forge of idols." As scholar Thomas Luxon has observed, this diagnosis puts Protestant Christianity in a bit of a fix, insofar as its "absolute success will be achieved only when 'that perpetual forge of idols' known as 'the human mind' is finally destroyed or exposed as the nothing all idols must always have been." (This, Luxon notes, "has not yet come to pass.") For Kakutani, the culprit is that by-now well-spanked bogey man, relativism, and its team of "fashionably nihilistic," postmodernist pushers, who have created "a climate in which concepts like 'credibility' and 'perception' replace the old ideas of 'objective truth.' "

Such arguments received an elongated (if retro) photo-op during the 2009 confirmation hearings of Supreme Court Justice Sonia Sotomayor, at which a host of (white, male) Republican senators dragged Sotomayor over the coals about her self-identification as a "wise Latina." To their minds, this self-identification was but a welcome mat into a "Brave New World" (as Senator Jeff Sessions put it) characterized by "relativism run amok" (Senator John Kyl). In this Brave New World, as Sessions explained in his opening remarks, the "firm belief in an ordered universe and objective truth" has been overthrown by the anarchic likes of Sotomayor, with her acceptance—her celebration, even!—of the notion that gender and ethnicity may play a role, however inscrutable, in what kind of judge she, or anyone, is. "I reject such a view, and Americans reject such a view," Sessions declared, on behalf of us all.

For the record, I believe James Frey was dishonest; I also believe that Sotomayor is a relativist (which seems to me—as Sotomayor herself explained eloquently—a condition of possibility for judging rather than an impediment to it). But so long as people like Kakutani keep using "fact" and "truth" as interchangeable terms that need no definition or clarification, and so long as they continue to smear out the differences between dishonesty and relativism, or between political lies aimed to bring us into an unjust war and, say, the art of creative nonfiction, no clarity of thought is likely to emerge.

Many artists have jumped into this debate, bending over backward to highlight their own truth-fetish. Armed with the Emily Dickinson mantra "Tell all the Truth but tell it slant," they argue that their profession offers better, deeper access to the Truth, albeit through back and side doors. "We all know that art is not truth. Art is a lie that makes us realize truth," Picasso famously pronounced. Or, as poet Anne Sexton put it, "[Truth is] what I'm hunting for when I'm working on a poem. . . . It might be a kind of poetic truth, and not just a factual one, because behind everything that happens to you, there is another truth, a secret life."

When it comes to art, I personally cannot see the use-value of these proclamations, nor of the related, superficially inverse claims that a culture's artists are somehow its "priests of truth." I don't mean to suggest that one isn't working toward *something* while working on a piece of art, something that could be called "truth" (though it might also be called "making it work," "aesthetic resolution," or some such thing). But to approach works of art or literature with the hope that they might deliver a referendum on truth, or provide access to Truth-truth, is to set up shop on a seriously faulty foundation. A work of art may tell us little about factual truth, or about Truth-truth, but that is no reason to banish or belittle it. So long as we exalt artists as beautiful liars or as the world's most profound truth-tellers, we remain locked in a moralistic paradigm that doesn't even begin to engage art's most exciting provinces.

By virtue of its being multiply sourced, art cannot help but offer up multiple truths. To a moralist in the market for "an ordered universe and objective truth," such an offering can be only a contradiction in terms. Worse still, because of its episodic nature, art offers the passing *impression* of truth, without the promise that the truth revealed will have any lasting power. For however powerful any given artistic truth might seem, a new, contradictory, or at least adumbrating truth might appear in the next instant, the next installment, the next frame, the next line, the next chapter, the next canvas.

Poetry is especially tricky on this account, as it sets forth aphorisms that, upon first encounter, can feel like dictums to live by. Take, for example, Williams's lovely line from his poem "The Ivy Crown": "The business of love is / cruelty which, / by our wills, / we transform to live together." Like most poetry forged from a good ear, this line convinces, momentarily, with no need of an argument. This is what poetic truths do: they blow in with the hot feeling of truth. You can then extract the line to read at an event (a wedding, a funeral, an inauguration, and so on) at which it makes sense, it marks the day. Everyone nods in assent, touched by how fitting, how wise, the words seem. Then you move on, the event moves on, life moves on. You turn the page.

I almost used Williams's line as the epigraph to this book, for example, simply because it sounded so good. But seeing as I could never figure out exactly what it meant, or definitively decide that it spoke any truth I believed in, I couldn't bring myself to use it. Did it hold some great wisdom, or did it simply derive its power from the kind of aesthetic logic that Brecht, among others, has force-fully, often convincingly, deplored? "Through artistic suggestion, which it knows how to exercise, [aesthetic logic] invests the most absurd assertions concerning human relations with the appearance of truth," Brecht wrote. "The more powerful it is, the more unveri-fiable its productions."

In other words, truth, in art, is but a feeling. An itinerant one. "Feelings are facts": an adage I've heard some set forth as sage therapeutic advice; others, as the defining belief of a psychopath.

For the fact is that Williams did not cast the business of love as cruelty all of the time, or even most of the time. Williams was a great love poet, whose most famous love poem, "Asphodel, That Greeny Flower," describes love as a "garden which expands," and credits his wife with showing him "a grateful love, / a love of nature, of people, / animals, / a love engendering / gentleness and goodness." I must admit, I have never been able to read this poem without tearing up. It really is that beautiful. Poet Joanna

Fuhrman thought so too, until a friend told her, "Yeah, Williams wrote his wife some nice poems, / but he was cheating on her the whole time. Everyone knew." Alas: the business of love may not be cruelty, but certainly it is complexity.

—

LIKE MOST artists charged with being cruel, or "cruel to be kind," photographer Diane Arbus always testified to having a greater fidelity to the so-called brutality of fact than to either cruelty or compassion. "I don't mean to say that all photographs have to be mean," Arbus said. "Sometimes they show something really nicer in fact than what you felt, or oddly different. But in a way this scrutiny has to do with not evading facts, not evading what it really looks like."

Unsurprisingly, Arbus supporters have tended to rally around this claim, casting her forays into various subcultures (nudist colonies, circus sideshows, the world of sex workers, homes for retarded adults, and so on) as those of a fearless and compassionate renegade. Meanwhile, her detractors have charged her with being "an exploitative narcissist," slumming it in communities in which she did not belong in order to generate provocative portraits that are fundamentally unkind to their subjects. (This fearless renegade/ narcissistic exploiter dyad also dogged Sylvia Plath, which is one reason why Arbus is sometimes dubbed "the Sylvia Plath of photography"; her suicide is another. Lest we forget, to be called the Sylvia Plath of anything is *a bad thing*.) In this polar version of events, Arbus's excursions to the "dark side" are either a record of adventuresome fellow-feeling or an extended exercise in callow, cynical coldness.

Sontag famously thought the latter—in her 1977 book *On*

Photography she roasts Arbus for "concentrating on victims, on the unfortunate—but without the compassionate purpose that such a project is expected to serve." In retrospect, it seems clear that the problem lies more in Sontag's standards than in Arbus's alleged cruelty. Changing times have not served Sontag's assessment well, as the so-called victims and unfortunates captured by Arbus that Sontag presumes we should pity—those lives Sontag assumes are defined by horrific pain—include drag queens, dykes, sex workers, sideshow performers, interracial couples, and others for whom pity does not now seem, a priori, the order of the day. Sontag also scolds Arbus for not being interested in "ethical journalism." But who ever said she was? Ethical journalism was probably about the last thing on Arbus's mind as she roamed about, photographing her freaks. Nor did Arbus shrink from admitting the stirrings of both cruelty and compassion within her. "And I photographed him then which was really cold," she wrote of her visit to her father on his deathbed. "But I suppose there is something somewhat cold in me."

Critics sympathetic to Arbus have worked overtime to absolve her of such coldness, often by recasting it as honesty. "Arbus knew that honesty is not a gift, endowed by native naiveté, nor a matter of style, or politics, or philosophy," one wrote in the catalogue essay to her 2003 retrospective, *Revelations*. "She knew rather that it is a reward for bravery in the face of the truth." But what truth could this critic possibly be talking about? That freaks look freaky? That anyone can be made to look like a freak? And since when is honesty a prize rather than a practice?

Whatever Arbus's stated intent, the fascination of her work for me is less about her ability to capture "what something really looks like," and more about its capacity to reveal how that "something" changes per frame—how many conflicting truths there might be within a singular image, moment, or person. Arbus's subjects typically look straight at the camera, but I know of no other photographer who draws so much attention to the disturbing split that can exist between two eyes in one gaze (or between two purportedly identical subjects, such as twins, or between two halves of an intimate couple, or even between two sides of a room). One eye of an Arbus subject might deliver the good news of fellow-feeling, while the other bespeaks the bad news of human isolation and pitiability. To insist that one cancels the other out, or to fault her inquiries for not meeting the requirements of "ethical journalism," is to miss the disconcerting schism of her vision. "I am like someone who gets excellent glasses because of a slight defect in eyesight and puts Vaseline on them to make it look like he normally sees," Arbus once explained, describing a late-breaking technique having to do with blurring. "It doesn't seem sensible but somehow I think it's right."

The artist standing bravely in the face of the (inconvenient, brutal, hard-won, dangerous, offensive) truth, the artist who refuses to "evade facts," or who can stare down "what the world really looks like"—what could be more heroic? Critics love the rhetoric used by artists such as Arbus and Bacon because it bolsters the sense that art and artists can rip off the veil, they can finally show us what our world is "really like," what *we* are really like. I mean it as no slight to these artists (both of whom I admire), nor to the practice of truth-telling (to which I aspire) when I say that I do not believe they do any such thing. Bacon shows us Bacon figures; Arbus shows us Arbus figures. This isn't to say that Bacon's paintings don't tell us quite a bit about the human animal, especially when caught in a spasm of despair or carnage, or that Arbus's photos don't communicate quite a bit about the human animal in its freakiness, loneliness, absurdity, or abstruse ecstasy. Their works do all this, while also remaining products of their notoriously particular view of the world. There is absolutely nothing strange about this paradox, unless you're looking to art to tell you "how things are," rather than give you the irregular, transitory, and sometimes unwanted news of how it is to be another human being.

At times, this news is familiar. "In every work of genius we recognize our own rejected thoughts: they come back to us with a certain alienated majesty," wrote Emerson, providing a memorable phrase for the grand, surprising pleasure we feel when a work of art returns or restates our own thoughts and feelings to us, however obliquely. At other times, however, the news arrives more alien than majestic, generating the perpetual undergraduate grievance, "I just can't relate." It behooves us, I think, to develop an openness to this latter feeling as well as to the former. If we're lucky, this openness may eventually grow into a hunger.

———

Our word is our bond: the phrase belongs to J. L. Austin, the British philosopher whose famous collection of essays, *How To Do Things with Words* (1962), focuses on something Austin called "performative utterances." These are instances in which words themselves act as deeds: "I thee wed," "I hereby christen you," "I dare you," "I declare war," and so on. As Austin explains, whether or not a performative utterance is successful (or "felicitous," to use his term) depends on the context in which it is uttered. A wedding ceremony conducted by someone not authorized to perform it causes a "misfire"; a promise made by someone who has no intent to fulfill its terms constitutes an "abuse"; and so on. The possible infelicities run the gamut—some involve political questions about social authorization (In which settings can the wedding vows of gay couples be called successful? What kind of action does a public apology—such as the Australian government's 2008 apology to the indigenous Aborigine people—actually perform?), while others stay tethered to the more personal matter of plain-old broken oaths ("But you promised you would love me and never leave me!").

Most important to our purposes here, however, is the one context Austin aims to exclude in entirety: the artistic context. As he explains, "A performative utterance will, for example, be *in a peculiar way* hollow or void if said by an actor on the stage, or if introduced in a poem, or spoken in soliloquy. Language in such circumstances is in special ways—intelligibly—used not seriously, but in ways *parasitic* upon its normal use—ways which fall under the doctrine of the *etiolations* of language." Many Austin readers—Jacques Derrida foremost among them—have found themselves intrigued and titillated by this notion of language-as-parasite, this doctrine of linguistic etiolation. For while Austin meant to partition artistic utterance off into the land of un-serious play (an impossibility, Derrida argues), it is precisely here—in the realm of the perverse, or the explicitly performative— that things get interesting.

For it is here that the question "Is it true?" falls off the table, and other questions move into view, such as "Does it work? What new thoughts does it make possible to think? What new emotions does it make possible to feel? What new sensations or perceptions does it open in the body?" (These are, not incidentally, the questions that Brian Massumi, translator of Gilles Deleuze and Felix Guattari's opus, *A Thousand Plateaus*, puts forth as the most pertinent to his subjects' wild philosophical endeavor.)

These questions are enthralling to me. But they are not enthralling to everyone. In fact, an emphasis on new thoughts, new emotions, new sensations, and new perceptions has struck some—the poet T. S. Eliot, for example—as completely wrongheaded. In his famous essay "Tradition and the Individual Talent" (1919), Eliot argues that the search for "new human emotions to express" is in fact a grievous error, and that such a quest for novelty leads only to "the discovery of the perverse." But, of course, for those of us who sense that there is more human hope and enlivenment to be found in the realm of the perverse than in traditions that have proved dull, restrictive, unimaginative, inapplicable, or unjust, Eliot's warning acts as a goad rather than a discouragement.

—

"IF YOU are unwilling to know what you are, your writing is a form of deceit," wrote Ludwig Wittgenstein. I agree. But what are we?

After all, a writer can be lying to herself as well as to the reader, and still convince herself, as well as the whole world, of her brutal honesty. I have heard many memoirists, for example, float the principle that "you can say anything you want about other people in your work as long as you make yourself look just as bad"—the cruel-to-oneself-obviates-cruelty-to-others fallacy. I've heard this equation tossed out at seminars and podiums and cocktail parties and interviews and classrooms. Often it is set forth as the secret solution to the essentially unsolvable ethical mess that is autobiographical writing.

Personally I think this equation a sham, a chicanery, one with its roots planted firmly in narcissism. Writing can hurt people; self-exposure or self-flagellation offers no insurance against the pain. And while I do not think all autobiographical writing is essentially an act of betrayal, as I've also heard it said, in my experience it does nearly always make someone feel betrayed. It doesn't have to be "brutal" to do so—all it has to do is offer the record of one person's consciousness, one person's interpretation of events that involved others, which is precisely what it cannot help but do. If and when it tries to speak for others, the sense of betrayal it provokes can be even stronger. Add to this the fact that a book's publication rarely coincides with the period in which it was written (and, by extension, with the self who wrote it)—a situation that can create a certain temporal dissonance, in which feelings from the past make their uneasy debut in the present, often in much-changed circumstances. This temporal dissonance—familiar to writers everywhere—can cause agonizing discomfort for current loved ones, and understandably so. There is no inoculation against these pains—only unsteady compromise, negotiation. If one is lucky, such dissonances can offer insight into the ways in which writing serves as a seismograph of feeling, an open-eyed charting of what has come down the river, rather than as a testament to unchanging emotional truths or desires.

Writing, especially autobiographical writing, can be a hothouse of self-deceptions, but it also has the uncanny ability to expose self-deceptions with the formidable exactitude of surgery. Most distressing, perhaps for writer and reader alike, is when both functions appear to be underway simultaneously. This is not rare. It could be one description of "the writing process." It is also a good description of the particularly acute vacillation between insight and self-delusion that characterizes addictive thinking, which is likely why it haunts Frey's drunkalogue, along with those of so many others.

I know of no writer who dramatizes this vacillation more

compellingly than Scottish writer Alexander Trocchi, particularly in his 1960 best-seller, *Cain's Book*. *Cain's Book* is an autobiographical, diaristic account of a junkie living on a barge in and around New York City. In his foreword to its 1992 reissue, critic Greil Marcus writes, "Trocchi's life was a cheap triumph. *Cain's Book*, written over the course of seven years, is not cheap. It is cruel." Marcus argues that despite attempts by well-meaning readers to rescue *Cain's Book* from itself, "You can't derive socially useful sentiments from lines like, 'She'd suck the fix out of your ass.'" True enough. But if the cruelty in Trocchi were simply a reiteration of the amorality and nihilism of a junkie's universe, it would be a bore. Trocchi's cruelty is of a more metaphysical variety: it is the cruelty of leading himself, and the reader, through passage after passage of compelling philosophical rumination and psychological insight, then snapping us back to nasty animal need—to score, to fuck, to flee, to forget—which is always standing by to nullify mind and heart.

Likewise, Trocchi's bluster would not be interesting or even all that cruel were it nothing but bluster. Dark as Trocchi's junkie narrator's mental whirlpool may be, it is also laced with clarity. Junk gives him the distinct impression that he is finally seeing things "as they are," but whether this insight is enlightenment or delusion cannot be settled: it is both, and it is neither. That is the inexorable, cruel struggle of being in thrall to a substance—especially one that alleviates pain at the same time that it causes it.

Here is Trocchi's narrator, for example, contemplating the "illusory sense of adequacy induced in a man by the drug": "Illusory? Can a . . . 'datum' be false? Inadequate? In relation to what? The facts? What facts? Marxian facts? Freudian facts? Mendelian facts? More and more I found it necessary to suspend such facts, to exist simply in abeyance, to give up (if you will), and come naked to apprehension." This sounds worthy; we are with him. We, too, are ready to live like Adam and Eve, feral and wide-eyed in the Garden. But in the next breath he admits, "It's not possible to come quite naked to apprehension and for the past year I have found it difficult to sustain even an approximate attitude without shit, horse, heroin." In other words, the addict, much like the artist, finds himself using artifice to strip artifice of artifice. The whirlpool grabs another limb.

In the end, the junkie narrator of *Cain's Book* does not so much cut through the veils of his self-delusion as he does give up the fight. "I am still sitting here, writing, with the feeling I have not even begun to say what I mean, apparently sane still, and with a sense of my freedom and responsibility, more or less cut off as I was before, with the intention as soon as I have finished this last paragraph to go into the next room and turn on." Writing hasn't changed a thing; when the writer puts down the pen, no matter how lucid or brutally honest his insights may have been, it is back to business as usual, which means, in this case, shooting up. This is depressing, but its honesty heartens me. It disallows the delusion that the act of writing necessarily connects us to humanity, that it will help us quit noxious substances, that it will restore us to love lost, or at least serve as a consolation. Literature is not, after all, self-help. "I am living my personal Dada," writes Trocchi. "In all of this there is a terrible emotional smear."

—

BUT WHAT about Bacon's earlier claim, that there exists some kind of intrinsic link between "facts" and the horrific, or the offensive? What kind of "fact" is Bacon talking about? Is it "fact" in and of itself, or a particular *kind* of fact that Bacon thinks so hard for us to hear, so hard for us to bear? Is it the news of our inevitable death, our animal-ness, "man's inhumanity to man," the endless wheel of suffering, our "situation of meat"? Or, in Trocchi's case, that of the dog-eat-dog nature of addiction? Does "fact" feel brutal only if and when we—either as individuals or as a populace—have grown accustomed to living in a realm of delusion or lies? Is there a relationship, as Bacon suggests, between honesty and brutality, or is "brutal honesty" but a shortcut to conjuring "direct and raw" feeling? Is it a shortcut that Bacon—along with many other so-called artists of cruelty—indulges?

"All cruel people describe themselves as paragons of frankness," a Tennessee Williams character once proclaimed. My own experience testifies to something of the same. I go down to the bookstore and skim shiny new memoir jacket after shiny new memoir jacket, until my mind starts to blur with blurb-speak testifying to each writer's brutal honesty, which is usually a close cousin of his or her "searing" or "unsentimental" prose, which, to be truly praiseworthy and dazzling, must also somehow shimmer onto the page "without a drop of self-pity." I wander out of the bookstore wondering, Is honesty paired with brutality a more winning, or at least a more marketable, combination? And why has self-pity become the specter to be avoided at all costs, in order to earn artistic seriousness, moral rectitude, and, perhaps, that all-important commodity, readers? ("How to avoid self-pity," Joan Didion chastens herself at the outset of her bestselling grief memoir, *The Year of Magical Thinking*, a book a friend of mine recently designated, without rancor, as "widow porn.")

For not all frankness is created equal. "Brutal honesty" is honesty that either aims to hurt someone or doesn't care if it does. ("No one wants to be friends with you," "You smell bad," "You've always been less attractive than your sister," "I never loved you.") While the two words often arrive sutured together, I think it worthwhile to breathe some space between them, so that one might see "brutal honesty" not as a more forceful version of honesty itself, but as one possible use of honesty. One that doesn't necessarily lay truth barer by dint of force, but that actually *overlays* something on top of it— something that can get in its way. That something is cruelty.

The fictional world of English novelist Ivy Compton-Burnett showcases this distinction with more alacrity—and, if you like, more cruelty—than I've found in any other place. If you pick up one of her drawing-room novels such as *Parents and Children* (1941) expecting it to depict only "the deadly claustrophobia within a late-Victorian upper-middle-class family," as its back cover says, beware. For Compton-Burnett's truer subjects are the deadly knots of honesty, brutality, and betrayal that can lie at the heart of both our language and our deeds.

Once I happily recommended Compton-Burnett's novels to a friend, who later told me that she had tried to read them but couldn't, because the things people said to each other in them were so unrelievingly cruel. Up until that point, I had felt only an unmitigated, cleansing pleasure in reading Compton-Burnett. And so I was forced to take pause and consider the possibility that I was either especially attracted to Compton-Burnett's particular brand of emotional sadism, blind to it, or both. There may be some truth here. But I think, at the end of the day, what I find so invigorating in Compton-Burnett is not her alleged cruelty, but her unwillingness to let anyone off the hook when it comes to the complexities of truth-telling. "I know you did not mean to be unkind, dear," says Eleanor, the mother in *Parents and Children*, to her daughter, who has just unintentionally insulted her mother's class status. "I do not indeed," her daughter insists. "I was only speaking the truth." "There isn't much difference," Eleanor replies. "Brutal frankness is an accepted term."

Accepted term or no, there is a difference. And one main task of Compton-Burnett's stringent dialogue is to lay it bare. Listen, for example, to this exchange between Eleanor and her young children:

> "Do you show your natural self, James?" said Eleanor, with one of her accesses of coldness.
>
> "No; yes; I don't know," said James, looking surprised and apprehensive.
>
> "Do you pretend to be different from what you are?"
>
> "Oh, no," said James, suddenly seeing his life as a course of subterfuge.
>
> "Do you, Venice?"
>
> "No, I don't think so."
>
> "Do you, Isabel?"
>
> "I don't know. I have not thought. And I do not intend to think. Probably most of us do the same thing."
>
> "That is not a gracious way to talk."
>
> "It was not that sort of question. It was one to make people admit what they had better keep to themselves."

By the novel's end, Eleanor's pitiless quest to merge honesty and "brutal frankness"—to make people admit "what they had better keep to themselves," and to project her own subterfuge onto others—has become one of the book's most repugnant displays.

The plot of *Parents and Children*, which is conveyed almost completely in dialogue (as is the case in most Compton-Burnett novels), is as follows: The father of Eleanor's nine children has gone on a business trip to South America, where he falls grievously ill. Eventually the family receives a missive saying that by the time this letter reaches them, he will be dead. The children begin grieving, and Eleanor hatches a fast plan to marry a close friend of her husband's named Ridley.

Quite some time after the father's purported death, however, one of his young sons, Gavin, thinks he sees him in town. He rushes home to tell his mother, but Eleanor—who by this point has planned not only to run off with Ridley, but also to leave her whole brood behind—is not interested in the news. After she brushes Gavin off, Gavin asks, in quiet despair, "Why do people speak to each other, if people don't listen?" "I heard what you said," Eleanor snaps. "You remember that I answered. But you must know you made a mistake." "I know that I saw him," Gavin says. "All my life I shall know." Later that evening, in the middle of dinner, a still-unbelieved Gavin announces to no one in particular, "I should like to die." When one of his sisters asks him why, he replies, "Because as long as you are alive, things can happen that you don't like. Even if you couldn't bear them, they would happen."

If you're looking for the brutality of fact, look no further. It was unbearable that Gavin's father died; now it is unbearable that his father has come back to life but no one believes it. Then, when the family is forced to believe it, things become more unbearable still. Here is Gavin, mulling over the effect of the revelation with one of his sisters (and Miss Pilbeam, their governess). He asks his sister:

"Would you mind as much, if he died now?"

"I shouldn't think it was as great a loss. But I should mind more. I couldn't ever bear it again."

"Would you die?" said Gavin, in a grave tone.

"If that is what people do, when they can't bear the things that have happened."

"Come, don't forget you are children," said Miss Pilbeam, who believed that this conversation had been unchildlike.

The fact of our inevitable deaths, and the pain that ensues for the survivors, begin to seem almost desirable when placed against the alternative laid out here: a scenario in which the return of a beloved only portends a future loss, one made more unbearable by virtue of anticipation and repetition.

And yet. The father's return does bring with it something utterly crucial, utterly clarifying. His reappearance rips through the subterfuge that has transpired in his absence. For Ridley knew his friend was still alive, but hid the fact in order to run off with Eleanor. In retaliation for his foiled marital plans, Ridley in turn wastes no time in revealing a paternity scandal that rips down the titular edifice, *Parents and Children*, like a house of cards.

And here we are delivered unto the cruel genius of Compton-Burnett's novels: they fixate so tightly on the parsing of spoken language that their characters and readers alike end up overlooking monumental acts of deceit that have taken place right in front of, or around, them—acts that, in the final hours, no amount of "brutal honesty" can undo or dispel. "I only ask that there should be honesty between us," Eleanor says to her son Graham at one point, to which Graham snaps back, "I would ask rarer and better things." Surely one of these "rarer and better things" would be the ability to distinguish between idiot honesty (i.e., "brutal frankness," honesty employed as a weapon, or as its own version of subterfuge) and an honesty that takes not only truthfulness as its standard, but also usefulness and intent.

This latter practice resembles what Buddhists call "right speech"—the third principle of the noble eightfold path—which is speech that is not only truthful, but also employed without the intent to divide, abuse, or be frivolous. Of course, "right speech" can be as misinterpreted or abused as any other principle—think of how many infidelities have flown under the cover of "I didn't want to hurt him," or of how many self-serving political lies circulate under the guise of protecting a populace ("the Iraqi regime is a threat to any American"—George W. Bush, January 3, 2003). Nonetheless, I find the principle an excellent one, in that it guides gently but firmly away from the fantasy that the most uncompromising, purest form of truthfulness must come at any price, while it also encourages as much honesty—with oneself and with others—as possible.

All the principles on the eightfold path (such as right thought, right livelihood, and right action—the latter of which includes refraining from stealing, sexual misconduct, and intoxicants) are quite obviously and inevitably open to interpretation. They require inquiry, experiment, and guidance to navigate over the course of a lifetime. The fact that such a navigation may be deeply worthwhile does not mean that it is always pretty. At times, it may even swerve away from the worthwhile. Think, for example, of Wittgenstein, who saw his lapses in honesty, however small, as his greatest defect, and in the 1930s went so far as to undertake a sort of world tour to rectify remembered instances of bad or duplicitous behavior. Like someone locked in a particularly grandiose version of the ninth step of Alcoholics Anonymous, Wittgenstein penned a long confession, then showed up on the doorsteps of friends, family, former pupils, and acquaintances to read it. He told his listeners that their attention to the matter was urgently required, and demanded a rapt audience.

Of course it was self-obsessed, self-serious behavior of this sort, more than the original "offenses," that often ended up infuriating, alienating, and sometimes hurting his friends, lovers, former pupils, and acquaintances. It is rare, after all, to experience an uninterrupted, unmitigated flow of love, respect, admiration, affection, and passion for an other over time, but few of us feel that if we fail to announce every dip or gradient in our feelings to that other, we are, in fact, "lying" to him or her. Wittgenstein, on the other hand, worried that these oscillations made him less truthful, and therefore often chose to employ a form of brutal honesty that at times laid waste to his personal relationships. The flagellating effects of Wittgenstein's self-flagellations on his loved ones are far more painful for me to read about than their effects on Wittgenstein himself. "If ever a thing could wait," one irritated friend remembered thinking, sitting across from him at a café table at which he read aloud his penance, "it is a confession of this kind and made in this manner." Or here is a letter from his lover Francis Skinner, in which Skinner is trying to dissuade Wittgenstein from his punishing course: "Whatever you have to tell me about yourself can't make any difference to my love for you. . . . There won't be any question of my forgiving you as I am a much worse person than you are. I think of you a lot and love you always."

Given self-flagellation's propensity to beget more of the same— not to mention our capacity to become attached, erotically or otherwise, to its punishment—it comes as little surprise that Wittgenstein's tour did little to purge him of his need to be purged. As his biographer Ray Monk reports, not long after he returned home, he wrote, "It is as though I had spent all that, and I am not far from where I was before. I am cowardly beyond measure."

—

"RIGHT SPEECH" adumbrates the concept of truth-telling by introducing questions of purpose and effect. A trickster/activist group such as the Yes Men joyously complicates the conversation by adding the phenomenon of the hoax—specifically, the hoax that has the power to underscore the brutality of facts that certain parties (i.e., the government, corporations, the military, the mainstream media, and so on) would prefer to keep spinning at will.

Many of the hoaxes orchestrated by the Yes Men replace the notion of "speaking truth to power" with impersonating power: while pretending to be certain officials, they make the humane and just pronouncements they wish the officials themselves would make. When the real officials come forward, as they must, to decry the hoaxers, they are thereby forced to reassert, in the renewed glare of the public eye, their inhumane and unjust policies.

One salient Yes Men hoax of this nature involved the catastrophic industrial disaster that occurred at a pesticide plant, then owned by Union Carbide, in Bhopal, India, in 1984. A toxic gas leak from the plant exposed up to 500,000 people, killing around 8,000 people in the first few weeks and more than 8,000 in the years since. As I write, up to 120,000 people in Bhopal continue to need and demand medical care and compensation—care and compensation that Dow Chemical, the company that acquired Union Carbide in 2001, has adamantly refused to provide. (Dow Chemical's official line is that Bhopal was indeed "a tragic event," but one for which it bears zero responsibility—this despite the fact that the purchase of Union Carbide included the purchase of its liabilities.)

On December 3, 2004—the twentieth anniversary of the disaster—one of the Yes Men, posing as a spokesman for Dow named "Jude Finisterra," managed to get an interview on BBC World News. (The Yes Men operate a number of fake Web sites pretending to represent various corporations and organizations; these Web sites provide contact information should the news media, a conference organizer, or any other party wish to get in contact with a representative.) In his BBC interview, Finisterra announced that Dow Chemical was pleased to announce that, on the twentieth anniversary of the Bhopal disaster, it had finally changed its course and decided to do the right thing: the company would "at long last compensate the victims, including the 120,000 who may need medical care for their entire lives," as well as assume responsibility for cleaning up the many tons of toxic chemicals that continue to pollute the groundwater in Bhopal, producing high rates of disease, disability, and death among the residents. By the end of the day, angry officials from Dow Chemical had alerted the BBC that Finisterra was an imposter with no relation to the company; Dow was thereby forced to reassert, on the twentieth anniversary of the Bhopal tragedy, that the company still had no intention of helping the people of Bhopal, or of detoxifying their land.

Given this deeply unflattering reiteration—and given how obviously and profoundly the people of Bhopal continue to suffer—the question remains, how would the media spin the hoax to diminish the brutality of the facts? Here's where the cruelty card comes in. The BBC ran its apology for broadcasting a false report under the headline, "Cruel $12 billion hoax on Bhopal victims and the BBC." The report focused on the alleged cruelty of the hoaxers, who unconscionably "raised then shattered" the hopes of the people of Bhopal for a half hour, during which time the residents thought Dow was finally going to distribute a $12 billion compensation package to them. In addition to trying to elicit sympathy for itself (as in, "cruel hoax played on the BBC"), the BBC (along with other networks) also attempted to elicit sympathy for Dow and its shareholders, repeatedly pointing out the fact that the hoax caused the company to have a tumultuous day on the stock market, as investors horrified at Dow's sudden willingness to take responsibility for the disaster drove down its share price for several hours.

The Yes Men have admitted that, after the BBC and other media outlets played the cruelty card, they too worried that their hoax might have had a negative effect on the people of Bhopal. So they went to Bhopal to ask the people themselves. Their conclusion? "For one thing, [the people of Bhopal] were much more sophisticated about their position in the world than a lot of people would assume," one of the Yes Men, who goes by the pseudonym Mike Bonanno, said. "Secondly, they basically just told us that they had been hoping for years that Dow would do something, so thinking it was true for less than an hour didn't hurt them at all. . . . They recognized that we weren't victimizing them—they knew who was victimizing them, they knew it all too well."

In subsequent hoaxes, the Yes Men have become savvier still about the charge of cruelty, and have in fact incorporated it into their stunts. In the months after Hurricane Katrina, for example, when it became clear that the U.S. Department of Housing and Urban Development (HUD) was not going to allow thousands of people who had previously lived in New Orleans public housing to return to their homes (but would instead be possessing or demolishing the homes, and turning the real estate over to the private sector), a Yes Man impersonated a HUD representative at a Gulf Coast Reconstruction Conference held on August 27, 2006. Speaking alongside New Orleans mayor Ray Nagin and Louisiana governor Kathleen Blanco, the imposter announced a total reversal of this policy; he also announced that oil companies would be investing billions of dollars to rebuild Louisiana's coastline. Both false proclamations were met with thunderous applause of the "it's about time someone did the right thing around here" variety.

This time, however, before the media could jump on the "cruel hoax" bandwagon, the Yes Men put out their own press release, which pretended to come from HUD itself and which described the Yes Men as cruel numerous times. "It is terribly sad that someone would perpetrate such a cruel hoax and play on the fears and anxieties of families who are desperate to return to their homes," the release read, before reiterating all the policy points HUD would like to make "perfectly clear, once and for all," such as "HUD will NOT let people come home simply because they want to, are part of the city, and constitute a much needed workforce," and "There is NO partnership between HUD, health departments and the CDC to provide adequate health care to low-income residents." Statements to the contrary, the press release insisted, are "all lies, monstrously cruel, generative of oceans of false hopes and sadness." By the time the release reaches its final line—"May God afflict the HUD perpetrators of this cruel hoax with all the varieties of damage they so amply deserve"—the hyperbole finally convinces the reader that the release is yet another hoax, one that takes direct aim at the notion that the alleged cruelty of the Yes Men could be said to exist in the same ballpark as that of official government policy.

Art may not be a lie that tells the truth. But, as the Yes Men demonstrate, a well-orchestrated hoax may, under the right circumstances, force the spinners and suppressors of certain facts out of the woodwork. The brutality of those facts must then hang anew, in open air, for all to see. This is not an exposure, precisely; the facts have typically been there all along. It is a means of re-attending to that which is already visible, of reconsidering that which we may already know. It is, in short, a recalibration of the function of knowledge itself. And here we find ourselves in yet another newly opened space—a space from which, as Eve Kosofsky Sedgwick has put it in *Touching Feeling*, we can finally move away from "the rather fixated question Is a particular piece of knowledge true, and how can we know? to the further questions: What does knowledge *do*—the pursuit of it, the having and exposing of it, the receiving again of knowledge of what one already knows?"

WHO WE ARE

———

WITTGENSTEIN NEVER became what might properly be called a religious believer, despite his self-cajolements to the contrary ("Go on, believe!" he wrote in a note to himself around 1944. "It does no harm"). Nonetheless, he remained as prone to self-doubt and self-abasement as any serious Christian. (It was arguably this propensity that drove him toward Christianity, rather than toward his Jewish roots.) For in Christianity, to "know what you are" means facing the wretchedness of one's original sin. In which case, the most correct apprehension of our situation on this swiftly tilting planet might be best summarized by the title of Jonathan Edwards's famous 1741 sermon, "Sinners in the Hands of an Angry God."

In this sermon, Edwards memorably describes the situation of all "natural men" (i.e., nonbelievers) as follows: "The wrath of God burns against them, their damnation does not slumber; the pit is prepared, the fire is now made ready, the furnace is now hot, ready to receive them; the flames do now rage and glow. The glittering sword is whet, and held over them, and the pit hath opened its mouth under them." Speaking directly to the unredeemed, Edwards warns, "The God that holds you over the pit of hell, much as one holds a spider or some loathsome insect over the fire, abhors you." To know "what we are" is to know our essential unworthiness, and to believe that is only by the grace of God that we are not dropping, right now, into the pit prepared for us.

This portrait of the human soul contrasts starkly with the one presented by a certain banner I drove by for a period of time in 2007, one that hung over the entrance to the Los Angeles County Museum of Art. The banner read, in large block letters, "IN VIOLENCE WE FORGET WHO WE ARE." I later learned that the quotation comes from writer Mary McCarthy, and was rendered into this banner by artist Barbara Kruger.

The intention behind the banner was, no doubt, virtuous. Nonetheless, every time I drove by I found myself in loose, if inchoate, disagreement. For many have argued precisely the opposite: that it is through violence that our souls come, as it were, into focus. Greek tragedy likes this idea; it is also a good description of our American mythos of regenerative violence. Sartre's introduction to Frantz Fanon's anticolonial classic *The Wretched of the Earth* sets forth something of the same—that it is through "irrepressible violence" that man "re-creates himself," that "the wretched of the earth" finally "become men." A well-known recruitment slogan for the U.S. Army underscores and expands the point, in its suggestion that to become a soldier is to "Be All That You Can Be."

Had she not starved herself to death in solidarity with the French Resistance in the 1940s, and had she somehow ended up an exile in Los Angeles, an elderly Simone Weil might have nodded in agreement while driving by Kruger's LACMA banner. For Weil's famous 1940 essay, "The Iliad, or the Poem of Force," argues that force is that which turns both its wielders and its victims into things. That is to say, under the guise of subject-object relations, violence actually works to construct object-object relations between otherwise sentient beings. This view stands in precise opposition to, say, the masculinist model set forth by Bertrand de Jouvenel (as quoted by Arendt in her 1970 book *On Violence*, which is dedicated, incidentally, to Mary McCarthy): "A man feels himself more of a man when he is imposing himself or making others the instruments of his will."

As much distaste as I have for this latter sentiment, and as much as I admire Weil, I must admit that I have never really understood the novelty or social efficacy of Weil's reversal. It may indeed come as a surprise to the abuser or the torturer or the soldier to find that the formula runs both ways—that he or she is made thing-like by the force he or she presumes to possess—but really it is part of the same package. The larger, crueler problem, it seems to me, comes from the conviction that violence is the privileged means by which we come into ourselves *or* lose ourselves as human subjects. It is quite banally human both to perpetrate violence and to find oneself a victim of it. And if, as Arendt observed, the "rage and the violence that sometimes—not always—goes with it" are human, to cure man of them would be to dehumanize him. And dehumanization is one means of forgetting who we are. But again, who are we? And what could it mean to forget who we are?

—

ANOTHER complication of the IN VIOLENCE, WE FORGET WHO WE ARE adage is that in many famed accounts of subjectivity—such as Freud's—a certain kind of forgetting—namely, repression—plays a critical role in structuring the mind. According to Freud, one of the most powerful repressed elements of the unconscious is the Oedipal complex, which places a fantasized or symbolic patricide at the center of the (male) psyche.

Freud was not known for his attention to female subjectivity or sexuality, the latter of which he famously deemed a "dark continent" for psychology. It therefore comes as no real surprise that he chose a founding myth for psychoanalysis that places the male subject, heterosexual desire, and patricidal fantasy at its core. Ironically, however, the trope of a psychically repressed matricide (or, more generally speaking, a gynecide) as the constitutive element of (male) psychic life crops up ubiquitously in art and literature. A trashy but lucid recent template for this trope can be found in the movie *Memento* (2000), whose main character is a man who has no memory and can make no new memories, but who is nonetheless trying to stay coherent enough to move ahead toward the avenging of the brutal rape and murder of his wife. As the film moves backward in time, however (the movie unfolds in reverse order), we become confused—as does the main character—as to whether he is aiming to avenge a heinous act committed by another, or whether he is on the run from an act he himself committed. (The movie also poses the possibility that his wife is alive but has left him—in which case the fantasy of her rape-murder stands in—as wish fulfillment?—for the pain of his rejection.)

Memento was, to my mind, essentially a pretentious gimmick, but it did have one memorable offering: this distilled portrait of male amnesia, coupled with its ubiquitous counterpart—a woman with her mouth slightly open, her eyes frozen wide with terror, her brutalized body left for dead in the clear plastic of a shower curtain—in short, in as positive a situation as the situation would allow. As with so many renditions of this narrative device (see, for example, any number of Clint Eastwood movies, from *Unforgiven* to *Mystic River*), the female is always already dead: that is how the plot begins. Indeed, there can be no plot without her death—

without it, what would there be to find out, explain, or avenge? Comic-book aficionados even have a stock phrase to describe this setup: they call it the "woman in the refrigerator syndrome," which derives from a *Green Lantern* comic in which the hero is set into motion by the discovery of his girlfriend's corpse in his icebox.

Hashed as it may be, this narrative structure continues to enthrall, seducing even those whom one might hope were too impatient with cliché to fall into its clutches. Brian Evenson presents a complicated case on this account, as he has at times wielded the trope with great success. I am thinking primarily of his excellent, dreadful, transporting novel, *The Open Curtain* (2006), which takes on the Mormon Church's repressed history of violence—specifically, the murderous practice known as blood atonement. The novel gets worrisomely bogged down at times by its (literal!) use of the rotting-corpse-in-the-fridge motif, and then, in its final hour, by a man-strangling-woman denouement lacking in the inventiveness of the preceding pages. But taken as a whole, the novel presents a surprisingly poignant, linguistically brilliant, and viscerally terrifying portrait of the dialectic of concealment and revelation that undergirds certain forms of individual and institutional violence.

Elsewhere, however—such as in the short story, "Desire with Digressions" (from 2009's *Fugue State*)—Evenson's wielding of the trope collapses into the hackneyed. "Desire" begins with a man leaving a woman after an unnamed, charged encounter. As he turns away from her, her humanity—signified here by her face—has already begun to slip away: "I felt that if her head were to turn toward me then I would not see her face but an unfeatured facelessness, as inhuman and smooth as a plate." The further he drives, the longer he stays away, the less he can remember about what happened between them: "What was it she had said to me, that day before she had abandoned me to sit beside the creek and grow strange? And how had I responded? Why could I not recall?"

When he finally makes it back to her, after a manly sojourn that has included an interminable trek through snow, the witnessing of a craggy old man's death, a bad case of frostbite, and a nightmarish hospital stay and escape, he finds the woman sitting by the creek, just as he had left her. But, to his horror, on closer inspection he sees that she is now but a rotting corpse: "what I had thought was her arm was only the bones that had once structured the arm, the flesh mostly gone. And I saw that a part of her on the other side, too, was in the process of grimly disarticulating itself with the aid of vermin and time, and I remembered what, out of love or hate, had happened, and why I had left in the first place."

Ah yes, that pesky thing I kept forgetting, O.J.- or *Memento*-style—I killed her! And then the final, disingenuous smearing of agency (not to mention the textbook repurposing of love as a constituent factor in gynecide): he remembers not what he did, but "what, out of love or hate, had happened." Of course, this story is narrated, and one could argue that Evenson intentionally created a narrator who suffers from these tired symptoms and self-deceptions. (One could also argue that the story leaves tantalizingly unclear "what, out of love or hate, had happened"—but given that the man speeds away from the primal scene unharmed, while the woman is left creek-side to rot, a certain ineluctable narrative shifts into view.) Such moments in Evenson drain the writing of its disquieting inventiveness. In short, while the woman or corpse may "grow strange" beside the creek, the story fails to do so.

—

GIVEN THE ubiquity of this storyline, it can seem as though matricide or gynecide stands somehow behind or before the Oedipal complex—perhaps as the repressed content of the Freudian repressed. (French feminist philosopher Luce Irigaray has gone so far as to call matricide "the blind spot of Western patriarchal civilization"; scholar Amber Jacobs has described it as the "death that will not deliver"—that is, a "non-concept" long denied any structural generativity by classical psychoanalytic thought.)

By this point, however, everyone from radical feminist theologian Mary Daly to psychoanalyst Melanie Klein to French philosopher Julia Kristeva has noted that it is a hallmark of patriarchal religion, culture, and psychology to have a repressed, symbolic matricide at its root—a matricide cast as necessary for the human subject to leave the mess of Nature and bodily dependency behind, and to become a full participant in subjectivity, language, and culture (all of which, in phallocentric discourse, are identified with the male). As Kristeva famously puts it, "For man and for woman the loss of the mother is a biological and psychical necessity, the first step on the way to becoming autonomous. Matricide is our vital necessity, the *sine qua non* of our individuation." Note that the subject here imagined doesn't simply outgrow or separate from the mother. It murders her.

One of the most shocking literalizations of such a matricide can be found in the Marquis de Sade's *Philosophy in the Bedroom* (1795), a drama in dialogue that tells the story of the corruption of a young teenage girl, Eugenie, by a team of libertines. Throughout *Philosophy*—which alternates between pornographic action and philosophical disquisition, as does most of Sade—the figure of the mother is the enemy of just about everything Sade holds dear. The unfolding tale of Eugenie's corruption is fairly jovial and enjoyable (depending on your tastes, of course), but the work's finale is decidedly one of the cruelest in literature that I've encountered. When Eugenie's mother finally arrives on the scene, she is gang-raped (her daughter both participates in the assault and cheers it on). She is then given the following death sentence: a man with late-stage syphilis (a disease that was uncurable and fatal at the time) is summoned to ejaculate into the mother's vagina and ass. Both orifices are then sewn together with needle and thread (without anesthesia, obviously), in order to keep the pestilence in, and likely as a symbolic, punitive measure—both for giving birth and for attempting to protect her daughter from the free exercise of carnal pleasure. The scene has a viciousness that never fails to take me by surprise—and this even compared to the many torturous rapes and murders in Sade's *120 Days of Sodom*.

Kristeva's term for this violent psychic expulsion of the maternal (dramatized in *Philosophy* as a sadistic, elongated matricide) is abjection. And while the abjection of the maternal may be necessary, according to Kristeva, to form a subject, its expulsion can never be seamlessly accomplished. The abjected maternal returns, via horror, repulsion, the uncanny, haunting, melancholia, depression, guilt, the inchoate but harrowing sense that one has lost, left, or killed something critical. (And here we might note that Evenson's first book of stories, *Altmann's Tongue*— the volume that got him in so much trouble at Brigham Young—takes its epigraph from Kristeva's *The Powers of Horror: An Essay on Abjection*.)

Personally I have no idea why this abjection or matricide (or the Oedipal complex itself, for that matter) need be the sine qua non of our individuation. As with most psychoanalytical concepts, the question of whether they are descriptive, prescriptive, transiently useful, or simply lunatic always strikes me as wide open. Nonetheless, it seems clear enough that many or most models of Western selfhood place a repressed crime (or the repressed desire to commit one) at their core. Indeed, modernity itself could in some sense be defined as that which privileges disassociation from—even the violent destruction of—that which has come before, rather than that which secures its reverent continuation (in which case murder, particularly of a parent, is a fitting trope).

In other words, in placing Oedipus at the center of his psychic modeling, Freud did much more than privilege patricide (and the subsequent sexual possession of the mother) as the defining desires of the (male) subject. He also placed the questions "What have I done?," "Am I a criminal?," and "Do my deepest and darkest desires make me a criminal?," at the heart of self-inquiry (see the plot of *Memento*). As Adam Phillips has put it (in *Terrors and Experts*), "Oedipus is so important in psychoanalysis because he does something that can be found out, something he can know about. . . . The fictional Oedipus becomes the paradigmatic seeker and avoider of truth, and therefore the sustainer of the idea that there are truths." No wonder this paradigmatic seeker and avoider of truth recurs so often in art and literature as our hero, or anti-hero. His circuitous journey toward and away from unbearable self-knowledge makes for compelling drama, as it turns our lives into detective stories; our innermost selves, into culprits.

While seemingly custom-made for Screenwriting 101, this version of both self and self-knowledge can have an utterly flattening, reductive effect on the myriad mysteries of being a human being. "After all," Phillips writes, "what else can we do with crimes—and with people—but find them out?" And here, Phillips explains, is where the Enlightenment Freud and the post-Freudian Freud part ways: the former is more interested in what the patient cannot afford to let himself know that he knows (the repression of which constitutes the unconscious); the latter recognizes that the acquiring of knowledge is but one means of knowing, and further, that knowing itself is but one mode of experiencing. In which case, as Phillips explains, psychoanalysis gets interesting when it shifts the focus from making us more intelligible to ourselves to helping us become more curious about how strange we really are. And so, I would argue, does art.

—

AFTER ALL, the assertion that we ourselves, or the business of love, or the universe at large, or a religion (such as Islam or Christianity), are essentially cruel or essentially compassionate, essentially "nice" or essentially "not nice," essentially peaceful or essentially violent, essentially optimistic or pessimistic, or essentially any one thing at all, is but an assertion—one whose pretension to certitude usually incites rather than terminates debate. Perhaps you could even call such an assertion a choice, albeit one mitigated by an amalgam of experience, education, genetic disposition, ideology, mood, chance, and will. But whatever it is, it cannot be an empirical measurement, or a verdict reached after all the evidence is in.

Freud knew this, which accounts for his ever-changing conjectures about the complex drives that propel and perplex the human animal. But that didn't stop him from making radical pronouncements throughout his career on the human condition—pronouncements that have, over time, been isolated from their contexts and congealed for many into "fact," as if their emanation from an entity named Freud miraculously stamped them with a lasting, objective authority. "Men are not gentle creatures who want to be loved," Freud famously wrote in *Civilization and Its Discontents* (1930). "They are, on the contrary, creatures among whose instinctual endowments is to be reckoned a powerful share of aggressiveness. As a result, their neighbor is for them not only a potential helper or sexual object, but also someone who tempts them to satisfy their aggressiveness on him, to exploit his capacity for work without compensation, to use him sexually without his consent, to seize his possessions, to humiliate him, to cause him pain, to torture and to kill him."

Men do these things, it is true. But men are also gentle creatures who want to be loved (see Hitler, nuzzling his cat). Due to Freud's own revelatory, relentless emphasis on ambivalence, his life's work, when taken together, ends up providing a portrait of the human animal that does more to explain "why we deplore cruelty in some cases and relish it in others" (see Richard Rorty) than that of almost any other thinker. The more compelling question becomes not "what" or "which" we essentially are, but why, how, and when we choose to believe that one aspect of the human condition edges out, invalidates, or annihilates another.

This question applies not only to the human condition, but also to that of the divine. "I cannot believe in a God who metes out hurt for hurt, pain for pain, torture for torture," writes Sister Prejean, in an attempt to explain her anti–capital punishment activism in light of Christian theology. "Nor do I believe that God invests human representatives with such power to torture and kill." Fair enough. But it's no wonder that more and more often Prejean finds herself "steering away from such futile discussions," and trying instead "to articulate what [she] personally believe[s] about Jesus and the ethical thrust he gave to humankind: an impetus toward compassion, a preference for disarming enemies without humiliating and destroying them, and a solidarity with poor and suffering people."

This belief is a choice, or a focus, and one with a purpose. It is essentially pragmatic, and I respect Prejean's willingness to put that pragmatism front and center. When we choose a belief and act on it, we change the way things are—or so said pragmatist William James. Prejean has been brilliant at utilizing this mode of belief and action, and it has served the world well. But as theology, it will likely convince no one. Which is fine, so long as one is willing to turn away from theology, and toward the bewildering but urgent maze of habits, choices, refusals, aspirations, and actions that constitutes a living ethics.

—

IN HER book *Lovingkindness*, Buddhist teacher Sharon Salzberg tells a story that offers a refreshing alternative to the saga of seeking the truth about ourselves, especially the truth of our inherent goodness or badness. "When I first practiced meditation with Sayadaw U Pandita, in 1984, I went through a period of disturbing memories about all the terrible things I had ever done. . . . I said, 'You know, I just keep thinking of event after event—all of these bad things I've done. I feel terrible. I feel horrible. I feel awful.' U Pandita looked at me and asked, 'Well, are you finally seeing the truth about yourself?' I was shocked at his response. Even though I was enveloped in self-judgment and criticism, something in his comment made me want to challenge it. I thought to myself, 'No, I'm not seeing the truth about myself.' And then he simply said, 'Stop thinking about it.' Only later would I understand the wisdom of his advice."

In short, attempts to nail down "who we really are" most often serve as rhetorical pawns in unwinnable arguments fueled by competing agendas (i.e., humans are "really" self-interested first and foremost, therefore a self-serving capitalism is the system most suitable for us; humans are "hard-wired" for aggression and conflict, therefore some form of warfare will always be with us; or, conversely, "the kind life—the life lived in instinctive sympathy with the vulnerabilities and attractions of others—is the life we are more inclined to live," as argued by Adam Phillips and Barbara Taylor in *On Kindness*). In light of this situation, Sayadaw U Pandita's advice to "stop thinking about it"—or, perhaps, to stop talking about it—can start to seem like the best advice indeed. At the very least, following such advice makes space for different conversations, different questions.

A SITUATION OF MEAT

F, AT the very least, we are human, we must concede that humans evidence an ongoing interest in becoming, at certain times and in certain contexts, things, as much as in turning other people into things. The spectre of our eventual "becoming object"—of our (live) flesh one day turning into (dead) meat—is a shadow that accompanies us throughout our lives.

Of course, this shadow is thicker for some than others. Certainly it was thick for Francis Bacon: "Every time I go into a butcher's, I'm surprised that it's not me hanging there," he once said. It was also thick for Simone Weil, which makes her critique in "The Iliad, or the Poem of Force" complicated. Weil's protest depends on her horror at force's capacity to turn human beings into things—either dead things (i.e., corpses, made by "force that kills") or "things with souls" (i.e., shells of humans, made by "force that does not kill, i.e., that does not kill just yet"—"a compromise between a man and a corpse," Weil calls the latter). Yet Weil's theological ruminations are saturated with the desire to dispense with subjectivity altogether, and to become completely emptied out, effaced, "thing-like," in order to get closer to God. "Once we have understood that we are nothing, the object of all our efforts is to become nothing.

May God grant me to become nothing," she wrote. "My meat is to do the will of Him that sent me."

When viewed through the lens of Christian theology, this complexity holds no paradox. For in Christianity, the crucifixion and resurrection of Jesus alchemize an otherwise brutal "situation of meat" into a scene of divine redemption—not just for Christ, but also for us if we become his followers. As Weil summarizes in *Gravity and Grace,* "The false God changes suffering into violence. The true God changes violence into suffering." This is one of Christianity's most gripping promises: that violence need not remain simply violence; it can be changed, via faith, into suffering, which, due to Christ's sacrifice on the cross, is never in vain.

The crucifixions of Bacon stand in direct opposition to the above narrative. As John Russell has pointed out, Bacon's crucifixions differ substantively from those of religious paintings in that Bacon has no designs on painting *the* crucifixion; rather, he is painting *a* crucifixion—which, for Bacon, is simply "a generic name for an environment in which bodily harm is done to one or more persons and one or more other persons gather to watch." "I know for religious people, for Christians, the Crucifixion has a totally different significance," Bacon explains. "But, as a non believer, it was just an act of man's behaviour, a way of behaviour to another." In short, if you remove the story of the Passion, if you remove the radiant, suffering face and body of Jesus, if you remove the specter of a miraculous Resurrection, you are left with an act of bald cruelty—a situation of meat—and some aggregate of its victims, perpetrators, witnesses, and accomplices.

In short, what looks like meaningful, divine suffering to one person often looks like brutal, preventable violence to another. Religious convictions do not insulate against this divide; many would in fact say they cause it. To take a particularly garish example, think of Mel Gibson's ludicrous bloodbath of a film, *The Passion of the Christ* (2004), which focuses about 100 of its 126 minutes on the torture, mutilation, and death of Christ's body. "I wanted [the violence] to be shocking; and I wanted it to be extreme," Gibson explained to Diane Sawyer in a February 16, 2004, interview, "so that [the viewers] see the enormity—the enormity of his sacrifice." Most critics remained unconvinced—if not downright horrified—by this logic, which claims the shock and awe of surround-sound ultraviolence as a worthwhile tool for bringing young people—including young children—to Christian faith. Many churches, on the other hand, knocked themselves out to support the film, offering everything from free tickets to discussion groups to private theater rentals to ensure its wide circulation, believing that "the film presents a unique opportunity to share Christianity in a way today's public can identify with" (as a certain Reverend John Tanner of Alabama explained).

One of the most wicked satires of the above logic can be found in Franz Kafka's exceptionally grim story from 1914, "In the Penal Colony." In the story, Kafka's officer—the operator of a torture/execution device called the Harrow—waxes rhapsodic about the glory days in the colony, when public torture and execution were a popular spectacle: "It was impossible to grant all the requests people made to be allowed to watch from up close. The commandant, in his wisdom, arranged that the children should be taken care of before all the rest. Naturally, I was always allowed to stand close by, because of my official position. Often I crouched down there with two small children in my arms, on my right and left. How we all took in the expression of transfiguration on the martyred face! How we held our cheeks in the glow of this justice, finally attained and already passing away! What times we had, my friend!" The surrounding story, as we shall later see, eviscerates the officer's interpretation of the execution, primarily by juxtaposing such monologues against the patently revolting situation of meat at hand (a situation epitomized, perhaps, by the recurring appearance of the felt gag the prisoner in the Harrow must wear— a gag saturated with the vomit of all those previously executed in the machine).

Bacon's *Three Studies for a Crucifixion* (1962) and *Crucifixion* (1965) offer scenes of similarly revolting (though perhaps unintentional) satire. In both paintings, the crucified figure resembles a split animal as much or more than a human, and appears upside down—"a worm crawling down the cross," as Bacon once put it, rather than a child of God getting ready to make his ascent. (An upside-down cross is also a coarse symbol of blasphemy.) The witnesses in the paintings are decidedly modern: no weeping or cradling of the meat here—just a woman who looks like she's passing by a bad traffic accident, two men who could be casually checking in on a brutalized detainee in their custody, and two men in fedoras who appear to be eating at a lunch counter, completely oblivious to the bloody action beside them. And then, of course, at the apex of the triangle, there's us, looking at the meat, and at the people looking or not looking (by now, a la Mendieta, a familiar architecture).

"For Bacon, the worst has already happened," writes John Berger in "Francis Bacon and Walt Disney," an essay that makes the intentionally jarring link between Bacon paintings and Disney cartoons. Berger here argues that Bacon's insistence on this postness—on this sense that all the viewer can do is stumble belatedly upon the carnage (rather than intervene, understand, participate, or prevent)—proposes that both "refusal and hope are pointless."

According to Berger, Disney cartoons have the same point, even if there "the ultimate catastrophe is always in the offing": both present worlds, Berger says, that could be captioned *There is nothing else*. Given how much Berger values refusal, hope, and unforeclosed possibility, this is a serious critique.

The problem here, it seems to me, lies in Berger's willingness to give Bacon's proposition such overarching power. For while the paintings may indeed propose that there is nothing else, their proposition remains just that—a momentary proffering. As one beholds them (at, say, Bacon's 2009 centenary retrospective at the Metropolitan Museum of Art), there is wall space between each canvas, there is space to walk around the room. One can come and go, look closely and then look away, stay for a long time or simply walk on by, en route to the bathroom or gift shop. Their depiction of belatedness or mindlessness—however claustrophobic—does not necessitate our acquiescence. They are paintings; our job is to behold them. There is no need, or even invitation, to submit to their terms.

It is true, as Berger suggests, that Bacon's subject is not consciousness. Nor is it empathy—or at least the kind of empathy that depends on consciousness. Bacon's crucifixions do not ask us to empathize. The victims offer up no faces shining with tortured beatitude for our spiritual contemplation. Instead we get, in *Crucifixion*, a central panel of a faceless, splayed pink carcass, its front two limbs taped down to the crucifying plane with unforgiving bandages. And yet, in looking at this painting, a fierce kind of empathy can arise. This is not the kind of empathy that stays on pause until we feel that we've understood the being that this meat belongs or once belonged to. We aren't waiting around to behold the same emotions we have felt reflected back to us in its eminently human face. (In fact, in Bacon's crucifixions, the onlookers typically have the more well-defined human faces, yet they seem more horrific than the disasters of flesh and blood in the room with them.) There is no attempt to shock us into feeling "the enormity of the sacrifice." There is no sacrifice. We do not have to understand or get to know Bacon's figures to feel their pain, nor do they need to represent the pitifully massacred children of God. They are animals on their way down, as are we; that's enough.

The figures that dominate Plath's late poetry, on the other hand, are almost always on the rise. But as with the spirit of "Lady Lazarus," who notoriously rises out of the ash in the poem's final lines to "eat men like air," their ascent is not usually very nice. Plath's resurrected figures have an effect eerily similar to that of Bacon's worms crawling down their crosses: they disallow the reassurances of martyrdom, rebirth, and resurrection just as brutally. But in doing so, they also reveal something else: the cruelties and complexities of resurrection, and its ties to potentially lethal forms of psychological or historical amnesia. In "Getting There," for example, Plath's speaker—who seems stranded somewhere between an unborn fetus and a wartime prisoner on a train bound for slaughter—is struggling to "get there": to rise from Adam's side, to "fly to a name, two eyes," to arrive at the destination which she describes as a "bloodspot, / The face at the end of the flare." She gets there—or somewhere—eventually; the poem's last lines read, "And I, stepping from this skin / Of old bandages, boredoms, old faces // Step to you from the black car of Lethe, / Pure as a baby." This is very bad, but one gets the sense that for this born-again—and perhaps for us, in greeting it—the worst is yet to come.

Elsewhere, Plath's ascensions are of a more metaphysical variety, as in "Fever 103°": "I think I am going up, / I think I may rise— /

The beads of hot metal fly, and I, love, I // Am a pure acetylene / Virgin / Attended by roses, // By kisses, by cherubim, / By whatever these pink things mean." In reference to this ascent, a critic once wrote, "This is bogus spirituality, and it has its admirers, who even seem pleased that Plath did not survive it." But I think it fairly clear from Plath's sarcastic tone ("whatever these pink things mean") that she means to tinge such ascents with the bogus, precisely to undercut any facile rebirth or purity typically associated with them. I, for one, am not particularly pleased that Plath did not live a long life, but I am pleased that, in the short life that she did, she managed to produce a poetry that relentlessly exposes the dangers of hoping against hope to step from amnesia ("the black car of Lethe") to an infantile purity ("pure as a baby").

—

MANY SEE the confrontation with the body-made-meat as dramatized in splatter films as fundamental to their psychological appeal, the idea being that such films provide an entertaining, over-the-top place to encounter our primal fears about the worst possible fates of our mortal coils. Surely it's no accident that a slaughterhouse occupies a central place in the *Texas Chainsaw Massacre* franchise, nor that many horror movies feature meat in their titles, as in *Dead Meat*, *The Midnight Meat Train*, *Meat Grinder*, and so on. (Think, too, of 2009's terrific sci-fi horror extravaganza, *District 9*, which meshes a futuristic plot with a relentless, gritty obsessiveness with meat, including cannibalistic feeding frenzies, aliens obsessed with cat food, the spectacle of man-flesh-becoming-alien-flesh, egregious organ harvesting, and more.)

Pornographic films are also often called "meat movies"—not on account of any dead meat per se, but on account of their insistent, intense focus on particular body parts (i.e., the parts involved in fucking), a focus that can have the effect of parsing the body into isolated chunks of meat, stripped of human subjectivity. (At times, the rhetoric between the two genres meets up, as in the term "fresh meat vixen," a term sometimes used to refer to the female stars of horror films.) As the infamous June 1978 cover of *Hustler* made clear, straight pornography has a long and fraught history of "making meat" of women (the cover features a woman being fed into a meat grinder, her legs sticking out the top, alongside a quotation by Larry Flynt which reads, "We will no longer hang women up like pieces of meat"—implying, one can only suppose, that from now on *Hustler* will grind them).

The meat-making aspect of pornography is regularly denounced by certain feminists and moralists as woman-hating, soul-sucking, and home-wrecking (at least for straight folks; the souls and homes of queers are presumably too damned to merit much concern). Books such as Carol J. Adams's *The Sexual Politics of Meat* and *The Pornography of Meat* take the argument further, in their effort to link up realms of sexual, economic, and ecological injustice. The advent of Internet porn has only hastened the charges, in that the Internet has made porn not only ubiquitous but also predatory: it tracks you down as much as you track it down, and even the most vanilla user is only ever about three clicks away from seeing a ten-year-old boy giving someone a blow job, or a woman being penetrated by a horse. (And don't forget to watch out for those decoys from Perverted Justice!)

Be all this as it may. But we miss something crucial about the meat-making of porn if we focus only on its most addictive, alienating, and misogynistic aspects. For ecstasy—as we are constantly being reminded—literally means being beside oneself, which means standing slightly apart from one's body and slightly apart from one's mind. From which vantage point, one might experience one's body—and perhaps even one's consciousness—as things. The transcendent parts of this smash-up are not typically captured on film; likely they are not capturable. Pornography leaves us, instead, with the spectacle of the meat.

Using camera work that can have more in common with laparoscopic surgery than with cinema, hard-core porn knocks itself out to get supranaturally close to the body's capacities for contact and penetration. The closer you go—that is, the more hard core it gets—the more abstract it becomes. And the more abstract it becomes, the deeper the mystery of why it works—why watching close-ups of throbbing pink body parts moving in and around each other instantly turns most of us on. "That is porn's greatest strength, its almost mystical dimension," Virginie Despentes observes.

Of course, not all "thingness" is created equal, and one has to live enough of one's life *not* as a thing to know the difference. (This may explain, in part, why the meat-making of gay male porn doesn't produce the same species of anxiety as that of straight porn: since men—or white men, at any rate—don't have the same historical relation to objectification as do women, their meat-making doesn't immediately threaten to come off as a cruel redundancy.) Even a literary masterpiece of masochism such as Pauline Réage's *Story of O* depends on the subjectivity of its protagonist to stay vital: the novel is compelling all the way through O's self-aware transformation into a thing, but once she asks Sir Stephen for death and is extinguished, the tension goes slack; the dream, as it were, has died. The Marquis de Sade solved this problem by allowing himself an endless supply of victims to be corrupted, frigged, tortured, and killed, but in doing so, he tipped his writing into comedy.

He also tipped it into tedium. Indeed, one of the most fascinating things about Sade's writing is its immense capacity to shock, and its equally immense capacity to bore. Such a coexistence is typical of pornography, but the sheer volume of Sade's work—combined with his habit of inserting a fifty-page diatribe about French politics into the middle of an orgy—gives this coexistence a whole new meaning. But perhaps the most profound tedium in Sade lies not in his penchant for voluminous or digressive discourse, but in his preference for meat over flesh. As Angela Carter puts it in *The Sadeian Woman*, "It is a mistake to think that the substance of which [Sade's] actors are made is flesh. There is nothing alive or sensual about them. Sade is a great puritan and will disinfect of sensuality anything he can lay his hands on; therefore he writes about sexual relations in terms of butchery and meat."

Sade's penchant for meat—like Bacon's—stems in part from his intense atheism. He is wholly against transubstantiation. In its place, you will find mechanistically executed penetration, cannibalism, necrophagy, coprophagia, and the like. This meatifying aspect of Sade differentiates him from many other transgressive pornographers, including Georges Bataille, whose blasphemy is always suffused by a mystical interest in the flesh made sacred (as is clear in the ritualistic sex-murders of clergy in Bataille's pornographic classic, *Story of the Eye*). As Sontag puts it in *Regarding the Pain of Others*, Bataille "links pain to sacrifice, sacrifice to exaltation—a view which could not be more alien to a modern sensibility, which regards suffering as something that is a mistake or an accident or a crime." (Bacon's crucifixions are a good visual aid for the latter, save for the fact that they provoke no consequent impulse for correction, for justice.) Bataille's interest in sacrifice differs profoundly, however, from Christian-

ity's (and Gibson's), in that Bataille thought the introduction of
God, salvation, and purgation to the event denied the act's most
sacred attributes: transgression, sadism, profanity, impurity, and
the death of God.

This meatifying aspect of Sade also differentiates him from the
Actionists, who regularly argued that certain forms of killing—
such as Nitsch's slaughter of three bulls during the *Six-Day Play*, or
Muehl's penchant for decapitating geese (as in *O Sensibility*, 1970,
in which Muehl puts the goose's neck stump to sexual use)—are
transformed, made sacred, by their employment in ritual. As Muehl
said of *O Sensibility*, "I became Jupiter, and [the goose] became the
symbol of woman. I became the priest who would not kill it in
order to devour it, but rather to carry out a kind of magic ritual
with it. . . . I do not condone animal murders. I show the sentimentality and hypocrisy. With tears in their eyes they gobble up their
geese! Actionism is provocation and performance, the representation of moral double standards."

Though my aversion to killing animals for art is likely not going
anywhere fast, a meat-making instance that holds more interest
for me arrives in the infamous "chicken fucking" scene of John
Waters's *Pink Flamingos*, during which Crackers (Danny Mills)
crushes a live chicken to death between his body and Cookie Mueller's during an unnerving sexual encounter. ("Even without their
heads they were a lively nasty bunch of fowl, flopping and kicking
with all their might," Mueller recalls in her terrific memoir *Walking through Water in a Pool Painted Black*. "I was getting hurt for
real. I'd underestimated these chickens, even while I was feeling
sorry for them.") In the years since filming *Pink Flamingos*, Waters
has not exactly appeased any of his critics with his oft-repeated,
Warholian reasoning that "we made the chicken's life better. It got

in a movie, it got fucked and it got famous." But at least this defense makes sport of the projection taking place (i.e., we all know that the chicken likely didn't care about getting fucked and famous, and we all know that Waters knows it too), rather than remaining seduced, a la Muehl, by the anthropocentric projection that a "magic ritual" has taken place, in which the male "became Jupiter, and [the goose] became the symbol of woman."

As for Waters, when asked (in 2001) whether he had ever felt the need to "pull back" from his provocations, he answered, "Would I today kill an animal in a movie? Probably not. I mean we ate them. We didn't have craft services, then, on *Pink Flamingos* you had to go find something in the woods, kill it and eat it. There was no 'lunch' or anything." Mueller concurs: "Later on, after we finished for the day, with the sun sinking beyond the horizon of winter's leafless trees, we roasted all those chickens, had a big feast for the whole cast and crew. Those chickens I'd felt sorry for earlier sure were delicious."

Meat recurs throughout *Pink Flamingos*, often in hilarious ways. Who can forget the close-up shot of Raymond Marble's genitals when he flashes a woman in a public park, revealing not just his penis but also a gnarled piece of sausage tied to it? The twinning of meats, along with the pathos of the uncomfortable-looking twine affixing them, happily renders the penis meat bound, deflated, a leftover among leftovers. (*Soll niemand mein Schwanz steif machen*, indeed.) Waters is just as perverse as Sade or the Actionists, but his perversity joyously extends to realms of sexuality in which the phallus is regularly downgraded to penis, a situation of meat characterized by bathos, comedy, and possibility rather than power struggles or turgid myth-making.

As *Pink Flamingos* makes clear, when the body-made-meat gets pushed to its extreme, the result can be quite funny, albeit in the darkest of fashions. (The first time I saw, in person, Bacon's bloodiest crucifixion—a triptych Bacon reports having painted in a drunken haze—I laughed out loud. Critic Jerry Saltz, in reviewing Bacon's 2009 centenary retrospective at the Metropolitan Museum, picked up on this humorous tone, noting that Bacon "may be the only artist sharing a name with one of his main subjects, meat.") Much physical comedy depends on the human body's vulnerability: slapstick, for example, makes its home here—although slapstick, by definition, takes pains to reassure the audience that no real harm is taking place. (The word "slapstick" comes from *battacchio*, an object used in Italian theater to produce a loud noise upon impact without hurting what it hits.) Comedy darkens when we begin to lose this reassurance, or when—as in *Family Tyranny*—the reassurance itself uncannily, inexplicably, ceases to reassure.

Things become more uncomfortable still when the comedy is unintentional. Consider, for example, the scene from Steven Spielberg's Holocaust epic, *Schindler's List*, in which a Nazi officer unexpectedly and suddenly shoots a Jewish woman in the head at point-blank range, sending her body crumpling awkwardly to the ground. In a regrettable incident in 1994, sixty-nine students from Castlemont High School in Oakland, California, went on a Martin Luther King Day field trip to see *Schindler's List* at a local movie theater. During the aforementioned scene, a group of the Castlemont students—who were mostly black and Latino—began to laugh, deeply offending other members of the audience (some of whom were apparently Holocaust survivors). The management ended up stopping the film and ejecting the students from the theater.

As one might imagine, in the weeks that followed, the students of Castlemont suffered through a storm of accusations of anti-Semitism, cultural insensitivity, cruelty of heart, and desensitization to violence. The episode culminated in their delivery of a public apology at a televised news conference, the development of a "Holocaust curriculum" at their high school, which included visiting lectures by concentration camp survivors, and so on.

I can't profess to know what generated the students' laughter, nor can I say that the subsequent conversation and measures taken were without value. What I do know, however, is that while I watched this sorry episode unfold in the media, I remembered that I had had a related reaction to this scene in the film. Its violence was utterly chilling, but its chill was laced with a discomfiting slapstick comedy, the kind that derives from watching a body go from flesh to meat in but an instant. (I imagine that for Spielberg, this effect was unplanned, whereas for someone like Quentin Tarantino, it is explicitly and repetitively conjured.) I doubt that I laughed out loud, but a certain nervous, appalled laughter was not out of the question.

For the ever-present possibility that our bodies could be made meat in but an instant—that this precious, big-deal life we imbue with so much spirit and meaning could be extinguished at any moment by, say, a speeding car or bullet—is frightening enough that laughing in its face can at times seem an understandable response. If and when this fear becomes a commonplace, our response may become more unpredictable still. As one sixteen-year-old Castlemont student explained to the *New York Times* on February 6,

1994, "We see death and violence in our community all the time. People cannot understand how numb we are toward violence."

—

THE BRILLIANT, mordant work of German artist Otto Dix may have captured the dark humor of human meat more relentlessly, and more trenchantly, than any other European artist of the twentieth century. Unlike Bacon, whose paintings deliberately eschew social or political context, Dix's war etchings—the *Der Krieg* cycle of 1924—depict images of grievously wounded faces, terrifying skin grafts, putrefying corpses, and the like, which derive explicitly from Dix's experiences as a soldier at the front in World War I. Despite their otherworldly, often cartoonish nature, the etchings remain tightly tethered to this context by documentary titles such as "Wounded Man Fleeing—Battle of the Somme, 1916," "Wounded Soldier, Autumn 1916, Bapaume," and "Buried Alive, January 1916, Champagne."

Dix's portrayal of the horrors of war is indelible and savage. And yet, as one considers his work over the next several decades, one cannot help but notice how the grotesque, caustic vision of *Der Krieg* extends to everything and everyone Dix ever painted. His sensibility definitively transports all figures and faces—be they those of fellow soldiers, his family, his friends, himself, or various dancers, prostitutes, johns, criminals, and children—into the world of Dix, which is characterized by bulging, demonic eyes, foreshortened limbs, a dog-like sexuality, and—in the case of the women—larger-than-life T & A, the likes of which would be at home in a cartoon by Robert Crumb.

In short, whether the subject is trench warfare, a Weimar sex club, a crime scene, or a seriously tongue-in-cheek Madonna and Child, one of the most remarkable things about Dix is his rabid employment of caricature without a spirit of mockery. One gets the sense, in Dix, that we are all in this situation together—that our desires, injuries, genitals, faces, illnesses, bravado, and vulnerabilities may be pathetic, ugly, inglorious, and often quite terrifying. But, as Dix's long career suggests, that is no reason not to celebrate them.

PRECARIOUSNESS

I<small>N</small> *On Beauty and Being Just*, Elaine Scarry argues that our first response to beauty, and by extension, to vulnerability (the link comes from beauty's fleetingness), is to protect it, to cherish it. My dance student's response was to hurl heavy objects at it. Sometimes, as we have seen, when faced with the radical vulnerability of another's body or soul, one might feel inclined to laugh at it (the recipe for much cruel humor, in art as in life). The schizoid nature of these responses reminds me of a child who plucks a beetle from the dirt, makes it a home in a dish, gives it a name, then squishes it to death, then cries because it's dead.

One means of understanding this volatile back and forth is provided by philosopher Emmanuel Levinas, who proposes that the perceived precariousness of an Other simultaneously provokes in us the urge to protect him and the temptation to kill him. For Levinas, the negotiation of these two opposing impulses—rather than the abolition of the latter—provides the foundation for ethical behavior.

This makes sense to me. But, as Judith Butler has noted, it also skips over an important question—namely, why would it be that apprehending an Other's precariousness would tempt me to kill him?

There are several ways of addressing this question. Pop psychology would likely have it that the precariousness of an Other reminds us of our own precariousness—a precariousness we may wish to disavow or deny out of fear, out of a (doomed) desire to be invincible, immortal. Feminists might add that since our fundamental precariousness has been feminized (as vulnerability, as weakness), a misogynistic ideology would naturally demand its suppression, abjection, or defeat. This latter version of events may help to explain the rage that can ensue when any given woman is revealed *not* to belong to something that could be called the "weaker sex." For when women cease to be the repositories of human vulnerability, the radical precariousness in which we all share jumps into focus and becomes everyone's burden to bear.

Many have not found, do not find, this burden bearable. This is too bad, especially if (as Adam Phillips and Barbara Taylor have put it) the very definition of kindness is "the ability to bear the vulnerability of others, and therefore of oneself." The whiff of cruelty is in the air.

———

Since the birth of the form, novelists have had a long love affair with the female heroine—specifically, with creating a likable, strong character who then gets smacked down by the prehensile tail of her vulnerability. The Victorian era featured a multitude of magnificent novels—often written by women—starring feisty heroines who get batted around by the cruel forces of finance and fate (George Eliot's Maggie Tulliver, Charles Dickens's Little Dorrit, Charlotte Brontë's Jane Eyre, and so on). Then, in 1880, Henry James's *The Portrait of a Lady* arrived.

The founding germ of the novel, according to James, was his

involuntary apprehension of a character—a particularly bright and engaging young woman who, like the "frail vessels" of George Eliot, would become one of those specimens of small "female fry" in literature who somehow "insist on mattering." *Portrait* introduces us to this woman in the form of Isabel Archer, arguably one of the most likable heroines in Anglo-American literature. After apprehending her character, James said his next job was to decide on the novel's driving question, which was, "What will she 'do'?" James saw the rest of the novel as charged with constructing a set of "right relations" in which to let both his character and this question loose.

Unsurprisingly, the question of "What will she 'do'?" soon boils down to "Whom will she marry?" The drama of the first half of *Portrait*, like that of most Victorian novels, circulates around Isabel's marital options. *Portrait* differs from these, however, in that Isabel is a fiercely independent American woman of means living in both the United States and Europe at the end of the nineteenth century. She therefore has an unprecedented sense of agency—not to mention a range of potential spouses—of more promising nature than is customarily allotted to small "female fry." Nonetheless, Isabel notoriously chooses quite badly—worse, even, than Dorothea Brooke's appalling commitment to the infirm, bitter Casaubon in Eliot's *Middlemarch*. For Isabel chooses a husband (Gilbert Osmond) who hates her, and who holds her unhappiness as his life's primary objective.

For the second half of the novel, Isabel is up against the difficult task of sifting through a maze of feelings and thoughts that she once took to be facts, or at least sound reflections of facts, but that now appear to be delusions by which she somehow duped herself into her miserable situation. "It was impossible to pretend that she had not acted with her eyes open; if ever a girl was a free agent she had been," James writes. "There had been no plot, no snare; she had looked and considered and chosen." In *Portrait*'s justly famous "Chapter 42"—which arguably invents "stream of consciousness" as a literary form—Isabel uses every ounce of lucidity she's got to cut through her self-deceptions, about Osmond and herself. She discovers, in the end, that her error was, in a sense, one of misinterpretation: "she had not read him right . . . she had mistaken a part for the whole." Learning to read well, for James, is no academic matter. A life's happiness can depend on it.

In a nasty (if dated) 1972 piece excoriating the "women's movement," Joan Didion scoffs at feminist readers who would skip over Isabel's status as a "free agent" and interpret her demise as a casualty of patriarchy. For feminists, Didion says, "Isabel Archer in *The Portrait of a Lady* need no longer be the victim of her own idealism. She could be, instead, a victim of a sexist society, a woman who had 'internalized the conventional definition of a wife.' " Jeer as Didion might, the fact remains that *Portrait* also bends over backward to show us how Isabel has "internalized the conventional definition of a wife"—not only for herself, but also for her husband's daughter, whom she considers marrying off "as you would put a letter in the post-office" in order to please her horrible mate. Further, Isabel eventually discovers that there was indeed a plot, or a snare: her marriage was fixed behind her back to provide cover—and funds—for her husband's illegitimate daughter. By the novel's end, Isabel is no longer ruing the results of her actions as a "free agent," but rather standing face to face with "the dry staring fact that she had been an applied handled hung-up tool."

The genius of *Portrait* is that it allows both versions of events— Isabel as "free agent," Isabel as "hung-up tool"—to be true. After all, it is not only cruel but also inaccurate to insist that people are the sole authors of their lives; to tell them so is, as Phillips has said, one means of punishing them. And yet another profound way of punishing people is to insist that they have no capacity to author their lives whatsoever. We live, with Isabel, in the balance.

———

THIS SUSPENSION is an interesting place. But be wary of the many male authors and auteurs who nail their empowered female heroines into this spot for sport. One of the most renowned practitioners of this formula is Dogma filmmaker Lars von Trier, whose "Golden Heart" trilogy provides ample opportunity to contemplate—should one be in the mood—its machinery.

The first film of the trilogy—and the most insidious to my mind (though 2000's *Dancer in the Dark* is up there)—is *Breaking the Waves* (1996). *Breaking the Waves* showcases the indestructible "goodness" of the lead female character, Bess (Emily Watson), as she moves from newlywed naif to bereft wife to sexual adventurer to prostitute to victim of a fatal sexual torture. She undertakes all this to please her husband, Jan (Stellan Skarsgård), who has been paralyzed and rendered impotent in an oil rig accident shortly after their wedding. Jan consequently encourages her, from his hospital bed, to engage in sexual transgressions and report on them to him. These transgressions build toward a brutal sexual encounter with two sailors that leaves Bess sliced up, facially disfigured, and screaming in agony on an emergency room table, where she eventually expires. To add to the horror, we never see what transpires on the boat with her rapist/murderers; we see only her entering the boat, then entering the ER in a pool of blood. The viewer is thus left to fill in the gaps of whatever forms of sexual torture might have caused such unbearable, fatal suffering.

All through the film, Bess's "sacrifices" to her husband have been figured as Christ-like, and as she dies in the ER, Jan miraculously rises from his hospital bed and begins to walk. As church bells ring over the ocean in the film's parting shot, announcing the glory of Bess's ultimate sacrifice and its redemptive effect on Jan, I sat in the dark theater, probably not unlike many viewers, feeling distraught to the point of destroyed. Then, as the first wave of emotion lifted, I felt angry. Then I felt disgusted. Finally, I felt bored. The brutal emotional impact of Bess's suffering aims to undo the viewer so profoundly that the film's final message—that her sexual torture serves as a necessary, redemptive good for the male, and further, that there is sublimity to be found in such a scenario—almost slips down the gullet whole. But who can truly swallow it? Von Trier's cruelty does not lie in any capacity to strip away cant or delusion, but rather in an ability to construct malignant, ultimately conventional fictions that masquerade as parables of profundity, or as protests against the cruelties of the man's world in which we must inevitably live and suffer.

Or, worse—and more likely—von Trier means to present these fictions with tongue so firmly in cheek that if we take them as parables of profundity, the joke may be on us. Von Trier imbues René Girard's notion of sacrificial violence with an ironic, perhaps even a campy sensibility. But unlike the campiness of, say, Paul McCarthy or John Waters, von Trier keeps his cards close to his chest, as if to preserve his right—and the culture's—to an entrenched, inevitable chauvinist malevolence. Of course, this approach has gone quite well for him, as it has for related others: David Mamet, Neil LaBute, Philip Roth, John Updike, Woody Allen, and so on. Judging by popularity and acclaim, these men are not "persisting in registering the dimmed signals of a bygone era," as Sam Tanenhaus says in his 2010 *New York Times* piece, of Abramović and Finley. Misogyny, when expressed or explored by men, remains a timeless classic.

I suppose, in the end, I remain grateful to *Breaking the Waves* for one thing: it spoke to a question I've had for some time—namely, what purpose could a female Christ serve in the (male) imagination? As writer Eileen Myles has put it, "What would be the point in seeing [a woman] half nude and nailed up? Where's the contradiction? Could that have driven the culture for 2,000 years? No way." The cruelty of *Breaking the Waves* is its revelation, intentional or not, that there could be no sustaining contradiction—that the redundancy of female victimization inflates into a sickening, fundamentally unbelievable martyrdom.

—

Breaking the Waves has male vulnerability and precariousness at its root, as it is Jan, not Bess, who has been rendered paralyzed and impotent. And yet the film works overtime to shift the burden of vulnerability to Bess's body, as if to prove how effectively the precariousness of the female body can distract from that of the male body, not to mention that of (heterosexual) masculinity itself. For up until her demise, Bess is uncommonly ambulatory and horny—two conditions that, perhaps on screen even more than in life, rarely go unpunished for the female subject. (See, for example, Michael Haneke's film *The Piano Teacher*, based on the novel by Elfriede Jelinek, for a particularly nasty rendition of this narrative.) This arc has for many years subsumed gay and transgendered characters as well, whose humanity was—until quite recently—typically allowed to come into cinematic focus so long as the characters died terrible deaths (as in the otherwise well-intentioned *Boys Don't*

Cry, Kimberly Peirce's 1999 film based on the murder of trans-man Brandon Teena, or the many films based on the 1998 murder of Matthew Shepard, or early AIDS films such as 1993's *Philadelphia*, and so on).

What a relief, in the face of such ghastly narratives, to shift one's attention to an image such as *Self-Portrait/Pervert*, the iconic 1994 self-portrait by photographer Catherine Opie. In *Pervert*, Opie is formally seated, facing the camera, her hands crossed in her lap, an ornate tapestry hanging behind her. A glossy black leather S/M hood encases her face; forty-six needles have been ritually inserted up and down her tattooed arms; and the word "Pervert" has been freshly carved, in ornate lettering, into the skin of her chest. Her body squarely presents itself to us as bleeding, resilient, imperial, and desirous.

Unlike Ono's *Cut Piece*, Mendieta's *Rape Piece*, or Abramović's *Rhythm 0*, *Pervert* is decidedly uninterested in what others might do to a passive female body. Opie's self-portrait speaks to the opposite: it broadcasts what Opie's body likes, what it wants—indeed, what it is: a pervert, stated brightly in flesh and blood. Its solidity, its composure, its reclamatory *Pervert* announcement, all say, The buck stops here. The meticulousness of the cutting and the needlework signifies intent, resiliency, and training; likewise, the mask indicates a gratified desire for effacement rather than a silencing. Opie bleeds when punctured, as do we all. But her bloodshed here signifies solidarity—a shared kinship with the queer leather community from which much of Opie's early work emanates, as well as with the work of gay male artists (such as Ron Athey, Opie's friend, subject, and collaborator), for whom the public shedding of blood—especially HIV-positive blood—during the height of the AIDS epidemic was experienced as an act of catharsis and defiance. Such a stance rejects the burden of abjected precariousness; as a result, the whiff of cruelty is nowhere to be found.

The work of an artist such as William Pope.L—who has adopted the epithet "The Friendliest Black Artist in America©"—takes up related problems, but with a wholly distinct sensibility. In lieu of reclamation or sturdiness, Pope.L repeatedly invents ways to inhabit and conjure precariousness, by means of a decades-long performance practice dedicated to analysis, abjection, and absurdity. As Barbara Pollack put it in a 2002 *Village Voice* article on Pope.L's work, "One idea that continually intrigues Pope.L is the use of physical vulnerability to unmask the public face worn by African American men—from the machismo of Puff Daddy to the respectability of Martin Luther King. 'The preachers in my church were the first men I saw who made use of this,' [Pope.L] says. 'Ordinarily, they were dressed dapper—handkerchief in their pocket, shine on their shoes. But when it comes to Sunday, they're on their knees, crying and making a mess of themselves. And everyone knows that the way you rate the sermon is how much of a mess they made of themselves.' "

For Pope.L, this mess also includes the lived reality or ever-present possibility, for many black American males (or BAMs, as Pope.L calls them), of being threatened, poor, powerless, homeless, lynched, humiliated, despaired, addicted, or imprisoned. This, Pope.L explains, is the flip side of the BAM as hypermasculine, righteous, menacing, overendowed. Neither side of this coin contains an untroubled claim to power or presence. As Pope.L sees it, in terms that would please (or perhaps even baffle) French psychoanalyst Jacques Lacan, "The BAM is a phallus looking for its body."

Pope.L is interested in how this volatile dyad gets foisted upon black men from without, and how it plays out in communities, families, and bodies from within. Speaking of his own patrilineal heritage, he says, "I would be remiss and arrogant to dismiss the shameful aspects and celebrate only the so-called good. It was the two in tango that made these men. If I celebrate poetry and carpentry, I must also celebrate rape and alcohol. If I denigrate domestic violence, I must denigrate the ethos of hard work and Christian character." This insistence on coexisting contradictions, no matter how disturbing or perplexing, characterizes Pope.L's thought, speech, and practice. Or forget coexisting contradictions—as he puts it, "There is no such thing as contradiction, only the fire that burns amidst the networks made up of them."

Some of Pope.L's best-known pieces propose his body as a site for these volatile networks, this fire. In *How Much Is That Nigger in the Window*, performed in the summer of 1991 (at Franklin Furnace in New York City), Pope.L stood, as if for sale, behind the gallery window, naked except for a coating of mayonnaise smeared all over his body. Over the course of the performance, the mayonnaise turned from an opaque white to a translucent, putrid oil evoking decay, transmutation. ("For me, mayonnaise is a bogus whiteness," he says. "It reveals its lack in a very material way. And the more you apply, the more bogus the act becomes. The futility is the magic.") In *Roach Motel Black* (1993), Pope.L meandered around New York City with a large roach motel stuck to his head, at one point lying down in the street covered with discs of roach bait—a literalized gambit about the black body as a pestilence requiring extermination. The piece's motivating force was Pope.L's question to himself: "What if I explored what whites think about black folks as a sort of truth?"

In one of his most arresting and entrancing performance pieces, *My Niagra* (1998), Pope.L transformed a gallery space (The Project, in New York City) into a sort of basement dungeon, lit by bare bulbs, punctuated by empty beer cans and other detritus, and lashed himself to a bed frame hanging at a vertical angle in the space. He was naked, save for a bright red ski mask (his glasses eerily poking through), heavy boots, a layer of white flour on his skin, and sheets of bright blue plastic tarp bunched around him. His bare belly was pressed against the bed frame's metal wires, his head affixed at an alarming angle, as if his neck might be broken. As Project gallerist Christian Haye remembers the piece, "He had his dick clamped to a pitcher. He would let people in two at a time. There was this really eerie light. It was fantastic. Literally, nobody who saw it forgot it. "

By most accounts, what was so unforgettable was the uncanniness of Pope.L's cadaver-like presence, and the unruly, conflicting effects of the materials at hand. For while the piece viscerally evoked the radical, savage violence that racist America has leveled at the black male body—a violence that has included dismemberment, disfiguration, immolation, and mutilation—his tableaux had an absurdist, clownish quality to it, palpable in its use of primary colors (yellow light, blue tarp, red ski mask), and its scrambling of the symbols of victimology (i.e., the ski mask evokes the criminal or the threatening, rather than a crucified innocent; his penis is affixed to the milk pitcher as if being force-fed whiteness, but what could that exactly mean?). As in much of Pope.L's work, the humor feels both trenchant and inscrutable. "In the case of humor," he explains, "it is not just about confronting, but also seducing and lubricating as well as confusing (intentionally). I am after the mixed signal."

One of the simplest, most effective employments of this mixed signal can be found in Pope.L's *Crawl* pieces, which he has been performing, using various costumes and locales, for over thirty years.

In one of their most well-known manifestations, Pope.L dresses up in a nice suit and, while holding a potted plant in one hand, attempts to crawl on his belly across a part of New York City. He wears the suit, he explains, so as to distinguish himself from other prostrate black men who might not normally garner any attention, so accustomed New Yorkers are to seeing black men in the gutter.

For Pope.L, the *Crawl* pieces are a means of reinhabiting the underclass from which he came, and whose radical precariousness he experiences as an ever-present possibility (he grew up in poverty in rural Florida; many members of his family are or have been homeless). "People who are forced to give up their verticality are prey to all kinds of dangers," he explains. "But, let us imagine a person who has a job, possesses the means to remain vertical, but chooses to momentarily give up that verticality? To undergo that threat to his/her bodily/spiritual categories—that person would learn something. I did." To give others the chance to do the same, Pope.L has from time to time organized "group crawls," inviting others to "give up their verticality," if only for a brief period.

As the eccentric pathos of the potted plant might indicate, the *Crawl* pieces are not meant to provide an object lesson, but rather a peculiar public spectacle around which prejudices, sympathies, uncertainties, and other unpredictable emotions might swirl. In the case of *Tompkins Square Crawl* (1991), the most salient emotion conjured was anger. The performance—for which Pope.L had engaged a (white) videographer—enraged an African-American pedestrian, who stopped to express incredulity and outrage, eventually demanding that the videographer stop filming or he would break his camera. The pedestrian was upset by the spectacle of a white man filming a black man in such a humiliating posture—an image he took as a personal insult. "I wear a suit like that to work!" he exclaimed.

Precariousness may indeed be a condition—indeed *the* condition—that unites us all; our primary vulnerability, as Butler has it, is undoubtedly a problem that "one cannot will away without ceasing to be human." But as *Tompkins Square Crawl* makes clear (as do Butler's own inquiries into what counts as a livable life and a grievable death), this condition is not perceived equally, either from within or from without. And it is not perceived equally because it is not distributed or constructed equally.

Part of Pope.L's genius has been to draw out these differences in the art world as well as on the street. As critic C. Carr has pointed out, Pope.L's *Crawl* pieces overtly echo Chris Burden's *Through the Night Softly*, but no one takes Burden's crawling as representative of the internalized masochism, existential precariousness, or economic humiliation of white people, nor were Burden's performances likely to be interrupted by a white person admonishing him as a traitor or embarrassment to his race. To underscore such differences—and to stake his claim on whatever artistic heritage he sees fit—Pope.L often explicitly engages with the work of white artists (such as Robert Ryman, who is most well known for his monochromatic white paintings), constructing performances that bring into focus what changes when a black man takes up related artistic activities. One example of such détournement might be Pope.L's 2000 piece, *The Hole Inside the Space Inside Yves Klein's Asshole*, which hearkens directly back to Klein's *Anthropometries* series. In *The Hole inside the Space*, which was performed at Concordia University in Montreal, Pope.L—wearing an African mask—smeared his ass in K-Y jelly and acrylic paint, then made "ass prints" on a piece of Kwanzaa paper hanging on the wall.

One of the things I find most intriguing about Pope.L's investigations into precariousness and "have-not-ness" is his willingness to link them up, at least rhetorically, with the discourse around lack that has (lamentably, and bizarrely) dominated discussion of female subjectivity and sexuality ever since Freud theorized that women suffer from "penis envy," and Lacan extended the formulation to conclude that women—having neither the penis nor the castration complex that purportedly accompanies it—are doubly stranded, in that they even "lack lack."

Pope.L repeatedly refers to blackness as lack, but as a "lack worth having"—a notion he has been working out in quizzical, sometimes hermetic writings gathered under the name "Hole Theory." In 2001, he began a related postering project that involved pasting fliers around Manhattan that read, "This is a painting of Martin Luther King's penis inside my father's vagina." In explanation of this somewhat cryptic provocation, Pope.L says he is trying to "involute" King's body and men's bodies in general. "I think one must say in all honesty, 'Boy, that Martin Luther King Jr. sure had a big vagina.' This, I think, says something. It gives the legacy of King's body as a (w)hole worth having. It digs him up from the catacombs of celebration and presence and places him in the lived moment of contraries where we all have to deal."

I agree: this says something. What on earth it says, I have no idea. I like it, though, because it bothers me, and I'm not sure why. It also makes me laugh, though I'm not sure if I'm laughing at the vagina or with it, whether it's a misogynistic insult to MLK to suggest he has a big one, a mockery of such, or an irreverent, scrambled act of insurrection, (dis)identification, and reclamation that I can truly get behind. Whatever it is, I agree that it places us in the "lived moment of contraries where we all have to deal." I'm not sure where this is, but I'm glad to be here.

INFLICTED

TRUTH CANNOT be imparted," says a character in Brian Evenson's novel *Dark Property*. "It must be inflicted." Inflict: from *fligere*, to strike. The statement brings to mind a famous quote by Romanian dramatist-of-the-absurd, Eugène Ionesco: "To tear ourselves away from the everyday, from habit, from mental laziness which hides from us the strangeness of reality, we must receive something like a bludgeon blow."

For his part, Francis Bacon often said he felt the need to "clarify" his paintings by lacerating or nailing down the figures that blob and lurk on his canvases. Almost in exasperation—and, perhaps, to avoid painting more crucifixions—Bacon at times took to pinning his figures down with hypodermic needles. "I've used the figures lying on beds with a hypodermic syringe as a form of nailing the image more strongly into reality or appearance," he explained. On other occasions, Bacon went without needles or nails, and simply hurled a blob of paint from his fist onto the figure to finish it off. "Pity the meat!" cried Gilles Deleuze, in the face of such painting.

If such recourse to inflictions appeared once in a blue moon, it might not seem so strange. But given how often it recurs, especially in twentieth- and twenty-first-century artistic rhetoric, I feel compelled to ask, what kind of knowing is this, that is supposedly accomplished by striking?

On the one hand, one could say that this "bludgeon blow," this infliction, is but a metaphor meant to indicate that "Eureka!" moment of freshness, of lightning-flash discovery—that moment at which, as Thomas Kuhn, author of *The Structure of Scientific Revolutions* (1962), would have it, a shift in paradigm occurs, a shift so revolutionary that it obliterates the old paradigm, rendering obsolete an entire mode of seeing, of understanding the world. Kuhn's theory about the role such paradigm shifts have played in the history of science has proved enormously influential well beyond the bounds of his field, largely because his story about science is also the story of modernity. Rather than valuing the accumulation of received wisdom, modernity values radical change, cleavage from that which has come before. And its name for this process is "progress," however teleological or nonteleological that progress turns out to be.

Christian traditionalists often cite the Bible as source and guarantor of the reverent preservation of tradition. But as many theologians and historians have observed, Christianity is also a fundamentally modern religion, in that it encourages radical cleavage from family and tradition, if necessary, in order to become a true follower. The New Testament is a hotbed of such incitements. See, for example, Matthew 10:35–37, where Christ says, "For I am come to set a man at variance against his father, and the daughter against her mother, and the daughter in law against the mother in law." Such counsel is no anomaly, but rather a recurring theme throughout the Gospels, as in Luke 14:26: "If any man come to me, and hate not his father, and mother, and wife, and children, and brethren, and sisters, yea, and his own life also, he cannot be my disciple." In light of such passages, one may find oneself agreeing with Annie Dillard when she asks, in an essay titled "The Book of Luke," "Why did [adults] spread this scandalous document before our eyes? If they had read it, I thought, they would have hid it. They did not recognize the lively danger that we would, through repeated exposure, catch a dose of its virulent opposition to their world."

In this scandalous document known as the New Testament, one of the major symbols of the cleavage brought about by Christ is that of his sword. As Jesus says in an infamous and hotly contested line (Matthew 10:34), "Think not that I am come to send peace on earth; I came not to send peace, but a sword." Christ makes good on this promise in the last book of the Bible, the Book of Revelation, in which he returns as a warrior riding a white horse, a sword in his mouth, ready to cleave the righteous from the wicked, and cast the wicked into the pit of hell. This cleavage has also been forecast in Matthew, in the so-called parable of the weeds, in which Christ tells of the day on which the weeds (i.e., evil and its doers) will be severed from the wheat (i.e., the righteous), and the weeds thrown "into the fiery furnace, where there will be weeping and gnashing of teeth."

Whether Christ's sword is best understood metaphorically, or whether it is to be taken as a literal instrument of violence to be employed in a holy war, has been the subject of much sermonizing and debate. History provides a clear abundance of the latter; as Dillard writes, with profound understatement, "What a pity that so hard on the heels of Christ come the Christians."

But before we harangue the Bible for this dangerous-seeming slippage between the metaphorical and the literal, we might note that the figure of the sword occupies a similar, pivotal place in Zen

Buddhism, where it has given rise to similar concerns and questions. Daisetz T. Suzuki discusses the matter in some length in an essay titled "Zen and Swordsmanship," which aims to explain the kinship between the art of swordsmanship (as practiced by samurai) and the figure of the sword in Zen. "The sword is generally associated with killing, and most of us wonder how it can come into connection with Zen, which is a school of Buddhism teaching the gospel of love and mercy," Suzuki writes. In explanation, Suzuki lays out the many differences between "the sword that kills" and "the sword that gives life," arguing that the latter is the one most appropriately associated with Zen. In a synchronic move, Suzuki suggests that this latter is "the kind of sword that Christ is said to have brought among us." Suzuki makes clear, however, that the sword that gives life is "not meant just for bringing the peace mawkishly cherished by sentimentalists." The sword of life, in other words, does not shrink from slaying its enemies when the time is right, on which occasion the sword "performs automatically its function of justice, which is the function of mercy." No room for idiot compassion here.

But what about the sword that brings not justice, but knowledge? This sword appears throughout the New Testament as well, most often as a figure for the word of God, which slices clear through to the soul. See, for example, Ephesians 6:17, "And take the helmet of salvation, and the sword of the Spirit, which is the word of God," or Hebrews 4:12, "For the word of God is quick and powerful, and sharper than any two-edged sword, piercing even to the dividing asunder of soul and spirit, and of the joints and the marrow, and is a discerner of the thoughts and intent of the heart." In Mahayana Buddhism, the figure of the sword symbolizes neither justice nor knowledge per se, but rather wisdom (in

Sanskrit, *prajna*). The sword of prajna is double-edged, in order to slice through all dualities, as well as the ego that purports to house them. In Buddhist iconography, the figure for prajna is the Bodhisattva Manjushri, who is most often depicted with a flaming sword in one hand and a sutra in the other.

Manjushri's flaming sword does not cleave weed from wheat, nor does it communicate the commandments of any God. Rather, its medium is its message. Its task is to keep slicing through all the ways in which we attempt to hold onto a sense of solid ground, all the ways in which we resist the fundamental impermanence of all things. The cutting itself—the practice of paring down, of becoming clearer and clearer, of hacking away at the ground under our feet not once, not twice, but always—is the practice of wisdom itself. If prajna brings one closer to anything, it is to shunyata (fundamental emptiness, or void).

As one might imagine, this type of cutting offers little to no reassurance. As Buddhist teacher Judy Lief puts it, "You could view all this as a bit of a warning: as soon as you enter the Buddhist path and start practicing meditation and studying the dharma, you are picking up this sword of prajna. Now that you have this sharp thing, this sword that skewers and cuts through ego trips of all sorts, you have to deal with it. . . . there's nothing left over, just this sword, slicing and slicing. . . . You're left nowhere, more or less."

The temptation to pair this intense penetration with "getting somewhere"—to justice, say, or revelation—can be as intense as it is self-defeating. Kafka's "In the Penal Colony" offers an exceptionally dismal and enjoyable satire of this affliction. The story circulates around an officer, an explorer, a condemned man, and an "apparatus," the latter being a torture device whose needles, collectively termed "the Harrow," inscribe the words of "whatever commandment the prisoner has disobeyed" on his condemned body. The Harrow begins by writing on the surface of the flesh, but over the course of twelve hours, it penetrates deeper and deeper into the body of the condemned, which is flipped over and over on a bed of cotton, so as to keep providing the Harrow with fresh parts of body to penetrate. Eventually, the Harrow pierces all the way through, and the prisoner perishes.

As the officer explains to the reticent but appalled explorer (who serves as a sort of stand-in for the reader, who is learning alongside him—to her horror—about the workings of the killing machine), "The first six hours the condemned man stays alive almost as before, he suffers only pain. After two hours the felt gag is taken away, for he has no longer strength to scream. . . . But how quiet he grows at just about the sixth hour! Enlightenment comes to the most dull-witted. It begins around the eyes. From there, it radiates. Nothing more happens than that the man begins to understand the inscription. . . . To be sure, that is a hard task; he needs six hours to accomplish it. By that time the Harrow has pierced him quite through and casts him into the pit, where he pitches down upon the blood and water and the cotton wool." The officer's speech reveals him to be quite mad, not only on account of his logorrheic, obsessive devotion to this antiquated, sadistic ritual, but also due to his almost mystical conviction that there is no reason to tell a condemned man what his sentence is, nor what crime he committed, nor even that he's been sentenced at all. "There would be no point in telling him," he asserts. "He'll learn it on his body."

As the story unfolds, this assertion—along with the officer's conviction that the apparatus brings a glorious and profound Enlightenment to torturer, tortured, and spectator alike—are revealed as the cruel shams that they are. First of all, the prisoner does not speak the language everyone else is speaking (French), and he presents throughout as a sort of cavorting idiot unlikely to understand any linguistic inscription offered by this motley crew, be it drilled into his body or not. Next, after the explorer tells the officer that he does not approve of the apparatus, and that he plans on sharing his disapproval with the powers-that-be in order to shut it down, the officer decides to exchange places with the condemned man, rather than survive into an era in which the apparatus is no longer used. The commandment that the officer programs into the Harrow to inscribe on his body is "BE JUST": a typical Kafka koan on which one could meditate for weeks, if not years, without coming to a conclusive interpretation.

Rather than being ceremoniously martyred, however, the officer is quickly mauled by the machine, which malfunctions terribly. "The Harrow was not writing, it was only jabbing, and the bed was not turning the body over but only bringing it up quivering against the needles. The explorer wanted to do something, if possible, to bring the whole machine to a standstill, for this was no exquisite torture such as the officer desired, this was plain murder." When the explorer finally manages to pry the officer off the spikes, he looks into the face of the corpse, and sees "no sign . . . of the promised redemption; what the others had found in the machine the officer had not found." This being Kafka, it's unclear whether the official might have reached the beatific state he so desired and admired had his machine not malfunctioned. The ambiguity manages to savage the idea of achieving redemption or justice through radical, tortuous penetration, while also preserving—via the fanatical, unwavering conviction of the officer—an ardent portrait of the temptation to keep on trying.

If one removes "In the Penal Colony" from its crime-and-punishment context, one can see that the temptation just described—and its frustration—also serves as an allegory, however inscrutable, for writing itself. It was Kafka, after all, who wrote in a now-famous letter that "we ought to read only books that bite and sting us. If the book we are reading doesn't shake us awake like a blow on the skull, why bother reading it in the first place? . . .What we need are books that hit us like a most painful misfortune, like the death of someone we loved more than we love ourselves, that make us feel as though we had been banished to the woods, far from any human presence, like a suicide. A book must be the axe for the frozen sea within us." Bite, sting, blow, hit, banish, hack: the terms echo those used by F. T. Marinetti, Ionesco, and a host of other modernists. Young Samuel Beckett, writing in Kafka's wake, had similar ambitions (though he took a more sculptural approach): "To bore one hole after another in [language], until what lurks behind it—be it something or nothing—begins to seep through; I cannot imagine a higher goal for a writer today," he wrote in a 1937 letter to his friend, Axel Kaun.

I, too, have often wondered whether there exists a greater pleasure than the feeling—however brief or illusory—that by writing, one is in fact incinerating layers of crap rather than tossing more of it onto the landfill. This can be a difficult feeling to achieve when the medium is language. One cannot simply offer up a white page and a stopwatch and produce the illuminating, cleansing effect of "silence," as John Cage did in *4'33"*. Nor can you easily do what artist Gordon Matta-Clark did: take out the BB gun, the handsaw, the chainsaw, the knife, and start making "core cuts" in the structures that surround us, in order to startle us into seeing new vistas or patterns of light. Each time I show a slide of Matta-Clark's "core cut" of an abandoned building at the Hudson River Piers—

an enormous half-moon which he sliced, with great difficulty and outrageous illegality, out of the corrugated tin wall of a mammoth industrial building on New York City's West Side in 1975—my students typically gasp, then erupt in laughter. That is how exciting and relieving the sensation of space transgressed and revealed can be.

But how to produce such an effect with words? They seem so small, compared to a sliced wall. Nor is it immediately obvious what remains when words have done their work of boring, of clearing.

No one suffered from this dilemma as acutely as Artaud. The longer he lived, the more fiercely Artaud longed for a form of expression that would constitute "no works, no language, no words, no mind, nothing," only "a fine Nerve Meter." The closer he got to becoming this "Nerve Meter," the more his life and work came to be seen, even by his most fervent admirers, as failures; his written body of work, a trail of fragmentary turds. "Talking, talking, talking, Artaud expresses the most ardent revulsion against talk," observed Sontag. To call this situation a contradiction brings us no closer to understanding Artaud's very real and very urgent predicament, which is the paradoxical predicament of any human who feels the need to awl through the strata of shit that so often seem not to obscure our world but to be our world, and who comes to feel that to do so, one must create.

The closest Artaud may have come to "cutting to the core"—or at least, the closest I have come through him—is his 1947 radio play *To Have Done with the Judgment of God*, which was commissioned by French radio but banned on the eve of its broadcast. When I first heard this recording, I did not understand the French, but I knew instantly that this was the voice of a madman living in a universe in which the concepts of "irony" and "sincerity" need not apply. His voice ate through such concepts like bile. His growls, whispers, and screeches seemed to be boring holes into something, but not language, as his voice seemed to have departed from the realm of language entirely. "No one knows how to scream anymore in Europe," he wrote in *The Theater and Its Double*. "People in the theater who can do nothing but talk and who have forgotten that they had a body have also forgotten the use of their throats." *To Have Done with the Judgment of God*, performed within a year of Artaud's death, is all throat, all body.

Years later, when I read a translation of the transcript, I finally learned what Artaud had been saying. He had been saying *to be someone, one must have a BONE, not be afraid to show the bone, and to lose the meat in the process*. He had asked, *Is God a being?* To which he answered, *If he is one, he is shit*. He had asked, *Do you know precisely what is meant by cruelty?* To which he answered, *Offhand, I don't*.

—

OF THE fiction writers working today, Evenson seems to have taken on this predicament most explicitly, and to inhabit it most relentlessly. "Writing for me is about moving through obstacles and establishing a trajectory inward, moving by way of intensities into more and more unsettling and revealing territory," he says, in echo of Kafka and Beckett both. "Anything that blocks the path you must cut through, including religion, including yourself." A harsh journey, this—one characterized, again, by hacking, by macheting one's way through the bush.

As with Artaud, this endless cutting can paradoxically leave quite a trail—which may explain why Evenson has published nine books of fiction, two chapbooks, and six works of translation since 1996. It may also explain why his stories offer an astonishingly long and varied catalogue of discomfiting excisions and penetrations: 2004's *The Wavering Knife*, for example, offers bullets fired into brains, teeth pulled out with pliers, eyes gouged out, syringes plunged into arms, flesh slit, stuffed, and sewn shut, body cavities sawed apart, and so on; *Altmann's Tongue* offers more, and in some cases, worse.

Unlike some writers whose work depends heavily on the visceral shock of ultraviolence (see Chuck Palahniuk, for example, author of *Fight Club*, who proudly keeps track of the number of faintings that have transpired at his public readings), Evenson is an intellectual, even conceptual, writer who is ready and willing to theorize about his work. Speaking of *Altmann's Tongue*, he describes the relationship between violence and religion as follows: "In positing a world beyond this world—a God, a transcendent heaven, moral absolutes—religion does violence to the present world. On a level of content, *Altmann's Tongue* insists that violence is meaningless and that justification of violence, controlled or not, is ultimately futile. Instead of doing violence to this world by positing transcendents, *Altmann's Tongue* does violence to the transcendents by refusing to acknowledge anything beyond this world, but offering characters who cannot even imagine the existence of a beyond."

Evenson knows, however, that as a writer, he's up against a sort of wall, insofar as language, like religion, "does violence to the immanent world by forcing the objects of that world to be understood in terms of generalities, by stripping them of their specificities and categorizing them." Language, in this version of events, accomplishes this feat by the simple act of naming, of representing—that is, when I say apple, I can no longer produce for you this specific apple, right here in front of me, even if that is what I meant to indicate; I must now rely on the constellation of letters that spells the term "apple," which must serve as a stand-in for the thing itself.

The fact that language cannot shed its representational function—or, at least, that it cannot play around with it in the same ways that, say, painting or sculpture can—has provoked strong feeling in many writers. At its most common and benign, the feeling is one of longing, as epitomized by poet Jack Spicer in *After Lorca*: "I would like to make poems out of real objects. The lemon to be a lemon that the reader could cut or squeeze or taste—a real lemon like a newspaper in a collage is a real newspaper." For others—such as Evenson—the feeling is more intense: he claims that linguistic representation *does violence* to the immanent world. Here, representation itself becomes a sort of villainous scythe, come to cleave world from word.

As Wittgenstein makes clear in the opening pages of *Philosophical Investigations*, there are many other ways to understand the functioning of language—ways that are not based on this Adamic naming, this dichotomy of signifier and signified. (Wittgenstein's famed notion of a "language game" comes out of this conviction: that before we generalize about what language is or what language does, we need to look at particular instances of its use, and ask *what game is being played*.) Despite the difference in their philosophical approaches, however, Wittgenstein and Evenson have one thing in common: both take imprecision as their enemy, and hope to counter its effects by using language as precisely as possible.

In Evenson's case, this urge sometimes comes off as a desire to fight fire with fire. For what lands Evenson's work in the genre of horror—and, at times, in the arena of camp—is that he gets so literal about this task: his writing doesn't just evoke the precision of slicing or cutting; his characters actually perform the deeds. When this literalness works, the work carries both visceral punch and intellectual heft. When it falls short, either the violence or the concept behind it seems suddenly naked, paltry, wrong. It is, in short, a gamble.

Often, as in the story "The Ex-Father," from *The Wavering Knife*, this gamble pays off tremendously. The first cut of "The Ex-Father" arrives after a foreboding but quiet opening, in which we are introduced to two young girls whose mother has recently suicided, and who are now residing with their remote father from whom they were previously estranged. After a series of blurry linguistic euphemisms offered by a visiting churchman about their mother's "passing on," we receive this sharp revelation: "Nobody knew that the oldest girl knew that *by her own hand* did not mean pills or exhaust fumes or anything like that, but that while they were at school the mother had taken a serrated knife and tried to hack her own head off with it. She had not managed to get the head off but had gotten pretty far, and the oldest girl had gone to Church herself for enough years to know that nobody who wanted to cut their head off as bad as that was going anywhere near heaven." Not just a knife, but a serrated knife. Not just a fact, but a fact held by a small girl, a mother's daughter, who alone witnessed the immediate aftermath of this horrific, if unbelievable, sawing. The rest of "The Ex-Father" is taken up with the older daughter's management of her burden.

Of course, the trauma has already occurred; it cannot be reversed or excised. It can, however, be restaged. Evenson calibrates the daughter's movement toward her final abreaction very finely, so that its horror is laced through with the daughter's poignant hope against hope that the restaging will "make everything right for good"—the perennial wish of any child who wishes to alter a primal scene that somehow went terribly, terribly wrong. In the end, the pleasure of the story's aesthetic perfection—that is, its own capacity to "make everything right," through language, through structure, through tone—stands in howling contrast to the characters' inability to do so. The effect is an unlikely tenderness that suffuses the story's variety pack of cruelties.

—

I HAVE been trying, for some time now, to understand if or how Plath's line is cruel. When I close my eyes and imagine one of her late poems, I see lines singed out of the page, or the thin red lines that so many adolescents have taken to slicing into their skin, be it for control or release. Then I open up Plath's *Collected Poems*, and see that her poems appear in lines like those of any other poet— some short, some long, all made of words, and so on. Then I start reading, and once again I feel the sear. And I realize that it comes from the combination of lines turned, shorn, or stopped with furious resolve, and the hyperactive sound Plath has enclosed within them—the meticulously coiled internal rhymes and consonance she folds like razor blades into crisply creased white paper. "I have suffered the atrocity of sunsets," she writes in "Elm," demon tongue dancing. "And this is the fruit of it: tin-white, like arsenic."

Perhaps because I find the prose of women writers such as Jean Rhys, Anne Carson, Lydia Davis, Marguerite Duras, Annie Dillard, Joan Didion, Octavia Butler, Eileen Myles, and their ilk often fiercer in form and effect than that of their male counterparts, from Ernest Hemingway to Raymond Carver, Western literary history's habit of aligning men with tough rigor and women with a hazy "écriture féminine" (or, analogously, Western art history's tradition of aligning men with the muscular decisiveness of line, and women with the spacey formlessness of color) has always struck me as odd: more of a prescription or fantasy than a description or observation. It is true, however, that when women push toward making "core cuts," the act may come across differently. If a body is already defined (by misogynistic culture) by its holes, where's the heroism—even if it's a nihilistic heroism—in "boring one hole after another, until what lurks behind begins to seep through"? As any ascetic can tell you, lucidity often arrives via subtraction, via impoverishment. But as any anorexic or self-cutter knows, it can be difficult to know when to stop chiseling.

Artist Eleanor Antin puts this problem on display with high irony in her 1972 piece *Carving: A Traditional Sculpture*. In *Carving*, Antin takes her own body as the living marble to be sculpted, and employs a thirty-six-day diet regimen to do the chiseling. Each day of her diet, she photographs herself from the front, the back, and both sides in front of the same white door frame. The resulting rows of photographs depict her stout, naked body, slimming almost imperceptibly over the days, her vacant stare prohibiting any happy before-and-after narrative. It is as if Antin had posed the question of if and how women might interact with an artistic tradition based on the shaping and marshaling of their bodies without literally diminishing themselves, and then stared it down, answer-less, with this unforgiving mug shot, this scraggly hair, these pendulous, broad-nippled breasts, all offered blankly, day after day, to the camera.

There is in fact an enormous amount of work by women that undercuts—or at least complicates—the heroism of penetration, and that dismantles—or at least complicates—the mythos of the devouring hole. After all, despite the elaborate fear, anxiety, and desire spun around the imago of the vagina as a sort of calamitous, even predatory void, most women are fully aware that the vagina does not resemble a whirling vortex, or a tunnel to the abyss. It, too, is a situation of meat—of blood vessels, of spongy walls, of mucus, of nerves, of pulse.

Mendieta's *Silueta* series, in which Mendieta makes a slit in the earth, often in the shape of her body, and fills it with either sand, water, twigs, flowers, pigment, gunpowder, or fire, comes to mind here, as does Louise Bourgeois's miraculous sculptural play with concave and convex forms. But perhaps the freakiest and most irreverent play of this nature can be found in the work of artist Yayoi Kusama, who has been obsessed with the polka dot—the ultimate hole that both is and is not a hole—for over forty years now. See, for example, Kusama's 1967 video, *Self-Obliteration*, which documents various obliterations—or ecstatic communions—accomplished via painting polka dots on the body, or wearing them while moving through a polka-dotted landscape. Here, Warhol's superficiality meets feminist wit (not to mention an outrageous obsessive-compulsiveness, for which Kusama has long been institutionalized). "We live amid surfaces, and the true art of life is to skate on them well," wrote Emerson. Is it true? If so, who can bear to believe it?

—

FROM THE legendary catastrophe of his working space, Bacon chiseled rings of action out of the piles of images strewn around his feet and affixed to his walls, and drew our attention to the game. The game, for Bacon, was to paint the human figure with inexorable precision and equally inexorable distortion. A smattering of arrows repeatedly draws our attention to certain smears of color, certain areas of the body or canvas, for no apparent reason other than to tell us that, however profound the distortion may be, we are not to be excused from the task of focusing. We are not to collapse, amid the loneliness, injury, or carnage, into a state of diffuse or shocked bewilderment. The paintings aim for "the right degree of bewilderment," as Henry James once put it, which, for James, most certainly did not mean allowing for sloppiness or randomness with bewilderment as an excuse. We are to remain alert. Alert pervs, alert detectives.

For James, this "right degree of bewilderment" meant a "precise ambiguity," one that could conjure, over hundreds of pages of dense, incandescent syntax, something of the glorious, shifting fog of human consciousness. For Bacon, it meant something quite different: it meant forcing precision and ambiguity to coexist in a sort of calamity, in which to clarify one aspect of a figure is to force the smearing, or implosion, of another.

In contemporary literature, the work of Mary Gaitskill presents one of the most riveting examples of this collision of cutting and smearing, incision and blur. Gaitskill's early stories, such as those collected in 1989's notorious *Bad Behavior*, are all about the cut. Language here—be it that of the descriptive fabric of the stories, or that of the dialogue exchanged by their characters—is most definitely a tool used to penetrate, to dismantle, to bore holes. But rather than burn through projections, delusions, cant, or miscommunications, language here bores through the self-esteem and dignity of the characters, along with any possibility of compassionate communication between them. In "A Romantic Weekend," a man and a woman who barely know each other go away together for the weekend, hoping to have some nasty S/M sex in an empty apartment. Before they've even boarded their plane, however, they find themselves wildly incompatible:

> They arrived at the bar an hour early. They went to a bar and drank. The bar was an open-ended cube with a red neon sign that said "Cocktails." There was no sense of shelter in it. The furniture was spindly and exposed, and there were no doors to protect you from the sight of dazed, unattractive passengers wandering through the airport with their luggage. She ordered a Bloody Mary.
>
> "I can't believe you ordered that," he said.
>
> "Why not?"
>
> "Because I want a bloody Beth." He gave her a look that made her think of a neurotic dog with its tongue hanging out, waiting to bite someone.
>
> "Oh," she said.

The open-ended cube in which these two miserable souls find themselves—and through which other miserable souls must pass, and be involuntarily subjected to our two main characters' mean scrutiny—is a good spatial example of Gaitskill's early fictive constructions at large. There is no shelter in them. The characters are fully exposed to the cruelty of the elements (which here means to each other, and, more crucially, to Gaitskill's merciless authorial voice), yet the stories are also lacking in fresh air, or any hope of it. The characters revolve in a stale atmosphere, repeatedly poisoned by nasty speech and corrosive projections, along with a sense that even the most quotidian details of the world are unbearably repulsive.

While waiting on the street for her weekend date to arrive, Beth thinks, "A large, distracted businessman walked by holding a half-eaten hot dog. Two girls passed, sharing cashews from a white bag. The eating added to her sense that the world was disorderly and unbeautiful. She became acutely aware of the garbage on the street. The wind stirred it; a candy wrapper waved forlornly from its trapped position in the mesh of a jammed public wastebasket. This was all wrong, all horrible." If a candy wrapper signifies this much ugliness and despair, one can only guess how Beth will feel after her weekend with a juvenile and obnoxious sadist who periodically burns her under her shirt with a cigarette lighter in a decidedly nonerotic fashion. Nothing here is nice at all.

The pitiless quality of these early stories was impressive, and Gaitskill justly gained fame for them. But it wasn't until her novel *Veronica*, published in 2005, that Gaitskill began to adumbrate this sear with extended experiments in blurring. In the earlier work, the principal task of intelligence—both that of the characters, and of Gaitskill—is to slice through the veil of cant and cliché to reveal the "all wrong, all horrible" nature of things. In *Veronica*, however, this version of intelligence is no longer enough. *Veronica* is narrated by Alison, an ex-model—once young and beautiful, now older, injured, and sick with hepatitis—thinking back on her salad days in New York and Paris, as well as about her friend Veronica, who died of AIDS years ago. "[Veronica] spent her last days alone," Alison bluntly tells us in the novel's opening pages. "I wasn't with her. When she died, nobody was with her."

Veronica has no shortage of such bluntness, a bluntness meant to highlight starkly the cruelty, suffering, and loneliness flowing through the lives of its main characters. But the novel takes equal care to emphasize the flow. When Alison recalls Veronica's story of being raped by a stranger in her apartment—a story Veronica ends by saying, "My rapist was very tender"—Alison has the following train of thought: "Smart people would say that [Veronica] spoke that way about that story because she was trying to take control over it, because she wanted to deny the pain of it, even make herself superior to it. This is probably true. Smart people would also say that sentimentality always indicates a lack of feeling. Maybe this is true, too. But I'm sure she truly thought the rapist was tender." What impresses me here, especially in contrast to Gaitskill's earlier work, is the space made by allowing there to be more than one way for "smart people" to respond, as well as the suggestion that while "smart people" might offer incisive, imposing diagnoses, they might also miss the boat entirely. That an intelligence focused solely on puncturing or mastery may end up deaf, dumb, and blind to other ways of knowing, of perceiving. Or that, at the very least, such an intelligence, with all its probing and psychoanalyzing, may miss the surface truth of what another is actually trying to communicate.

Veronica doesn't really "work" as a novel, at least not in the conventional sense, in that the proposed relationship between Alison and Veronica—which is seemingly meant to serve as a kind of saving grace for our narrator—never really rings true. The novel's truer triumph lies in its rendering of the rushing whirl of *things going on*, and the quiet ecstasy of feeling one's body, mind, and personal history to be but a small, momentarily congealed piece of matter in a glorious, fluctuating whole. If anything delivers Alison to the achievement of her last line—"I will be full of gratitude and joy"—it is her repeated, deepening experience of this blurring, this experience of herself as a "grain or a grass or a stone, a tiny thing that knows everything but can't say anything."

This blurring begins in the first few pages, when Alison sets out for a walk: "my focus slips and goes funny. . . . It's like I get sucked out of normal life into a place where the order of things has changed; it's still my life and I recognize it, but the people and places in it are sliding around indiscriminately." And it continues throughout her memories of her life as a model: "I walk down a hallway crowded with gorgeous people. Lush arms, gold skin, fantastic flashing eyes, lips made up so big and full, they seemed mute—made not to talk but only to sense and receive. So much beauty, like bursts of violent color hitting your eye together and mixing until they were mud. . . . A girl met my eye and I was amazed to see her face emerge with such clarity." The face here functions as a miraculous shimmer of individuality, albeit one always on the cusp of being made mud, or resubmerged into a crowd (or, as in a modeling career, into the sea of other models' equally extraordinary faces). Alison knows this, and as the novel comes to its climax, she finds in it no small measure of satisfaction and bliss: "I had succeeded. I had become like this music. My face had been a note in a piece of continuous music that rolled over people while they talked and drank and married and made babies. No one remembers a particular note. No one remembers a piece of grass. But it does its part. I had done my part."

This passage may sound familiar to readers of Virginia Woolf's *To the Lighthouse*, which culminates in a justly famous passage celebrating the dynamic relation between form and flux—a relation of paramount concern to Woolf. The last paragraph of *To the Lighthouse* describes painter Lily Briscoe's final reckoning with her canvas in progress: "There it was—her picture. Yes, with all its greens and blues, its lines running up and across, its attempt at something. It would be hung in the attics, she thought; it would be destroyed. But what did it matter? she asked herself, taking up her brush again. She looked at the steps; they were empty; she looked at her canvas; it was blurred. With a sudden intensity, as if she saw it clear for a second, she drew a line there, in the centre. It was done, it was finished. Yes, she thought, laying her brush down in extreme fatigue, I had had my vision."

Veronica's meditation on flux and form may echo Woolf's genius classic, but it is new to Gaitskill, a writer who is, after all, far more captivated by cruelty, nastiness, and callousness than Woolf ever was. Speaking about *Veronica* in a 2009 interview in *Bomb* magazine, Gaitskill says, "We come into these physical bodies . . . whatever we are takes this shape that is so particular and distinct—eyes, nose, mouth—and then it gradually begins to disintegrate. Eventually it's going to dissolve completely. It's a *huge* problem for people; we can understand it, but it breaks our hearts." A younger Gaitskill might have satirized the savagery of this situation. At present, she seems more interested in the ways in which specificity and precision coexist with—or eventually give way to—disintegration and dispersal: that completely natural, inevitable process that, as she herself notes, regularly breaks our hearts.

FACE

OWING IN large part to the work of philosopher Emmanuel Levinas, the face has received a lot of attention in recent years as a site of ethical activity. In her book *Precarious Life*, Judith Butler makes extensive use of Levinas's notion of "the face of the Other," which serves, for Levinas, as the locus of ethics. As Levinas puts it, "The face of the other in its precariousness and defenseless-ness, is for me at once the temptation to kill and the call to peace, the 'You shall not kill.' "

Unlike the many ethical systems that advocate beginning with the self and then extrapolating out to include an Other (epito-mized, again, by the Golden Rule), Levinas begins with the reverse presumption—that "the other's right to exist has primacy over my own, a primacy epitomized in the ethical edict: you shall not kill, you shall not jeopardize the life of the other." The face of the Other delivers this edict, which can be understood as a kind of divine imperative. "If the Other, the Other's face . . . at once tempts me with murder and prohibits me from acting upon it, then the face operates to produce a struggle for me, and establishes this struggle at the heart of ethics."

This struggle would have come as no surprise to Francis Bacon, who customarily referred to the distortions he performed on the faces of his subjects as "injuries," and preferred to work from photographs so as to "practice the injury in private." He preferred, too, to work from images of friends, especially friends whose faces he found beautiful. "If they were not my friends, I could not do such violence to them," he said. One primary object of this violence, for Bacon, was the subtraction of the face from the head, so that the head could be made meat.

For those of you with five minutes to spare and a curiosity about the head-made-meat, I recommend Otto Muehl's 1967 film *Kardinal*, as it is one of the most efficient, unsettling renderings of such that I've ever seen. The film is remarkable for its bold proposal of the human head as a canvas for Action painting, and its performance of a disconcerting, minimalist brutality, complicated by the apparent consensuality of the event. The film begins with the hands of a male figure binding a human face and head (its eyes shut) with twine and a clear plastic-like tape. After the face is bound, the male figure—whose body flickers in and out of the frame—begins performing a series of mistreatments, applications, and effacements on it.

He starts by violently slapping a gloppy red substance onto the bound cheeks, then he chugs dark liquid from a bottle and spits it all over the face and scalp. He then pours gallons of a clear syrupy substance over the crown of the head, creating a wall of fluid that flows down over the front of the face like a shroud. Then he hits and smears the scalp and face with a thick, yellowy dough which leaves a plaster of sorts, through which it looks almost impossible to breathe, before slapping more red, blue, and green slime over the doughy plaster, packing it into the orifices. He finishes off by smacking yellow, red, and blue powder all over the subject, which is, by this point, a caked, dripping, unrecognizable mass. This is the first two and a half minutes; the second two and a half depict three naked bodies crawling over and under each other as the same substances—slime, dough, powder—rain down on their orgy: another form of meat-making, to be sure, but one whose effect is far less sinister, and far more comedic—all those silly butt cracks!— than the effacement that precedes it.

—

"AND I have no face, I have wanted to efface myself," says Plath's hospital-bed-bound speaker in "Tulips," putting words to the desire that so often makes her poetry a horror show. For the head stripped of its face—because it never had one, because it has been sliced or burned off, because it has been covered, slimed over, because it still exists, but elsewhere (in a jar, on a different part of the body, in a mirror)—is a staple both of our nightmares and of Plath's vision. If Bacon's paintings evoke artist-as-butcher (and Muehl's *Kardinal*, artist-as-sadistic-baker), Plath shows us what it means to be artist-as-surgeon, with the face at the center of the action. As a doctor reports of the body under his hands in the poem "The Surgeon at 2 a.m.," "As usual there is no face. A lump of Chinese white / With seven holes lumped in."

No one and nothing in Plath's poetry escapes effacement—not the moon, not the clouds, not herself, not those she loves, not children. "And my child—look at her, face down on the floor, / Little unstrung puppet, kicking to disappear . . . She'll cut her throat at ten if she's mad at two," she writes in "Lesbos." Sometimes this effacement in Plath is placid: a speaker in a maternity ward gazes on a row of infants thinking, "I think they are made of water; they have no expression. / Their features are sleeping, like light on quiet water." But lo, when a child wakes, "her little head is carved in wood, / A red hard wood, eyes shut and mouth wide open. (. . .) It utters such dark sounds it cannot be good." It is not good, indeed. Everything is not nice here at all.

As with Bacon, who sometimes painted faces on pedestals or in mirrors, standing eerily apart from the human figures to which they once presumably belonged, sometimes in Plath missing features of the face show up elsewhere ("His fingers had the noses of weasels"), or appear punitively removed and isolated: "[The mouth] had been insatiable / And in punishment, was hung out like brown fruit / To wrinkle and dry." And sometimes, most famously, in poems like "Lady Lazarus," Plath dramatizes her own effacement and invites the reader in to watch. After scandalously describing her face in "Lady Lazarus" as "featureless, fine / Jew linen," she taunts: "Peel off the napkin / O my enemy. / Do I terrify?— // The nose, the eye pits, the full set of teeth?" She terrifies, indeed—and perhaps nowhere more so than in the poem's final, menacing, post-incineration lines: "Herr God, Herr Lucifer / Beware / Beware. // Out of the ash / I rise with my red hair / And I eat men like air." There is hair, there is mouth, but still no face. Like Bacon's monstrous creatures crouching wickedly in his *Three Studies for Figures at the Base of a Crucifixion* (1944), this speaker has pushed beyond the human. "She is the Phoenix, the libertarian spirit, what you will," Plath said politely of the speaker of "Lady Lazarus" in a 1962 BBC interview. "She is also just a good, plain, resourceful woman."

—

THE FINAL lines of Plath's poem "Elm" push beyond the chilling and into the slap-happy: "What is this, this face / So murderous in its strangle of branches?— // Its snaky acids kiss. / It petrifies the will. These are the isolate, slow faults / That kill, that kill, that kill." "Elm" can be read as a sort of riddle: what is this, this face? Probably, an owl. But the force of the last stanza has little to do with the solution of a puzzle, and more to do with the biting audacity of its sibilance, and the hammering repetition of "that kill, that kill, that kill"—sounds that have all the subtlety of Norman Bates's knife in the shower. These are the hooves; listen to their merciless churn.

At such moments, Plath's linguistic melodrama nearly pushes her over into camp. Nearly, but not quite—like Bacon, she remains suspended between high seriousness and the ridiculous. A filmmaker such as Fassbinder immerses us in the tremendously exciting space that can open up when high seriousness and the ridiculous collapse into one another, each rendering the other unrecognizable, thereby creating a whole new tonal palette. In fact, a Fassbinder film such as *In a Year with 13 Moons* (1978) is able to hit tonal nuances that, I have to admit, can make both Bacon and Plath seem nearly Neanderthal in comparison.

In a Year with 13 Moons houses an abundance of surface cruelty: within the first five minutes of the film alone, we see our heroine— the tragically self-castrated, alcoholic, perpetually scorned, and ineluctably moving-toward-death Elvira (played by a beefy, chalky skinned Volker Spengler)—get beat up in a public park by a group of hustlers angered by the discovery that she has no penis, then get verbally and physically abused at home by her lover, Christoph, who calls her a walrus, a person with no soul, and a superfluous lump of meat, all the while forcing her—by yanking her hair—to behold herself in the mirror, so that she can see what a hideous, bloated cow she has become, and why he's leaving her.

The cruelty is unrelenting, but it is feathered by a number of formal factors: principally, the cinematography, which showcases hallways and foyers in astonishingly crafted lighting set-ups, rather than the kind of point-of-view and reaction shots that would normally suggest or deliver psychological identification. (Indeed, throughout the movie, at Elvira's most humiliated or despairing moments, her suffering face or body is lodged in a corner or cul-de-sac of the screen, her sobs only a fraction of a complex soundscape that includes the noise pollution of whatever television, music, or video game happens to be nearby.) When Christoph finally exits the apartment in the initial scene, we feel some relief, in that the terrible berating has finally come to an end. But Elvira is not relieved—like any good addict, she is alarmed, and runs after him into the street, begging him not to leave her. She ends up throwing herself onto the windshield of his car, after which he hits the gas, leaving her sprawled on the street. The movie has truly begun.

The action and language here are tough, but their affect is inde-terminate, largely because Fassbinder has uncoupled this tough-ness from the set of signifiers that normally indicate how much—or even if—we are supposed to care. The spectrum is reset: no longer are we moving between tragedy and farce, melodrama and real-ism, empathy and coldness. Instead, we are set free to roam about in a landscape defined by not knowing, non sequitur, a radical uncoupling of cause and effect, and visual wormholes that lead us from one extraordinary location to the next. No sooner is Elvira dumped on the street, for instance, than she is swooped up by her prostitute friend Zora (Ingrid Caven), who drags her into a stun-ning gilded café, then into an even more stunning black-and-white tiled and mirrored bathroom. In the bathroom, Elvira tells Zora that in a previous life, she was trained as an animal slaughterer, a job she now misses. Zora shudders, calling the slaughter of animals "against life." "No, it *is* life," Elvira counters—and off they go to the slaughterhouse, as if to decide the case.

The slaughterhouse scene in *13 Moons* is nothing short of incredible—and this precisely because it is the most credible, "realest" scene in a film that is otherwise quite phantasmagoric. Elvira and Zora stroll leisurely along the slaughterhouse floor, while Elvira, in voice-over, tells the story of her earlier marriage (to a butcher's daughter) with whom she fathered a child, and of her current unhappy affair with the brutish Christoph. Their heels click along in the deep background, while in the foreground, dozens of cows get stunned, guillotined, hung by their feet to bleed out, stripped of their skin, and eventually strung up for market. The intensity of the bloodshed makes it almost impossible, at least upon first viewing, to take in anything Elvira's voice-over is saying, even though she is delivering presumably crucial backstory. What can one say or think while watching an unthinkable amount of blood—real blood—steam forth from a swinging row of decapitated cows? Elvira is reciting a scripted monologue, while we are staring at the everyday machinations of a killing floor. It is as if Fassbinder were saying, nothing I could ever script or invent could possibly compare to the raw intensity of this scene, which is repeated all around the globe, every day: welcome, and behold.

Nothing as visually upsetting occurs again in *13 Moons*, but it doesn't need to. We have already been catapulted into a world in which hackneyed versions of empathy have no truck. In this world, humans behave in a schizoid and unpredictable fashion toward one another's suffering. For instance, when Elvira's wife, Irene, pays a visit to Elvira's apartment and finds her passed out (which the viewer knows to be the result of a fitful session of autoerotic asphyxia), Irene is frantically concerned. As soon as Elvira revives, however, Irene's tenderness evaporates on a dime. In a disturbing echo of the nasty Christoph, Irene begins berating Elvira severely about a magazine interview Elvira gave that Irene didn't like.

Similarly, much later in the film, when Elvira stumbles upon a man preparing to hang himself in an abandoned building, Elvira treats him cordially enough, sharing her weird, quasi-religious picnic of baguette and wine with him and engaging him in philosophical small talk. Eventually, however, Elvira interrupts the man, and suggests that he might as well get on with the business of hanging himself, as she's no longer interested in talking to him. A moment later, Elvira breathlessly rushes to report (to a woman working elsewhere in the building) that a man on the floor below has just hung himself. When the woman laughs it off, explaining that suicides happen all the time in the building, Elvira shrugs it off as well, and continues about her business—business that will lead, soon enough, to her own suicide, which, in turn, no one will try to prevent.

How, then, are we to feel about the suffering and eventual demise of our heroine? It's hard to say. The insults, humiliation, and abandonments Elvira experiences seem cruel and excessive, but she is also one of those human souls seemingly immune to assistance—a suicidal, alcoholic masochist whose self-mutilation and death cannot rightly be blamed on anyone in particular, not even on the "cruelty of the world." (The fact that the film was made in the wake of the suicide of Fassbinder's lover, Armin Meier—a former butcher—deepens the psychological stakes of blame, guilt, and identification at play.) But in a sense, this whole line of questioning is off the point, as the systematic stylistic alienations of the film disallow projective identification with Elvira to be its engine. The film's import lies elsewhere—in its shrewd thematic layering, in its visual and temporal fascinations, and, perhaps above all, in its sustained tone of irreverent, unpredictable, and deeply enjoyable grimness that nearly defies linguistic description.

In this context, the many close-up shots of Elvira's face become not windows into her soul, but perches onto the inscrutable. Her face is neither wholly male nor wholly female, neither attractive nor completely repulsive, neither uncommonly expressive nor uncommonly remote. Over the course of film it becomes, in its unrelenting suffering, both an invitation to contemplate our common humanity, and a pasty, vaguely repellent block of flesh. Elvira's face—like *13 Moons* itself—strands us somewhere between caring and not caring. But regardless of our feelings about her, we do end up caring about the movie itself very much—and with good reason, as it is a film that rewards and perhaps even demands multiple viewings. As with its unforgettable slaughterhouse scene, if we can abide our discomfort long enough—and Fassbinder is more than happy to give us the time—the sight becomes riveting in unforeseeable ways.

"Who will love me through the blur of my deformity," asks one of Plath's speakers in "Three Women," a harrowing poem in three voices set in a maternity ward. Throughout *13 Moons*, Elvira tries to answer this question, with increasing desperation; it also haunts Alison, the narrator of Mary Gaitskill's *Veronica*. For not only is Alison aging, sick, and primarily on her own, but also she is suffering the ongoing physical effects of a car accident that threatened to leave her disfigured. Her first question to a nurse, upon coming to, is "Is my face all right?" Then, as she's wheeled into the X-ray room, she fights with the technician who is trying to remove her earrings, saying, "If you fuck up my ears, I swear I'll sue you. I'm a model and I can't have fucked-up ears." To which the technician replies, "Why not? You got a fucked-up head." Of course, it's her fucked-up head—the head-made-meat, not the specificity of her beautiful face—that brings her to whatever redemption she eventually finds.

As for Plath, she was seemingly unable to answer the question posed in "Three Women," either in her poems, or in her life. Nonetheless, it is a good one. It points to a place beyond cruelty.

—

GAITSKILL RETURNS to the face in "The Agonized Face," a story from her 2009 collection, *Don't Cry*. This story features Gaitskill at her best, insofar as it combines the take-no-prisoners ferocity of her earlier stories with her more recent interest in formlessness and space-making. Whereas *Veronica* performs a communion of these two modes, here they smash up in a collision made all the more fraught by the story's focus on feminism and its discontents.

The story's two protagonists are our narrator—a divorced mother and sharp-tongued journalist who has been sent to cover an unbearably self-serious literary conference in Toronto—and "the feminist author," a charismatic star of the conference who incites a host of chaotic feelings, prejudices, and sympathies in the narrator. Gaitskill lays out the conflict in bold terms in the opening paragraph, in which the narrator describes the feminist author as "one of the good-looking types with expensive clothes who look younger than they are (which is irritating, even though it shouldn't be), the kind of person who plays with her hair when she talks, who always seems to be asking you to like her. She was like that, but she had something else too, and it was that 'something else' quality that made what she did so peculiarly aggravating." The rest of the story pulses around what this "something else" might be.

At times, it is the "feminist author"'s feel-good championing of the sex work of her youth, which she calls "a fight against patriarchy." Other times, it's her purportedly liberating contention that "women can enjoy sexual violence, too!" or her impassioned, clichéd speeches to the conference about the danger of denying other people their humanity, and therefore "impoverishing and cheating ourselves of life's complexity and tenderness" (a literary conference mainstay). But mostly this "something else" is the "soft, reasonable" manner in which the feminist author addresses things that, to the narrator, cannot and should not be talked about in a soft or reasonable manner. As the story goes on, the symbol for these things becomes the "agonized face," which, the narrator explains, is "a face of sex and woman's pain," a face of "disgrace and violence, dark orgasm, rape, with feeling so strong that it obviates the one who feels it."

As the narrator meditates on this agonized face, she experiments with taking all sides in relation to it. At moments she sides with the feminist author, thinking, "Can you blame her for trying to put a good face on it? For talking so loudly about things that have been used to shame women for centuries? . . . Sometimes you want to be on the side of a smart-aleck middle-aged woman who thumbs her nose at the agonized face and fellates a snotty, sexy man, just for a dumb little thrill. Sometimes you wish it could be that easy." Other moments she comes down hard, with no small measure of brutality: "To tell those stories and pretend there's no agony—it makes you want to pinch her, like a boy in a gang, following her down the street while she tries to act like nothing's wrong, hurrying her step while someone reaches out for another pinch. It makes you want to chase her down an alley, to stone her, to force her to show the face that she denies."

In the end, the latter is the tack the narrator decides on, at least publicly: she publishes a piece about the feminist author so scathing that it creates an uproar among the younger women at the newspaper, who decry the article as mean-spirited and unfair. The narrator responds, "I almost agree that it was not fair. But fair or not, I was right. The agonized face and all it means is one of the few mysteries left to us on this ragged, gutted planet. It must be protected, even if someone must on occasion be 'stoned.' " To agree with our narrator here is to get on board for an indefensible embrace of literal or metaphorical violence; on the other hand, the case she's made throughout for the sanctity of the agonized face is affecting, the way any well-worded appeals to the primal, the animal, the sexual, and the ineffable tend to be.

But, as the narrator elsewhere explains, the agonized face "is not only about rape and pain." To prove her point, she embarks on a long description of sex with her ex-husband, which she describes as follows: "Afterward, we smiled, rolling in each other's arms, laughing at ourselves, laughing at the agonized face. But we couldn't laugh at the emptiness. It was like entering an electrical current, passing first into a landscape of animate light, and then into pitching darkness, warm with invisible light, the whispering voices, the dissolving, re-forming faces of ghosts and the excited unborn. Everything horrible to us, everything nice to us."

Who would want, the story suggests, a world in which everything nice were partitioned off from everything horrible, thereby draining the world of its wild, nearly unnavigable paradoxes? And who would want a feminism—or any form of social justice—that lessened our apprehension of such difficult coexistences, or diminished our access to this electrical current? The genius of "The Agonized Face" is that while its narrator eventually decides—in print, at any rate—that such contradictions are unsustainable, the story at large sustains them.

RINGS OF ACTION

———

A RTISTS SUCH as Plath and Bacon aimed to access "the brutality of fact" without providing any narrative to house it, and
yet also without courting abstraction. This is an intriguing aim,
albeit one bound to produce not only formal but also political
difficulties.

For many would argue that art which aims to extinguish the
story behind the suffering and focus on the suffering itself partakes
in a different, more insidious cruelty—that of depoliticization, of
stripping cruelties from their contexts so that they seem pitiable,
sensational, or inevitable, rather than contingent, avoidable, or
explicable. (This was Brecht's argument about most theater; it is
also Sontag's, in her critique of Arbus, and John Berger's, in his of
Bacon.) "The most politically indoctrinating thing you can do to a
human being is to show him, every day, that there can be no change,"
says filmmaker Wim Wenders. For the most part, I agree. And if
one suggests that the thing that cannot change is the very thing that
is causing suffering, the indoctrination can be all the more toxic.
Such forms of expression can seemingly act as an accomplice, even if
unwittingly, to this cynicism, which turns its back on the hard work
of ferreting out the reasons why a particular cruelty has occurred,
who is responsible for it, who gains from it, and who suffers.

Perhaps this is why I felt a wave of disappointment after viewing the Metropolitan Museum's 2009 retrospective of Bacon. My disappointment did not stem from the paintings themselves, but rather from the room devoted to the many visual sources from which Bacon derived images to paint. These clippings went beyond the expected homoerotic wrestling strips by Eadweard Muybridge and the film stills of the screaming lady from Sergei Eisenstein's *Battleship Potemkin*. They also included innumerable clippings of dead, disfigured, or mutilated people from any number of twentieth-century conflicts, from World War II to the Algerian War.

The disappointment I felt while beholding these clippings alongside Bacon's postcards of Michelangelo, Velázquez, and Rodin prints perplexed me. I already knew that Bacon was an omnivorous collagist who made no distinctions between so-called reality and representation as he went about isolating the screams, injuries, and physical deformations and configurations he wished to paint. I already knew that Bacon was especially keen on arenas in which human suffering and conflict are somehow both performative and real, such as in boxing matches.

And yet something about the documentary photos of bodily carnage—particularly those of rebel Algerian body parts, which came from a book of 1950s French propaganda called *The True Aspects of the Algerian Revolution*—gave me pause. After looking at them for some time, I found I wasn't in the mood to look at Bacon's paintings any longer. I felt a longing for Otto Dix, whose perversity and invention coexist raucously with named historical event. I also felt a weird longing for Andy Warhol—one of the few contemporaries Bacon admired, to the surprise of those who would pit Warhol's catatonic sheen against Bacon's muscularity and gore. At least Warhol's mining of newspapers for his *Death and Disaster* series (1967), which includes car crashes, plane crashes, suicides, electric chairs, celebrity deaths, and so on, was clean and clear—without pretension, without existential apparatus.

In retrospect, it occurs to me that part of the intensity of Bacon's paintings may in fact stem from their own status as cutouts, as isolated rings snipped from the social fabric and sea of images from whence they came. This likely would have been Theodor Adorno's take: in his essay "Lyric Poetry and Society," Adorno argues that the lyric I—that is, the sound of an individuated self, in all its privacy, individuality, and autonomy—is always but an excision; it is always formed by a rupture, or break, from "the collective and the realm of objectivity." "The more heavily social conditions weigh, the more unrelentingly the poem resists, refusing to give up any heteronomy, and constituting itself purely according to its own laws," Adorno writes, unwittingly providing a good description of the solitary, pressurized environments created by Bacon's rings of action, or Plath's fiercely personal mindscapes.

—

THE ARTIST who has become most well known in recent years for cutting figures—almost literally—from the psychosocial fabric of history is Kara Walker. Walker works primarily with silhouettes—black figures cut out of paper and arranged on white walls in phantasmagoric tableaux set in the antebellum South. These tableaux depict a panoply of brutalities and perversions played out in the context of the singularly cruel institution of American slavery. The pornographic violence of her imagined scenes contrasts sharply with the aesthetic neatness of her chosen form. But despite Walker's elaborate, almost baroque gestures toward the historical—which have included a meticulous engagement with the typeface, rhetoric, literary production, and handicraft of the period at stake—her work still engenders charges of narcissism, of being "more of an excursion into her personal hang-ups than an exorcism of the country's racial psychosis," as Howard Halle put it in a review of Walker's widely traveled 2007 show, *My Complement, My Enemy, My Oppressor, My Love.*

Halle's criticism doesn't come out of the blue—as the above title suggests, Walker is as insistently self-referential as she is referential of history, often casting herself in her work as "The Negress" (as in the "Negress of Noteworthy Talent," or the "Negress of Some Notoriety"). Truth be told, I find myself more politically interested in the phenomenon of Walker than aesthetically compelled by the work, as its formal properties often leave me cold. That said, the conflict Halle here poses between "an excursion into her personal hang-ups" and "an exorcism of the country's racial psychosis" interests me a great deal. I'm not saying one can't tell the difference between the two, but how?

We might all happily nod at the well-worn adage "the personal is political," but what has happened when we feel as though someone has abused or appropriated history in a "too personal" way? What, or who, demarcates the boundaries of such a meshing? Or is it not the boundaries themselves that are at issue, but rather the sensibility with which they are transgressed? When does the imbrication of intimate subjectivity and historical record come off as revelatory, and when does it bring us to Halle's conclusion: "[Walker's] cotillion of horrors—the pickaninnies trailing feces, the Negroes choking on massa's cock—grabs you by the throat, but to what end? As an object lesson in history, or as a form of elitist titillation? I'll leave it to others to enjoy Walker's visual equivalent of erotic asphyxiation, but as Samuel Goldwyn once remarked, include me out"?

Perhaps the confusion lies in the "personal is political" formula-tion itself, which offers but a simple copula where there actually exists a multitude of possible relations. As Jacqueline Rose has put it in *The Haunting of Sylvia Plath*, it isn't just that "the personal is political—for a long time feminism has insisted that what goes on in private is a political matter that concerns us all," but rather that "psychic life in itself will not be relegated to the private, it will not stay in its proper place. It shows up on the side of the historical real-ity to which it is often opposed." It's this inappropriate "showing up" that interests me—a kind of crashing of the party that cannot be stopped, only contended with, when it occurs.

I agree, for example, that reading about the inspiration Walker derived from an "on-again, off-again complicated relationship with a white man" whom she suggests, in a 2007 *New Yorker* pro-file, was "a sadist, a racist, a misogynist . . . and perhaps less cred-ibly, Satan himself," alongside work such as *Why I Like White Boys, an Illustrated Novel by Kara E. Walker Negress* (2000), begins to feel like an overshare, if such a thing could be said to exist in art. ("I am easy. / and that is why White boys like me, and black / boys, suspect me of liking white boys. / funny loop," she writes, in a series of notes collected in 2003's *Narratives of a Negress*.) But after decades of hearing the bad news from Spike Lee, Eldridge Cleaver, Amiri Baraka, and countless others about the nearly psychotic dynamics they perceive operating between black men and white women (see Lee's *Jungle Fever*, Cleaver's testimonial to raping white women as "an insurrectionary act," Baraka's monstrous white-woman-vil-lain creation in *Dutchman*)—not to mention centuries of literature and art by white men that gives free expression to a catastrophic erotic preoccupation with "the Negress"—why, or how, does an African-American woman artist's exploration of her feelings about white men come off as an overshare, speaking more of her personal tastes than of historical legacies?

The assertion that "the personal is political" is surely one of feminism's major achievements. Even so, predictably enough, women still struggle to lay their claim to it. The weird combination of narcissism, self-critique, and historical hyperbole that laces Walker's work seems to me symptomatic—not in wholly uninteresting ways—of this problem.

Perhaps Walker's more egregious stance has been her association of the workings of the art world (or, more particularly, her place within it) with the institution of slavery—an association many have found patently offensive, especially considering Walker's privileged status as the youngest recipient ever of a MacArthur "genius grant," and the recipient of solo shows at both the Whitney and the Met before she turned forty. Walker has addressed this conflict repeatedly in her work, with no small amount of self-loathing, as in this snippet from *Texts* (2001): "Dear you insufferable cunt . . . Why do you insist on tormenting yourself, as well as your loved ones, with Ingratitude? . . . You are given 'chances,' 'opportunities,' 'inches,' as well as Miles. And you take them all. And spit, spit in those faces, bite those hands defecate on heads from your bare branch perch." While witty in its way, this doesn't necessarily get her off the hook with those who think, as Halle puts it, that "she draws a rather outrageous parallel—that life as a famous artist is just like being a slave—in order to star in her own institutional critique."

Halle is here referring to the parallel Walker draws in her 2005 video *8 Possible Beginnings or: The Creation of African-America, A Moving Picture by Kara E. Walker*, in which a slave—referred to as "Bess, A Comely Negress," and played by a woman other than

Walker (but who stands in as a sort of double for her)—cuts out a black paper silhouette portrait of her master. Such parallels recur throughout Walker's writings, often by way of particularly loaded word choice (as when she talks about being driven to "auction" herself off—"teeth and hair, tits and ass"—"auction" having a strong association with both the history of slavery and the art world).

Similar indictments have hounded Plath, whose invocations of Jewish identity and the Holocaust amid her psychosexual dramas have seemed, to many, the height of irresponsible trivialization and self-aggrandizement. Unsurprisingly, the reactions to such provocations have been fierce. Speaking of Plath's notorious poem "Daddy," in which Plath's speaker says, "I think I may well be a Jew," and compares her father to a Nazi, critic Leon Wieseltier (whose parents were Holocaust survivors) scolds, "Whatever her father did to her, it could not have been what the Germans did to the Jews. The metaphor is inappropriate." Feminist critic Jane Marcus weighs in similarly: "For some of the suffering young, the murder of six million Jews is exactly equal to the rage felt twenty years later at a father's death. . . . Plath's capacity as a poet to enshrine private pain and suffering in terms appropriate to the suffering of millions appeals to that special audience which needs to feel that its private suffering is unique and colossal."

What's striking to me here is the repeated critical claim that each artist is drawing a one-to-one ratio that "exactly equates" her private situation with the public suffering of millions of others (others whose privacy and individuality have, by now, in the minds of many, been safely blurred into the great march of history). But does Walker really say that life as a famous artist is "just like" being a slave? Does Plath really say that the murder of six million Jews is "exactly equal" to her pain or rage? (And in what way could *historical event* be comparable to *private sensation* anyway, given that they are, in some real sense, apples and oranges?) The work of Walker and Plath makes ugly parallels, outrageous associations, and occasionally appalling speculative identifications. But why collapse these various operations into "exact equivalences," even if just for critical panache? And why ring the "appropriateness" alarm, when the injunction to behave appropriately—as both Plath and Walker know well—is but a death knell for art-making, especially for women?

There's no denying the fact that both Plath and Walker have an appetite for self-mythologizing, which can be, at times, seriously annoying. Both remain seemingly more transfixed by the psychology—and erotics—of oppression than of liberation (see, for example, Plath's incendiary lines from "Daddy": "Every woman adores a Fascist, / The boot in the face, the brute / Brute heart of a brute like you"—lines that reverb with Walker's infamous contention that "all black people in America want to be slaves a little bit"). We don't have to agree, and we don't have to like it. But why let it extinguish our capacity to differentiate between the many possible kinds of association that art sets into motion, such as metonymy, metaphor, simile, synecdoche, analogy, and allegory?

Blurring out such distinctions delivers us into a world made up of simplified resemblances and amplified divergences—in short, a world deprived of its wide array of relationality. "Really, universally, relations stop nowhere," Henry James once wrote. "The exquisite problem of the artist is eternally but to draw, by a geometry of his own, the circle within which they shall happily *appear* do so." That's the artist's exquisite problem. Ours, in turn, is to grapple as alertly as possible with the proposed nature of these relations, along with the contours of the circle that momentarily circumscribes them.

As far as Walker's work goes, the two interpretive lenses that Halle offers for it—that it is "an object lesson in history" or "a form of elitist titillation"—leave out a third term, which strikes me as the more accurate: that of psychological fantasia. In his 1925 poem "Heritage," Countee Cullen famously asked, "What is Africa to me?" Walker's work gives imaginative rein to the same question, along with its implicit twin: *What is America to me?* For both Cullen and Walker, the "to me" part of the question remains crucial, the point of generation.

The tongue-in-cheek opening sequence of *8 Possible Beginnings* (a rendition of Middle Passage in which some black bodies are marked "authentic" and others, "wannabe") already announces its historical apparatus as a sort of sham, or playpen—a loaded backdrop for present-day terms and preoccupations. The video's most disturbing layering of this sort occurs in a later scene, in which a cutout of a young African-American girl is being followed, or prodded, into the woods by a cutout of a menacing, haggish white man. The voice-over here is performed by Walker and her young daughter, who repeat, in staggered rhythm, lines such as "I wish I were white," "I think he's going to hurt me," "I wonder what it will feel like," "I guess this is what happened to Abby," "I wish I could get this thing off me," and, perhaps most chillingly, "Go with the flow."

Walker's use of her own daughter's voice to read such lines—lines that clearly prefigure the child's violation—is stunning. Perhaps it is stunningly cruel—though, once again, to whom, exactly, I cannot say; one can easily imagine that the daughter made it through the recitation unscathed. The impulse here seems to be to take one's worst fears—either for oneself now, for the child one was once, or for the child one is now charged with protecting—

and to smear oneself and one's child into them, even if by a reenactment laden with distances. ("They're only paper dolls," and so on.) The scenario evokes the plot of *Beloved*, in which Toni Morrison showcases how the charge of maternal protection was wickedly obstructed by slavery and profoundly complicated by subsequent racism. But Walker's engagement of her own daughter, in 2005, has a nastier edge. It seems gratuitous, almost evil. For instead of (or in addition to) reenacting a fear, it seems to construct a trap, insofar as it hoists a nefarious legacy into the mouth of a young girl before it's clear that she herself will be haunted by similar fears, legacies, or fantasies. The drive to undertake such a smearing becomes the fascination, as much or more than the historical incidence of such violations.

—

MANY COMMENTATORS on Bacon's "rings of action" have read in them a psychological ambivalence, a simultaneous need to love and murder his subjects, including himself. "Love is the instinct which creates that figure and nurtures it to fulfillment; murder, the instinct which pins it down and finishes it off," Russell writes. There is probably some truth here, especially insofar as it relates to the Levinas spectrum of murderous action on the one end, and instinctive protection on the other (not to mention to Bacon's own S/M proclivities). It is not, however, an interpretation that held much interest for Bacon. When asked by David Sylvester whether he considered his distortions "both a caress and an assault," he replied, "I think that is too logical. I don't think that's the way things work. I think it goes to a deeper thing: how do I feel I can make this image more immediately real to myself? That's all."

What is "deepest" for Bacon is sensation, not psychology. And the peeling away of psychology from sensation occasions a certain sort of pain—the pain of extinguishing the story behind the suffering, and of contending directly with the sensation of suffering itself. This process might be likened to the Buddhist instruction to focus first and foremost on the wound made by an arrow that has pierced your heart, rather than on the direction or bow from which it came. Focusing on the latter is sometimes termed frivolousness, insofar as it distracts from the pain, instead of leading you further into it. "It is obvious that, when you are really squashing frivolousness, you should feel pain, because there is a certain attraction toward the occupation of being frivolous," Chögyam Trungpa writes. "By squashing it you are completely taking away the occupation. You begin to feel that you have nothing to hold onto anymore, which is rather frightening as well as painful." What on God's earth, after this squashing, does one do next? "Then you must not live on your heroism, on having achieved something, but just dance with the continuing process of energy that has been liberated by this destruction."

Plath, too, knew how to do this dance. She too liked to keep moving. "And you, great Stasis— / What is so great in that!" she writes in "Years." "What I love is / The piston in motion— / My soul dies before it. / And the hooves of horses, their merciless churn." Plath also loved the feeling of going from zero to ninety, as in her famous fire arc of a poem, "Ariel," which begins with "Stasis in darkness," and ends with her hurtling like "the arrow, the dew that flies / Suicidal, at one with the drive / Into the red // Eye, the cauldron of morning."

Many have wondered whether this inexorable drive—Plath's infamous "blood jet"—had to have an element of cruelty to it—a cruelty that, in Plath's case, eventually took the form of self-murder.

Many have asked why she couldn't have loved the piston without having her soul "die before it," why the churn of the hooves had to be "merciless," why the arrow or the dew or the drive had to be "suicidal," why the jet had to be made of blood. Often I think people ask these questions because they are afraid that there is no drive that, when pushed to its outer limits, does not invite or at least graze its extinction. This seems to me a reasonable fear.

Bacon was one of those who insisted that humans will always suffer, no matter how just their circumstances, and that to argue otherwise is to deny a fundamental aspect of the human condition. He was right, of course, which is why any commitment to social justice that cannot acknowledge the existence of basic pain—that is, suffering that will exist for the human subject no matter how equitable or nourishing its circumstances—will end up haunted by bewilderment and disillusionment. (This is the narrator's main point in Gaitskill's "Agonized Face.") But to obliterate, happily and eagerly, the distinctions between avoidable pain and basic pain is another story. It speaks of a different taste—that of wanting to amplify basic pain, valorize it, court it, exalt it. (Case in point: art historian John Richardson recalls that, after homosexuality was decriminalized in Britain, Bacon—who was gay—once wished that they would "bring back hanging for buggery," a wish that makes clear how much pleasure Bacon derived from risk, taboo, and the threat of punishment.)

Of course, in art as in life, pain doesn't typically arrive wrapped up in neat boxes, some labeled "pain from preventable injustice," others, "pain from basic suffering." Think of the pain of being poor, of being raped, of being enslaved, of being gay-bashed, of being forced into exile, of losing everything in a natural disaster, of suffering from an illness such as HIV or cancer (or any illness, especially if one does not have access to health care to treat it): such experiences swirl all kinds of human-made and primordial sufferings together. But that doesn't mean one can't become a student of the swirl and learn how to make useful distinctions in its midst. (Reinhold Niebuhr's Serenity Prayer, known to twelve-steppers everywhere, comes to mind here, as does Buddhism's attention to discerning the differences between three categories of pain: "all-pervading pain," "the pain of alternation," and "the pain of pain.") The increased ability to make such distinctions is one means of wising up to our various styles of imprisonment, should one wish to lessen their grip.

It can be exciting and worthwhile when art assists in this wising up. For some—such as Brecht—it is art's duty. Perhaps that is one of the main differences between ethically scrupulous endeavors and so-called art of cruelty: the former is beholden to this sense of duty, while the latter can be more concerned with communicating the felt sensations—on all sides—of injustice or trauma, come what may. You might even see some art of cruelty as a division of trauma itself, in that one of trauma's most troubling cruelties lies in its tendency to replicate itself—Freud's "compulsion to repeat" writ reckless and large. "Beauty brings copies of itself into being," Scarry writes in *On Beauty*. Alas, the same must be said of trauma, as trauma can notoriously suffuse its sufferers with the desperate (if unconscious) desire to make others feel as bad as they have felt. The consequent wheel of suffering—often appropriately termed a "cycle of violence"—accounts for much of what is despicable in this world. It is also, for better or worse, the drive behind some of its art.

You want people to know how bad something feels, either for you, personally, or for a larger community—a family, a people, a race, a class, a gender, and so on. The urge might be strong enough that you want the mean satisfaction of producing, in another, bona fide pain. Some end up trying to bludgeon their audience into understanding. Think, for example, of Fernando Meirelles's 2002 film *City of God*, a fictionalized portrait of life in the ultra-violent, ultra-poor, ultra-corrupt Brazilian slum, or *favela*, known ironically as Cidade de Deus. *City of God* marries this bludgeoning impulse with the more noble desire to bring the bad news of radical poverty and its attendant miseries to both the elites of Brazil and the MTV generation worldwide. Its popularity depended on this union, and on the in-your-face, hyperkinetic, relentlessly violent aesthetic that it used to deliver it—an aesthetic designed to exhilarate as much as brutalize its audience. "Tarantino with a social conscience," several reviewers called it. You do indeed walk out of the film palpably terrorized—I felt jumpy and queasy for hours, and struggled to differentiate this sick feeling from that produced by other Tarantino-like experiences by telling myself that perhaps Meirelles was trying to inject into audiences who would otherwise have no conception of what it feels like to live in a place like Cidade de Deus but a drop of the knowledge—a drop that might stay with someone beyond the 130 minutes the movie takes to blow its wad. This possibility seemed potentially worth the film's many attendant risks: desensitization, glamorization, exploitation, misrepresentation, and so on.

Nonetheless, I almost walked out of the film during the scene in which a gangster is terrorizing a toddler at gunpoint, forcing him to choose whether he wants his hand or foot blown off. (At long last, the little boy chooses his foot, which the gangster promptly shoots off.) The cruelty of this scene felt like too much to bear, in part because the child at hand appeared too young to discern the difference between being terrorized at gunpoint for a film and simply being terrorized, and thus I had the bad feeling in my gut that I was watching a cruelty that was only partially simulated. This feeling was complicated by the fact that most of the actors in the film were residents of the *favelas* themselves, so if one tried to rid oneself of the bad feeling by telling oneself that this boy's life was probably chock full of similar terrors, and therefore the desire to protect him from this simulated one was as naive as it was useless, the argument brought about but a new breed of bad feeling. But really none of this mattered to me at the moment I felt the need to bolt. What mattered was the door clanging shut inside me, the door that clangs shut whenever I feel absolutely certain that neither I nor the world will be a better place if I ingest a particular cruelty. (Then, of course, I ingested it anyway, as per the implacable imperative of the cinema, especially the cinema of cruelty. *Bam*.)

—

WHAT KIND of circle is it, that aims to represent all sides of a horrible act? Does drawing such a circle provide the most ethically thorough and fearless approach to a heinous deed, or is "true" ethical clarity achieved only when one privileges the experience of the victim? Does focusing on the POV of a perpetrator re-perform a cruelty, under the guise of a far-reaching empathy? How to cultivate the difference between an all-inclusive compassion, with freely given forgiveness at its base, and idiot compassion, which fails to assign or take responsibility or to protect us adequately from those who have done or would do us harm?

Jenny Holzer's *Lustmord*—a project made in response to the systematic rape and murder of women during the war in former Yugoslavia, and made manifest by Holzer in various forms between 1993 and 1995—addresses itself to this question with controversy and variety. The basis of *Lustmord*—which is a German word meaning "sexmurder," or rape-and-murder—is three written texts, each of which tells the story of the *Lustmord* of a Bosnian woman from a different perspective: that of the woman being raped and murdered, that of the rapist/murderer, and that of a witness to the act. In 1993, Holzer presented this work as an insert in the *Süddeutsche Zeitung Magazin*, Munich's principal newspaper. (The November 19 cover of the magazine was taken over by Holzer's words: "DA, WO FRAUEN STERBEN, BIN ICH HELLWACH"—"I am awake in the place where women die"; more text followed inside.)

The controversy arose not only due to the disturbing nature of Holzer's text, but also due to the accompanying announcement that the words had been printed in an ink made partially of women's blood, which stirred up a very literal anxiety over their unsanitary nature. *Lustmord* has since appeared in a variety of different forms and settings. There was a 1994 installation at Barbara Gladstone Gallery in New York, in which Holzer presented the text in three distinct formats: as LED texts spinning around a dark, leather-lined module into which the viewer must step in order to read the words; as inscriptions on metal bands tied around human bones, all taken from female skeletons and lined up on a wooden display table; and in a series of photographs of the words printed on human skin, in ink that resembled blood, or branding. Pieces of *Lustmord* have also been projected, via laser, onto Leipzig's Monument to the Battle of Nations (1996); they have also appeared in various forms at museums and galleries in Germany, Norway, and Switzerland.

Holzer says she conceived of *Lustmord* as "a memorial to protest violence perpetrated against women." She has also said that, after reading the three texts, she "hopes the viewer will come down on the right side." But, as one can imagine, the most disturbing aspect of *Lustmord* is its unholy trinity of perspectives, and its use of the same poeticized language in each. I personally find the brief text of *Lustmord* some of the most upsetting, confusing, and indelible material quoted in this book. To take but a few examples: from the perpetrator, "I WANT TO FUCK HER WHERE SHE HAS TOO MUCH HAIR." "HER SWALLOW REFLEX IS GONE." "THE COLOR OF HER WHERE SHE IS INSIDE OUT IS ENOUGH TO MAKE ME KILL HER." From the victim, "I AM AWAKE IN THE PLACE WHERE WOMEN DIE." "I HAVE THE BLOOD JELLY." "I TRY TO EXCITE MYSELF SO I STAY CRAZY." And from the observer, "SHE SMILES AT ME BECAUSE SHE IMAGINES I CAN HELP HER." "SHE IS NARROW AND FLAT IN THE BLUE SACK AND I STAND WHEN THEY LIFT HER."

This is audacious, sickening, and troubling business, which has rubbed many the wrong way. Holland Cotter of the *New York Times* called the moral position of Holzer's work "so calculatedly opaque as to come across as sensationalist"; Laura Cottingham of *Flash Art* called *Lustmord* a "pseudo-poetic text" that "de-brutalizes, romanticizes, and eternalizes rape—a naturalization made complete by the installation's complete lack of historical specificity"—a judgment related to the distaste I felt for Bacon after seeing his collages of Algerian body parts. Nonetheless, despite what Brecht might have hoped, the "Always historicize!" imperative that has held sway in academia for some time now is not an easy import into the field of art-making, nor should it necessarily be.

Personally I don't feel capable of testifying to *Lustmord*'s work in the world as a political intervention (as was intended by its appearance in *Süddeutsche Zeitung Magazin*), nor do I feel particularly interested in charting the aesthetic differences between its appearance in spinning LED versus engraved on a bench, and so on. My interest in *Lustmord* remains tethered to its bare text, for the simple reason that I almost cannot read it. The prospect of deeply internalizing its 500 words frightens me more than the psychic effects of a hundred copies of *Altmann's Tongue* or *120 Days of Sodom* combined.

This response may be in part a reaction to something politically rotten about the work. After all, *Lustmord* could easily be accused of "vicarious possession," artist Adrian Piper's term for the "inappropriate level of imaginative involvement" that characterizes the attempt to speak for others, especially others who have been deprived of the right to speak for themselves. But I also suspect it due to other things, some of which I'm not even sure I want to touch. One has to do with coming into visceral, intimate contact with one's deepest fears for no obviously salutary reason, while simultaneously recognizing that countless others—such as the girls and women who were detained and tortured in the rape camps that operated throughout the Bosnian war—lived those fears, often dying in the process. Another has to do with the fact that, despite what we may want or need to believe, the perpetrators of such crimes are human beings, with human consciousness and human hearts, and further, that their experience is equally available for poetic rendering. Another has to do with the fear—or the conviction—that certain consciousnesses or hearts or events should *not* be rendered poetically (or "pseudo-poetically," whatever that may mean), a la Adorno's 1949 proclamation (later revised) that writing poetry after Auschwitz was barbaric. Yet another has to do with the worry that if and when one attempts such a rendering, the inhabitation of the perpetrator's consciousness will inevitably annihilate (or re-annihilate, as the case may be) the voice of the victim (who is, after all, much easier to deal with once she has been silenced). "I HOOK MY CHIN OVER HER SHOULDER. NOW THAT SHE IS STILL I CAN CONCENTRATE."

Cottingham takes the latter route, arguing that "even as [Holzer] claims to be presenting three perspectives on rape, she presents only one: that of the perpetrator." But why is this so? Or rather, must it be? Is it because the victim in *Lustmord* is, like most victims, too frightening to identify with? After all, the victim's script has few to no lines of heroic defiance, save "YOU CONFUSE ME WITH SOMETHING THAT IS IN YOU. I WILL NOT PREDICT HOW YOU WANT TO USE ME." But this one attempt at differentiation is definitively overwhelmed by testimony of ruinous invasion: "YOUR AWFUL LANGUAGE IS IN THE AIR BY MY HEAD." "HAIR IS STUCK INSIDE ME." "WITH YOU INSIDE ME COMES THE KNOWLEDGE OF MY DEATH." And while the observer's account begins with fearless tenderness ("I WANT TO LIE DOWN BESIDE HER. I HAVE NOT SINCE I WAS A CHILD. I WILL BE COVERED BY WHAT HAS COME FROM HER"), it soon gives way to an overwhelming sense of repulsion and horror: "SHE ASKS ME TO SLEEP IN THE HOUSE BUT I WILL NOT WITH HER NEW BODY AND ITS NOISE." "I WANT TO BRUSH HER HAIR BUT THE SMELL OF HER MAKES ME CROSS THE ROOM." "SHE FELL ON THE FLOOR IN MY ROOM. SHE TRIED TO BE CLEAN WHEN SHE DIED BUT SHE WAS NOT. I SEE HER TRAIL."

I don't profess to know why Holzer focuses so much of *Lustmord* on the abjection of the victim's body, but it seems clear from her deployment of *SZ Magazin* that she at least meant to disallow the abject from remaining abjected. She meant literally to force the bloodshed of women, however sickening, into people's living rooms. (The fact that the day's paper would likely go out with the trash, almost in reenactment of people's incapacity to know what to do with news of horrific events occurring around the world, may have unintentionally complicated the gesture.) Whatever one makes of the stunt, it is too bad that the editor of *SZ*, Tibor Kalman, couched the piece, in his explanatory essay, in the prototypically masculinist, violent, and aggrandizing terms of the avant-garde: "Jenny Holzer's art is an act of terrorism. . . . Jenny puts the gun to your head: think about it! . . . are we the assailants or the victims? Are we the strong or the weak? Are we the man or the woman?" Assailant/victim, strong/weak, man/woman, hero/victim: Kalman's rush of binaries—along with his suggestion that good thinking comes from having a gun held to your head—almost flatten Holzer's text beyond repair. But, alas, years later, it still pulses here beside me, in all its bewildering, spare, perhaps unforgivable horror.

—

"SYLVIA PLATH could not distinguish between herself and the facts of say, Auschwitz or Hiroshima," a critic once diagnosed. "She was victim, killer, and the place of horror, all at once." This critic did not mean this as a compliment. I, on the other hand, see this blurring as one of Plath's most salient poetic achievements. The intense, first-person drive of Plath's poems gives the sense that their speakers are hurling blame like thunderbolts from the heavens, so it may come as a surprise to realize that the Plath poems that seem, on the surface, to cast the most blame, when attended to closely, often offer but blame-blurs, which stand out like wonky smears amid her obsessive technical precision.

The main subject of Plath's controversial poem "The Rabbit Catcher," for example, is neither the sadistic trapper nor the victimized animal, but rather the "place of force— / The wind gagging my mouth with my own blown hair, / Tearing off my voice, and the sea/ Blinding me with its lights." Likewise, when she writes in "The Jailer," "How did I get here? / Indeterminate criminal, / I die with variety— / Hung, starved, burned, hooked," the speaker may be the criminal, but she could just as easily be addressing her jailer as such: it is, as the poem says, indeterminate. And even if the jailer were definitively to blame, Plath's use of the passive voice for the hanging, starving, burning, and hooking still smears out any neat assignment of agency. "How did I get here?" Plath's speaker wonders in "Getting There"; "Who has dismembered us?" she asks in "Event." These are not questions that Plath answers.

Perhaps because Plath did not, and cannot now, answer them, her readers have often done so for her. And the two primary answers—as critic Jacqueline Rose has pointed out—are that "she did it all—only—to herself" (pathology), or "he did it" (in which case "man, meaning Hughes or the male sex he stands in for, is to blame—the woman internalizes, turns against herself, the violence of the world outside"). Again, the problem isn't that neither answer holds any water. Both do. The problem, as Rose points out, is that "in neither [option] is it acceptable that there might be a component of psychic negativity with no singular origin, which no one will take away for us, for which no one can be blamed."

Tough news, this. No wonder that, in the face of it, we might run around trying to smear this negativity onto other sources, including onto itself. "It is easy to blame the dark," Plath tells us elsewhere. Plath herself took the more unpopular route: she asserted, without apology, in her journal on June 20, 1958, "I have a violence in me that is hot as death-blood." (See Kara Walker: "Rage is fun.")

This is an especially discomfiting admission for a woman to make. For a woman who claims this hot death-blood is no gladiator or emperor, but a hellish Fury (yet a woman who protests against it too ardently has not yet come to terms with the cruel "ways of the world"). A woman who delves into the relation between Eros and Thanatos is not typically regarded as someone making a transgressive, probing move, but as a self-abasing traitor aiding and abetting rape culture. Likewise, a woman who explores the depths of her despair or depression isn't typically valorized as a hero on a fearless quest to render any "darkness visible," but is instead perceived as a redundant example of female vulnerability, fragility, or self-destructiveness. A woman who lives, as did Artaud, like a mad animal at the furthest reaches of her sanity, isn't a shamanistic voyager to the dark side, but a "madwoman in the attic," an abject spectacle. "Her hair gave off a strong smell, sharp as an animal's," said a visitor to Plath's London flat, one month before her winter suicide.

Plath set up shop in "this blackness, / This ram of blackness," anyway. Then, with steely serenity, she went about sketching the landscape she found there. "This is the light of the mind, cold and planetary. / The trees of the mind are black ... And the message of the yew tree is blackness—blackness and silence." Perhaps you do not recognize this landscape, or perhaps you would prefer not to stay too long in it. Perhaps you do not like the starkness of its message. Plath does not care. Plath cares about telling us, over and over again, how it is to live in "the O-gape of complete despair." That is her suffocation, her dark generosity.

To perch in the O, to sit with its blackness and silence without demanding the immediate amelioration of either, to resist the urge to make ourselves or anyone else definitively to blame for its existence, to sketch its contours with patience, with exactitude, with eyes open—these are not easy feats. Perhaps they feel, at times, like cruelties, or like an acquiescence to cruelties. Once your eyes adjust to the darkness, however, you might be surprised to feel a sense of relief. "I know the bottom," Plath wrote. "It is what you fear. / I do not fear it: I have been there." At least there is a clarity here, a sense of clearing.

RARER AND BETTER THINGS

O F COURSE, the frustrating thing about Plath—as with so many artists of cruelty—is that she wields her scimitar of clarity without letting any air into the room. As with Compton-Burnett, Trocchi, Bacon, McDonagh, and many others who appear in these pages, whatever "rarer or better things" may exist in the universe ultimately remain but shadows outside their gates. As a consequence, entering their worlds can bring about the sensation described by Anne Carson (in *Decreation*) in a poem about reading Beckett: "You know that sense of sinking through crust, / the low black *oh no* of the little room / with walls too close, so knowable." One may love, respect, and admire the work, but one may not always feel like hanging out in its little room, or feeling the press of its walls. One may have to be, as they say, in the mood.

In Plath's case, I don't see this airlessness as the mark of any reprehensible shortcoming (be it chemical, moral, or aesthetic), but more likely a result of the fact that she died too young to explore the voluptuousness or complexity of her cruelty, much less to ventilate it. She died, after all, at thirty—an age at which Bacon, for example, had hardly begun to paint. And Bacon's early paintings are, unsurprisingly, his most over-the-top—he got to paint for four more decades after rendering his most horrific screams, his bloodiest carcasses.

Even Bacon's harshest critics agree that one of his best paintings is *Jet of Water*, from 1988, made when Bacon was seventy-nine years old. Ditto *Blood on Pavement*, made that same year, a gorgeous, nearly abstract painting that brings to mind both Cy Twombly and the crime-scene photos of Weegee. I don't personally subscribe to the belief—explicitly or unwittingly expressed by so many critics and curators—that a movement toward abstraction marks some kind of commendable, teleological progress in an artist's career, or in the history of art itself. Nonetheless, I would have been very curious to see equivalent work made by a seventy-nine-year-old Plath; I would have loved to have seen Plath's *Jet of Water*.

Am I suggesting that, in some sense, cruelty is a young person's game? Certainly an artist who stays fixated on it runs certain risks. Bacon's centenary retrospective was greeted by a surplus of back-lash reviews lambasting him as a cartoonish one-trick pony—as an overrated "illustrator of exaggerated, ultimately empty angst," as Jerry Saltz put it. Von Trier's *Antichrist* (2009), for which he went so far as to hire an official "misogyny consultant" (Danish journalist Heidi Laura), seems to have scraped the bottom of whatever gynophobic trough he's been drinking from for decades. (As the UK's *Telegraph* reported, "Recently, [von Trier] was asked directly whether *Anti-Christ* was misogynistic. Disarmingly, he replied: 'I don't know about that. I often wonder what would happen if I just came out and said, "I hate women." ' " Of course, nothing much would change at all.)

McDonagh has gone from penning linguistically riveting plays to directing derivative Hollywood shoot-'em-ups loaded with the banality of visual gore, such as 2008's *In Bruges*. His 2010 play *A Behanding in Spokane*—his first set in America—was laden with racist drivel, and panned by most as a sordid flop. Michael Haneke's

American remake of *Funny Games* seemed profoundly misguided, its scenes of a blonde and bound Naomi Watts jumping around in her underwear undercutting, for many, every highbrow thing Haneke has ever said about his pleasure-prohibiting representations of violence. (Haneke has since redeemed himself in the eyes of many critics with 2009's *White Ribbon*, primarily due to the film's restraint: "You expect harm to befall [the characters], like a plague, but, for once, it stays its hand," Anthony Lane wrote in the *New Yorker*.) Paul McCarthy is doing quite well into his sixth decade, but his beat has always been abjection, dark comedy, and taboo-busting rather than cruelty.

Some writers—such as Elfriede Jelinek—are able to sustain and invent upon their cruel and claustrophobic worlds so relentlessly over the years that their stamina rather than their affective range becomes the wonder. ("My writings are limited to depicting analytically, but also polemically, the horrors of reality," Jalinek has said. "Redemption is the specialty of other authors." It may also bear noting that Jelinek is a famous agoraphobe, who didn't even venture out for the 2004 Nobel ceremony at which she won the prize in literature.) Others, such as Gaitskill, evidence, over time, a certain expansiveness that feels thrilling rather than slack. Others still—such as Mendieta, Schneemann, Abramović, Walker, Bowles, Ono, Finley, Antin, Kusama, Akerman, Compton-Burnett, and so on—are, to my mind, still waiting to be adequately contended with, heard, understood.

And, of course, there are the many, many others whose work did not appear in these pages, but easily could have (Gina Pane, Valie Export, Maria Lassnig, Cindy Sherman, Rebecca Horn, Marlene McCarty, Chloe Piene, Nathalie Djurberg, Eileen Myles, Darcey

Steinke, Peggy Ahwesh, Wanda Coleman, Dennis Cooper, Harmony Korine, Jean Genet, Pier Paolo Pasolini, Amos Tutuola—to name but a few). The most interesting of this work—past, present, or future—is or will be that which dismantles, boycotts, ignores, destroys, takes liberties with, or at least pokes fun at the avant-garde's long commitment to the idea that the shocks produced by cruelty and violence—be it in art or in political action—might deliver us, through some never-proven miracle, to a more sensitive, perceptive, insightful, enlivened, collaborative, and just way of inhabiting the earth, and of relating to our fellow human beings. For as Arendt puts it succinctly in *On Violence*, "The practice of violence, like all action, changes the world, but the most probable change is to a more violent world."

And then, of course, there are madmen such as Artaud, who neither crash and burn nor "grow up," nor provide anything close to a usable blueprint for the future of art, life, human happiness, the revolution, or the planet, but who simply radiate, pulse, and magnetize across space and time, reminding us of what the outer limits of being human might be.

"There's a way that I always disbelieve Artaud," says writer Rick Moody, in a June 2009 piece in *The Believer*, "especially now that I am twenty years from my own time in the psychiatric hospital. In my disbelief, sometimes he seems *just* a sick person, and I want to say that I am no longer willing to be sick for my own art— it's a young man's game." I can't personally say that I've ever been tempted to believe or disbelieve Artaud—as Sontag once wrote, the one thing you cannot do with Artaud is apply him; likely you cannot believe him either, at least not in the sense of becoming a follower. What's there to believe or follow in his later poetry, in which he calls himself "Artaud the Momo," coins the term "Boss-Pussy," and worries incessantly about people stealing his semen and excrement? Artaud's last fragment of written work reads, "And they have pushed me over / into death, / where I ceaselessly eat / cock / anus / and caca / at all my meals, / all those of THE CROSS." In the face of such anarchic, blasphemous transmissions, I can only revel in their strangeness, and try to open myself up—when possible—to their incitements, inspirations, comedy, and terror, their spasms of agony and joy.

Perhaps as a sort of unwitting warning, my used copy of *The Theater and Its Double* arrived to me bearing the following inscription: "In art and dream may you proceed with abandon. In life may you proceed with balance and stealth." I have since learned that this quotation comes from punk legend Patti Smith—no stranger to abandon, balance, or stealth. Over the years, I have come to think of this quotation as a prayer, or aspiration—one that draws a ring of action around art and life, acknowledging their tight tether, while also sagely differentiating between them. The quotation reminds me of something Richard Foreman says in *Unbalancing Acts*, in the midst of a Brechtian diatribe against the attempt to create a flow of love or empathy between stage players and audience members. "Art should not be a substitute for real life," Foreman writes. "Love should be between people." I agree. Taking such pressure off art frees up both art, and loving.

—

So, to return to my rejected Williams epigraph, which takes love as its subject: "The business of love is cruelty, / which, / by our wills, / we transform / to live together." It still sounds good—but what could it mean? I don't particularly agree with its temporal proposition—that the business of love begins as a form of cruelty, which can be subsequently (heroically?) altered, until we all get along. I do, however, like its calm admission of the coexistence of love and cruelty—its acknowledgment that they can exist within one another, rather than at opposite ends of the spectrum, or locked in an oppositional embrace. That there might be an alchemical, rather than a conflictual, relationship between them. That the possibility of transformation is always alive, and always ours.

Such a proposition is in keeping with the work of British psychologist D. W. Winnicott, who concerned himself primarily with the needs and behaviors of infants and small children. Winnicott differed from Freud, Melanie Klein, and other analysts in that he did not customarily term an infant's "business of love" sadistic, no matter how aggressive the behavior; he thought such a term attributed more malice to the infant than was plausible. But Winnicott did spend a great deal of time thinking and writing about the intense dance between vulnerability and ruthlessness that begins when we are infants and persists, in its way, for the rest of our lives—our grappling with desires so fierce one fears that they might overwhelm or obliterate others, others that we may desperately not want to lose—indeed, that we cannot afford to lose.

For Winnicott, it was crucial and normal that a mother feel hatred for her baby, and equally so that the baby be able, in turn, to hate her. Love occurs, he thought, when the infant is able to test the love object, often via aggression, and the object survives, proves itself able to withstand the testing. One of Winnicott's most well-known images for the balancing act of parent and child has to with holding: the baby must be held loosely enough to experience freedom, but tightly enough so that it does not fall. Love, in this case, is a container—a "holding environment"—with the right amount of space provided. Or—and here is Winnicott's generosity—if not exactly right, "good enough."

Such an image echoes that offered by John Cage, in a 1966 piece of writing titled "Diary: How to Improve the World (You Will Only Make Matters Worse)." Here Cage writes: "The most, the best, we can do, we / believe (wanting to give evidence of / love), is to get out of the way, leave / space around whomever or whatever it is." These lines have always struck me as an admirable mantra to live by, if not an exceedingly difficult—perhaps at times impossible—one, given the ruthlessness of our desires, the fraught apprehension of our dependency, the heavy, chaotic experience of jealousy, and the radical undone-ness that can attend both loss and communion.

What a relief, then, to return to this Cage piece and find that its very next line reads, "But there is no space!"—a protest of the previous line's serenity. And so we are returned to negotiation, to paradox. A similar dynamic animates Cage's title: "How to Improve the World (You Will Only Make Matters Worse)," which first acknowledges the desire to change the world, then pulls the rug out from under it. Such gestures are in keeping with one of Buddhism's most enlivening paradoxes: that we can dedicate our lives to ending suffering, while acknowledging the first noble truth, that life is suffering. Such paradoxes are ours to keep.

A paradox is more than the coexistence of opposing propositions or impulses. It signals the possibility—and sometimes the arrival—of a third term into a situation that otherwise appeared to consist of but two opposing forces. Roland Barthes elaborates this third term—which he calls the Neutral—with the utmost of beauty and intelligence in his 1977–78 series of lectures titled *The Neutral*. Barthes's Neutral is that which throws a wrench into any system (*doxa*) that demands, often with menacing pressure, that one enter conflicts, produce meaning, take sides, choose between binary oppositions (i.e., "is cruel! / is not!") that are not of one's making, and for which one has no appetite.

As it disrupts such demands, the Neutral introduces responses that had heretofore been unthinkable—such as to slip, to drift, to flee, to escape. In a world fixated on the freedom to speak and the demand to be heard, the Neutral proposes "a right to be silent—a possibility of being silent . . . the right not to listen . . . to not read the book, to think nothing of it, to be unable to say what I think of it: the right not to desire." It allows for a practice of gentle aversion: the right to reject the offered choices, to demur, to turn away, to turn one's attention to rarer and better things.

Preserving the space for such responses has been one of this book's primary aims. Of equal importance has been making a space for paying close attention, for recognizing and articulating ambivalence, uncertainty, repulsion, and pleasure. I have intended no special claim for art or literature—that is, no grand theory of their value. But I have meant to express throughout a deep appreciation of them as my teachers. For, as Barthes suggests, insofar as certain third terms—however volatile or disturbing—baffle the oppressive forces of reduction, generality, and dogmatism, they deserve to be called sweetness.

ACKNOWLEDGMENTS

THE THOUGHTS in this book belong as much to my beloved and brilliant Harry Dodge as they do to me. I am beyond grateful for our dialogue, and for the unimaginably rich business of our love. The luck is mine, everyday. *Jackpot*.

My sincere gratitude to PJ Mark (of Janklow & Nesbit) and Alane Mason (of W. W. Norton), for their intelligence, encouragement, and guidance, all of which has made this a much better book. I thank them both for their profound role in bringing it into being. Thanks also to Denise Scarfi and all others at Norton who worked on this book's behalf.

Thanks also to the John Simon Guggenheim Memorial Foundation; my friends and colleagues at CalArts, especially Dean Nancy Wood, and my students from the 2007 and 2010 Art of Cruelty seminars; Ali Liebegott, Beth Pickens, and Michelle Tea of RADAR Lab, for providing such a beautiful place for me to finish, and for others to flourish; and friends Cort Day, Wayne Koestenbaum, Aaron Kunin, and Anthony McCann, for the immeasurably smart and helpful leads, inspiration, and advice they offered along the way.

Finally, to little Lenny: may he always carry the sword of Manjushri.

BIBLIOGRAPHY

Adorno, Theodor. *The Adorno Reader*. Ed. Brian O'Connor. Oxford: Wiley-Blackwell, 2000.

Arbus, Diane. *Revelations*. New York: Random House, 2003.

Arendt, Hannah. *On Violence*. New York: Harvest Books, Harcourt Brace, 1969, 1970.

——. *The Portable Arendt*. Ed. Peter Baehr. New York: Penguin, 2003.

Artaud, Antonin. *Selected Writings*. Ed. Susan Sontag, trans. Helen Weaver. Berkeley: University of California Press, 1988.

——. *The Theater and Its Double*. Trans. Mary Caroline Richards. New York: Grove Press, 1958.

——. *Watchfiends & Rack Screams: Works from the Final Period*. Trans. Clayton Eshelman with Bernard Bador. Boston: Exact Change, 1995.

Austin, J. L. *How to Do Things with Words: The William James Lectures Delivered at Harvard University in 1955*. Oxford: Oxford University Press, 1970.

Badiou, Alain. *Conditions*. Trans. Steven Corcoran. New York: Continuum, 2008.

Barthes, Roland. *The Neutral: Lecture Course at the College de France (1977–1978)*. Trans. Rosalind Kraus and Denis Hoiller. New York: Columbia University Press, 2005.

Bataille, George. *Erotism: Death and Sensuality*. Trans. Mary Dalwood. San Francisco, CA: City Lights, 1986.

——. *Literature and Evil*. Trans. Alastair Hamilton. New York: Marion Boyars, 2006.

——. *Story of the Eye*. Trans. Dovid Bergelson. San Francisco, CA: City Lights, 2001.

Beauvoir, Simone de. "Must We Burn Sade?" Trans. Annette Michelson. In *The 120 Days of Sodom and Other Writings* (Marquis de Sade). New York: Grove Press, 1966.

Benjamin, Walter. *Illuminations*. Trans. Harry Zohn. New York: Schocken Books, 1968.

Berger, John. *About Looking*. New York: Vintage, 1992.

Bey, Hakim. *The Temporary Autonomous Zone, Ontological Anarchy, Poetic Terrorism*. New York: Autonomedia, 1985.

Blocker, Jane. "Aestheticizing Risk in Wartime: The SLA to Iraq." In *The Aesthetics of Risk*. Ed. John C. Welchman. Volume 3 of the Southern California Consortium of Art Schools symposia. Zurich: JRP/Ringier, 2006.

———. *Where Is Ana Mendieta? Identity, Performativity, and Exile*. Durham, NC: Duke University Press, 1999.

Bowles, Jane. *My Sister's Hand in Mine: The Collected Works of Jane Bowles*. New York: Farrar, Straus & Giroux, 2005.

Bradford, William. "Of Plymouth Plantation," 1630–50. In *The Norton Anthology of American Literature*, 3rd ed., vol. 1. New York: W. W. Norton, 1989.

Brecht, Bertolt. *Brecht on Theatre: The Development of an Aesthetic*. Trans. John Willett. New York: Hill & Wang, 1964.

Burden, Chris. "Untitled Statement (1975)." In *Theories and Documents of Contemporary Art: A Sourcebook of Artists' Writings*. Ed. Kristine Stiles and Peter Selz. Berkeley: University of California Press, 1996.

Butler, Judith. *Precarious Life: The Powers of Mourning and Violence*. New York: Verso, 2006.

Cage, John. *Conversing with Cage*. Ed. Richard Kostelanetz. New York: Limelight Editions, 1988.

———. *X: Writings '79–'82*. Middletown, CT: Wesleyan University Press, 1983.

———. *A Year from Monday: New Lectures and Writings*. Middletown, CT: Wesleyan University Press, 1967.

Carson, Anne. *Decreation*. New York: Vintage, 2006.

———. *Glass, Irony, and God*. New York: New Directions, 1995.

Carter, Angela. *The Sadeian Woman: And the Ideology of Pornography*. New York: Pantheon Books, 1978.

Clark, T. J. *The Sight of Death: An Experiment in Art Writing*. New Haven, CT: Yale University Press, 2006.

Compton-Burnett, Ivy. *Parents and Children*. New York: Penguin, 1941, 1970.

Davis, Angela. "Sexual Coercion, Prisons, and Female Responses." In *One of the Guys: Women as Aggressors and Torturers*. Ed. Tara McKelvey. Berkeley, CA: Seal Press, 2007.

Deleuze, Gilles. *Coldness and Cruelty*. Trans. Jean McNeil. In *Masochism: Coldness and Cruelty and Venus in Furs* (Leopold von Sacher-Masoch). Brooklyn, NY: Zone Books, 1991.

———. *Francis Bacon: The Logic of Sensation*. Trans. Daniel W. Smith. Minneapolis: University of Minnesota Press, 2004.

———. *A Thousand Plateaus: Capitalism and Schizophrenia* (with Felix Guattari). Trans. Brian Massumi. Minneapolis: University of Minnesota Press, 1987.

Despentes, Virginie. *King Kong Theory*. Trans. Stephanie Benson. New York: Feminist Press, 2010.

Didion, Joan. "The Women's Movement." In *The White Album*. New York: Farrar, Straus & Giroux, 1979.

———. *The Year of Magical Thinking*. New York: Alfred A. Knopf, 2005.

Dillard, Annie. "The Book of Luke." In *The Annie Dillard Reader*. New York: HarperCollins, 1994.

———. *For the Time Being*. New York: Vintage, 2000.

Edwards, Jonathan. "Sinners in the Hands of an Angry God," 1741. In *The Norton Anthology of American Literature*, 3rd ed., vol. 1. New York: W. W. Norton, 1989.

Ehrenreich, Barbara. "Foreword: Feminism's Assumptions Upended." In *One of the Guys: Women as Aggressors and Torturers*. Ed. Tara McKelvey. Berkeley, CA: Seal Press, 2007.

Eliot, T. S. *Selected Prose*. Ed. Frank Kermode. New York: Mariner Books, 1975.

Emerson, Ralph Waldo. *The Portable Emerson*. Ed. Carl Bode in collaboration with Malcolm Cowley. New York: Penguin, 1981.

Evenson, Brian. *Altmann's Tongue*. Lincoln, NE: Bison Books, 2002.

———. *Dark Property*. New York: Thunder's Mouth Press, 2002.

———. *Fugue State*. Minneapolis, MN: Coffee House Press, 2009.

———. *The Open Curtain*. Minneapolis, MN: Coffee House Press, 2008.

———. *The Wavering Knife*. Tuscaloosa, AL: Fiction Collective 2, 2004.

Finley, Karen. *A Different Kind of Intimacy: The Collected Writings of Karen Finley*. New York: Thunder's Mouth Press, 2000.

Foreman, Richard. *Unbalancing Acts: Foundations for a Theater*. New York: Theater Communications Group, 1993.

Freud, Sigmund. *The Freud Reader*. Ed. Peter Gay. New York: W. W. Norton, 1995.

Gaitskill, Mary. *Bad Behavior*. New York: Vintage, 1989.

———. *Don't Cry*. New York: Pantheon Books, 2009.

———. *Veronica*. New York: Vintage, 2006.

Girard, René. *Violence and the Sacred*. Trans. Patrick Gregory. Baltimore: Johns Hopkins University Press, 1979.

Graeber, David. *Possibilities: Essays on Hierarchy, Rebellion, and Desire*. Oakland, CA: AK Press, 2007.

Griffith, David. *A Good War Is Hard to Find: The Art of Violence in America*. New York: Soft Skull Press, 2006.

Holzer, Jenny. *Lustmord*. Excerpts reprinted in *Witness to Her Art*. Ed. Rhea Anastas with Michael Brenson. Annandale-on-Hudson, NY: Center for Curatorial Studies, Bard College, 2006.

Howe, Fanny. *The Wedding Dress: Meditations on Word and Life*. Berkeley: University of California Press, 2003.

Jacobs, Amber. *On Matricide: Myth, Psychoanalysis, and the Law of the Mother*. New York: Columbia University Press, 2007.

James, Henry. *Portrait of a Lady*. New York: Penguin, 2003.

———. *Literary Criticism: French Writers, Other European Writers, Prefaces to the New York Edition*. Volume 2. New York: Library of America, 1984.

Kafka, Franz. *The Complete Stories*. Ed. Nahum N. Glatzer. New York: Schocken Books, 1971.

Kester, Grant. *Conversation Pieces: Community and Communication in Modern Art*. Berkeley: University of California Press, 2004.

Koestenbaum, Wayne. *Andy Warhol* (Penguin Lives). New York: Viking, 2001.

Kristeva. Julia. *The Powers of Horror: An Essay on Abjection*. Trans. Leon Roudiez. New York: Columbia University Press, 1982.

Kuhn, Thomas. *The Structure of Scientific Revolutions*. Chicago: University of Chicago Press, 1996.

Laing, R. D. *Knots*. 1970. New York: Vintage, 1972.

Levi Strauss, David. *Between Dog and Wolf: Essays on Art and Politics*. Brooklyn, NY: Autonomedia, 1999.

Luxon, Thomas H. *Literal Figures: Puritan Allegory and the Reformation Crisis in Representation*. Chicago: University of Chicago Press, 1995.

Marinetti, F. T. "The Founding and Manifesto of Futurism." In *Manifesto: A Century of Isms*. Ed. Mary Ann Caws. Lincoln: University of Nebraska Press, 2001.

McDonagh, Martin. *The Pillowman: A Play*. London: Faber & Faber, 2004.

Monk, Ray. *Ludwig Wittgenstein: The Duty of Genius*. New York: Penguin, 1991.

Morrison, Toni. *Beloved*. New York: Alfred A. Knopf, 1987.

Mueller, Cookie. *Walking through Water in a Pool Painted Black*. New York: Semiotext(e), 1990.

Nietzsche, Friedrich. *Beyond Good and Evil*. Trans. R. J. Hollingdale. New York: Penguin, 1973.

Phillips, Adam. *On Kindness* (with Barbara Taylor). New York: Picador, 2010.

———. *Terrors and Experts*. Cambridge, MA: Harvard University Press, 1997.

———. *Winnicott*. Cambridge, MA: Harvard University Press, 1989.

Plath, Sylvia. *The Collected Poems*. Ed. Ted Hughes. New York: Harper & Row, 1981.

———. *The Unabridged Journals of Sylvia Plath*. Ed. Karen V. Kukil. New York: Anchor Books, 2000.

Pope.L, William. *The Friendliest Black Artist in America* (monograph). Ed. Mark H. C. Bessire. Cambridge, MA: MIT Press, 2002.

Prejean, Sister Helen. *Dead Man Walking: An Eyewitness Account of the Death Penalty in the United States*. New York: Vintage, 1994.

Rancière, Jacques. *The Emancipated Spectator*. Trans. Gregory Elliott. New York: Verso, 2009.

Réage, Pauline. *Story of O*. Trans. Sabine d'Estrée. New York: Ballantine Books, 1965.

RETORT. *Afflicted Powers: Capital and Spectacle in a New Age of War*. New York: Verso, 2005.

Rorty, Richard. *Contingency, Irony, Solidarity*. Cambridge, England: Cambridge University Press, 1989.

Rose, Jacqueline. *The Haunting of Sylvia Plath*. Cambridge, MA: Harvard University Press, 1992.

Russell, John. *Francis Bacon*. New York: Thames & Hudson, 1993.

Sade, Marquis de. *Justine, Philosophy in the Bedroom, and Other Writings*. Trans. Richard Seaver and Austryn Wainhouse. New York: Grove Press, 1965.

Saint-Point, Valentine de, "Manifesto of Futurist Woman," 1912. In *Manifesto: A Century of Isms*. Ed. Mary Ann Caws. Lincoln: University of Nebraska Press, 2001.

Salzberg, Sharon. *Lovingkindness: The Revolutionary Art of Happiness*. New York: Shambhala, 2004.

Scarry, Elaine. *On Beauty and Being Just*. Princeton, NJ: Princeton University Press, 2001.

Schneemann, Carolee. *Imaging Her Erotics: Essays, Interviews, Projects*. Cambridge, MA: MIT Press, 2003.

Sedgwick, Eve Kosofsky. *Epistemology of the Closet*. Berkeley: University of California Press, 1990.

———. *Touching Feeling: Affect, Pedagogy, Performativity*. Durham, NC: Duke University Press, 2003.

Sontag, Susan. *Against Interpretation and Other Essays*. New York: Picador, 2001.

———. *Antonin Artaud: Selected Writings* (editor). Berkeley: University of California Press, 1988.

———. *On Photography*. New York: Picador, 2001.

———. *Regarding the Pain of Others*. New York: Picador, 2004.

Suzuki, Daisetz T. *Zen and Japanese Culture*. Princeton, NJ: Princeton University Press, 1959.

Sylvester, David. *Interviews with Francis Bacon*. New York: Thames & Hudson, 1987.

Trocchi, Alexander. *Cain's Book*. New York: Grove Press, 1993.

Trungpa, Chögyam. *The Collected Works of Chögyam Trungpa*. Volumes 3–4. Boston: Shambhala, 2003.

Virno, Paolo. *A Grammar of the Multitude: For an Analysis of Contemporary Forms of Life*. Trans. Isabella Bertoletti, James Cascaito, and Andrea Casson. New York: Semiotext(e), 2004.

WACK: Art and the Feminist Revolution (exhibition catalogue). Ed. Cornelia Butler and Lisa Gabrielle Mark. Cambridge, MA: MIT Press, 2007.

Walker, Kara. *Narratives of a Negress*. Ed. Ian Berry, Vivian Patterson, and Mark Reinhardt. Cambridge, MA: MIT Press, 2003.

Warhol, Andy. *POPism* (with Pat Hackett). New York: Mariner Books, 1990.

Weil, Simone. *Gravity and Grace*. Trans. Emma Crawford and Mario von der Ruhr. New York: Routledge Classics, 2002.

———. "The Iliad, or the Poem of Force." Trans. Mary McCarthy. In *War and the Iliad* (with Rachel Bespaloff). New York: New York Review of Books Classics, 2005.

Williams, William Carlos. *The Collected Poems of William Carlos Williams*. Ed. Christopher MacGowan. New York: New Directions, 1991.

———. *In the American Grain*. New York: New Directions, 1956.

Winthrop, John. From *The Journal of John Winthrop, 1630–1649*. In *The Norton Anthology of American Literature*, 3rd ed., vol. 1. New York: W. W. Norton, 1989.

Wittgenstein, Ludwig. *Culture and Value*. Ed. G. H. von Wright, trans. Peter Winch. Chicago: University of Chicago Press, 1980.

———. *Philosophical Investigations*. Trans. G. E. M. Anscombe. Oxford: Blackwell, 1953, 1958.

Woolf, Virginia. *To the Lighthouse*. San Diego, CA: Harvest Books, 1981.

Žižek, Slavoj. *The Ticklish Subject: The Absent Centre of Political Ontology*. New York: Verso, 2009.

———. *Violence*. New York: Picador, 2008.

INDEX